STUDY GUIDE

Thomas F. Jorsch
Ferris State University

AMERICAN STORIES
A HISTORY OF THE UNITED STATES

VOLUME II

SINCE 1865

H.W. Brands
University of Texas

T.H. Breen
Northwestern University

R. Hal Williams
Southern Methodist University

Ariela J. Gross
University of Southern California

PEARSON

Upper Saddle River, New Jersey 07458

PREFACE

Our goal in writing this study guide is to make your study of American history, using *American Stories: A History of the United States*, more effective and rewarding. We hope this study guide will help you

- develop the study skills you need to learn history inside and outside the classroom.

- master the text material and demonstrate your knowledge on tests and quizzes.

- develop a clear understanding of the main trends and recurring themes within American history.

To achieve these goals, we have gathered an assortment of study tips, exercises that require factual answers, and broader "thought questions"—all of which should help enhance your knowledge of the text and America history. These study aids can be divided into two general classes: essays and review exercises designed to improve your study skills and chapter-by-chapter review materials.

REVIEWING THE TEST CHAPTER BY CHAPTER

Each chapter in this study guide corresponds to a chapter in your text. Each chapter of review materials includes a chapter summary, learning objectives, glossary of terms, and self-test questions that include identification, matching, completion, true/false, multiple choice, and thought questions.

- The *Summary*, which is organized around the heads and subheads within the chapter, highlights the most important points and will help you review your reading of the chapter.

- The *Learning Objectives* pinpoint the most important themes or ideas of the chapter, themes and ideas you should take away from your study. Refer back to this list as you review the text chapter and as you complete the self-test exercises to see how well you have mastered the material.

- The *Glossary* contains a number of terms that may be unfamiliar to you. Besides a definition, we have supplied a quote from the chapter that shows you how the word can be used in a sentence. Learning these words and terms will expand your vocabulary, which will help you in this and other courses in the social sciences.

- The *self-test exercises* cover both specific details and broad concepts. (An answer key for these questions is at the end of the text). *Identification* items ask you to identify key phrases and explain their significance. *Matching* exercises are intended to help you distinguish between similar but different people, locations, or events. By asking you to fill in the blanks, *Completion* exercises will help you relate specific items to their context. *True/False* and *Multiple Choice* questions will give you valuable practice for objective tests and help you check your knowledge of key points.

- *Thought Questions* are designed to meet the objective of helping you develop a clear understanding of the main trends and recurring themes within American history. Answering these questions will help you tie together your classroom lecture notes and the text coverage; this will also help you study for essay tests, a feature of most history courses.

- *Critical Thinking Exercises* are designed to help you learn to analyze and compare primary source documents through a series of readings and analytical questions.

For best results, try to use the chapter-by-chapter review materials in a consistent manner. Read the chapter and then begin working through the chapter's review materials, using the "Summary" and "Learning Objectives" to focus your study. After you have completed the self-test exercises, check your answers against the answer key. When you understand why you missed a question and determine areas of weakness, focus your attention on reviewing those sections. If you do this faithfully, both your knowledge and pleasure in American history should increase. We hope you find your efforts worthwhile and your confidence in your ability to learn and enjoy history enhanced. If so, we will have accomplished our goals.

CHAPTER 16

The Agony of Reconstruction, 1863–1877

SUMMARY
After the Civil War, the South and the nation as a whole faced a difficult period of rebuilding its government and economy and of dealing with the newly freed African Americans.

The President versus Congress
In the absence of constitutional guidelines, the president and Congress struggled over how best to reconstruct the Union. The fight was colored by a debate over how far the federal government should go to secure equality and civil rights for the four million African Americans freed by the war.

Wartime Reconstruction
By 1863, Lincoln and Congress had begun to debate two divisive issues: the reconstruction of the southern states and former Confederates and the status of the freedmen. Lincoln proposed a moderate program to restore the southern states to the Union, but by 1865 showed some willingness to compromise with Congress's more radical plan for reconstruction. With Lincoln's death, the issue of Reconstruction remained unresolved.

Andrew Johnson at the Helm
The ascent of Andrew Johnson, a Southerner, to the presidency eventually led to a bitter clash with Congress. Though Congress and Johnson agreed that slavery should be abolished and that the power of the planter class had to be broken down, Congress supported federal guarantees for black citizenship while Johnson insisted that the South should be permitted to reestablish white supremacy.

Congress Takes the Initiative
Determined to crush the old southern ruling class, the Republican-led Congress extended the life of the Freedmen's Bureau and passed a civil rights bill to grant equal benefits and protection to the freedmen. Fearing that Johnson would not enforce the civil rights act, Congress passed the Fourteenth Amendment guaranteeing equal rights under the law to all Americans and defining national citizenship. After Johnson vetoed the two Reconstruction bills and the southern states rejected the Fourteenth Amendment, Congress initiated its own more radical program.

Congressional Reconstruction Plan Enacted
Often called Radical Reconstruction, Congressional Reconstruction began with the passage of the First Reconstruction Act of 1867 over Johnson's veto. This act temporarily placed the South under military rule and allowed for the re-admittance of southern states, only once African-American suffrage was legitimized. Congress assumed that once freedmen could vote, they could protect themselves.

The Impeachment Crisis

When the president obstructed the plan's implementation, Congress retaliated with an attempt to remove him from office. Johnson narrowly avoided removal, preserving the office from congressional domination, but insuring also that Congress would have the upper hand in the reconstruction process.

Reconstructing Southern Society

The South was devastated and demoralized after the war. Though slavery was dead, the region was dominated by southern whites who strived to deny all rights to freedmen. At the same time, southern blacks tried to make their freedom meaningful by becoming land owners, acquiring education, and exercising the right to vote. These two opposing goals resulted in chaos and violence.

Reorganizing Land and Labor

Despite the desire of some radical Republicans for land redistribution, Congress failed to enact such a program, except among a very few families. Facing vast tracts of land with no one to work them, Southern landowners initiated a contract labor system that forced freedmen into virtual peonage. While some ex-slaves resisted returning to work for their former masters, most had no alternative. Evolving alongside of and eventually supplanting the contract labor system, sharecropping became the dominant agricultural system in the South. Although African Americans initially viewed sharecropping as step up from wage labor, they soon learned that it trapped them in a cycle of poverty and dependence.

Black Codes: A New Name for Slavery?

While sharecropping extended black servitude and economic dependence on the farm, African Americans in southern towns and cities found themselves increasingly segregated from whites by Black Codes, community pressure, or physical intimidation. At their root, the Black Codes were meant to control the black population and insure white supremacy and privilege.

Republican Rule in the South

Politically, Reconstruction established southern governments made up of Republican business people (many of whom were from the North), poor whites (many of whom had been Unionists during the war), and the freedmen. Although often corrupt, these radical regimes initiated significant progressive reforms, including establishing the South's first public school systems, democratizing state and local governments, appropriating funds for an enormous expansion of public services, constructing internal improvements, and fostering economic development. They failed, however, to achieve interracial equality, and contributed to the hostility of southern whites toward southern blacks.

Claiming Public and Private Rights

Outside of the political process of Reconstruction, southern blacks also reconstructed their lives in various ways, giving meaning to their freedom. They negotiated with employers and utilized the Freedmen's Bureau and the courts to assert their rights against whites as well as other blacks. In the private realm, they established their own families, churches, political organizations, and community institutions and sought education for themselves, and more importantly, their children.

Retreat from Reconstruction

Serving during one of the most difficult periods in American history, Grant lacked the strong principles, consistency, and sense of purpose to be an effective administrator. His election marks the beginning of the end of Reconstruction as other political issues moved to forefront of Americans' minds.

Final Efforts of Reconstruction

Republican efforts to secure black rights culminated in the passage of the fifteenth amendment. The legislation was weakly-worded, however, leaving a great deal of room for violation of the spirit of the law. The amendment also split the age-old tie between black rights and Woman rights and effectively divided the women's suffrage movement. Many feminists were irate that women were denied the right to vote even as suffrage was extended to black men.

A Reign of Terror Against Blacks

In the South, Grant's administration failed to sustain black suffrage against violent groups bent on restoring white supremacy. Organizations like the Ku Klux Klan used terrorism, insurrection, and murder to intimidate southern Republican governments and prospective black voters. With the Fifteenth Amendment and Republican rule in the South severely threatened, Congress passed the "Force" Acts, allowing the president to use military force to quell insurrections.

Reunion and the New South

The reconciliation of the sections came at the expense of southern blacks and poor whites, and despite the rhetoric of the New South, the region remained poor and open to exploitation by northern business efforts.

The Compromise of 1877

In the 1876 presidential election, Samuel Tilden, the Democratic candidate, won the popular majority as well as the uncontested electoral vote. But disputed returns in the three Republican-controlled southern states threw the election into turmoil. The Compromise of 1877 ended military rule, insured that conservative "home rule" would be restored in the South, and effectively abandoned southern blacks to their former masters. With southern Democratic acquiescence, Republican candidate Rutherford Hayes assumed the presidency, though he did so under a cloud of suspicion.

"Redeeming" a New South

In the South, upper-class "Redeemers" took power in the name of white supremacy and laissez-faire government, initiating a "New South." As industrialism gained strength in the 1880s, the southern economy became dominated by northern capital and southern employers, landlords, and creditors. Though Redeemer governments were more economical than their Republican predecessors, cutting back funding for education and other public services, they were no less corrupt. Most hurt by the Redeemers were southern blacks and poor whites who were caught in the poverty of sharecropping.

The Rise of Jim Crow

Beginning in 1876 and culminating in the 1890s, southern governments began codifying the de facto segregation and discrimination of southern blacks through the enactment of the infamous Jim Crow system. Economic and physical coercion, including hundreds of lynchings in the name of southern white womanhood, effectively disfranchised people of color while the convict-lease system reduced blacks convicted of petty crimes to a system of forced labor that was often more cruel than slavery. After the passage of the Civil Rights Act of 1875, the federal government did little to stem or even alleviate racial oppression in the South and the Supreme Court effectively condoned it through a series of court decisions including *Plessy* v. *Ferguson*.

Conclusion: Henry McNeal Turner and the "Unfinished Revolution"

Some blacks like Henry McNeal Turner became justifiably bitter at the depth of white racism and the lack of action on the part of the federal government. They supported black nationalism and emigration to Africa as a solution. Most blacks, however, chose to struggle for their rights within American society. By the 1880s, Reconstruction was over, the nation was reunified, and blacks were sentenced to oppression that would not be challenged for another century.

LEARNING OBJECTIVES

After mastering this chapter, you should be able to:

1. Contrast the presidential and congressional wartime reconstruction programs.

2. Explain how Andrew Johnson's background shaped his attitudes and policies on Reconstruction.

3. Describe the processes by which Andrew Johnson lost support in Congress and the Radical Republicans gained control of Reconstruction.

4. Summarize the goals of Radical Reconstruction and evaluate the success with which these goals were achieved.

5. Define the sections of the Fourteenth Amendment and understand why its enforcement was crucial to Reconstruction efforts.

6. Describe the Radicals' attempt to remove President Johnson from office. Analyze the important results of the impeachment crisis on the federal government and the Reconstruction process.

7. Define the southern systems of contract labor and sharecropping with emphasis on their effects upon African Americans.

8. Analyze the failings of the Fifteenth Amendment. Consider how it might have been improved.

9. Identify the social and economic adjustments in the South during the Reconstruction years.

10. Identify the major groups that made up the southern Republican governments, then evaluate their achievements and list the reasons for their ultimate failure.

11. Explain the nature of the political crisis involving the election of 1876 and discussion the terms and result of the "Compromise of 1877."

12. Discuss the Black Codes. How were they like slavery? How were they unlike slavery?

13. Describe the social and political effects of the "Redeemer" regimes in the New South.

14. Discuss the meaning of freedom for African Americans. How did they experience Reconstruction in the public and private spheres?

15. Discuss the role of violence and groups like the Ku Klux Klan in Reconstruction.

16. Discuss the enactment of Jim Crow laws and their impact on the South.

17. Evaluate Reconstruction in terms of its successes and failures for the nation as a whole and for black Americans in particular.

18. Evaluate historians' changing views of Reconstruction.

GLOSSARY

To build your social science vocabulary, familiarize yourself with the following terms:

1. **crop lien** use of a farmer's crop as collateral for a loan. "... the notorious 'crop lien' system ..."

2. **disfranchisement** the act of depriving a citizen of the right to vote. "Full-scale disfranchisement ..."

3. **impeachment** the act of bringing charges against a government officer for official misconduct. "... to call for his impeachment."

4. **Jim Crow** segregated. "... black, or 'Jim Crow,' cars ..."

5. **laissez faire** government noninterference in the economy. "... advocated strict laissez-faire economic policies ..."

6. **patronage** political control of the distribution of jobs and other favors. "... the corruption breeding patronage system ..."

7. **referendum** the practice of referring a matter to the electorate for adoption or rejection. "... served as a referendum to the Fourteenth Amendment."

8. **specie** coined money, usually of gold or silver. "... redeemed in specie payments."

9. **amnesty** a pardon granted for past crimes. "... a Proclamation of Amnesty and Reconstruction ..."

10. **habeas corpus** a legal writ used to protect individuals against unlawful detention. "... suspend the writ of habeas corpus ..."

11. **rider** a clause added to a bill as it passes a legislative body. "... a rider to an army appropriations bill sought to limit Johnson's authority to issue orders to military commanders."

12. **revisionism** proposing a revised historical interpretation. "The most powerful example of this early revisionism was W. E. B. Dubois's *Black Reconstruction in America.*"

13. **provisional** temporary, until a permanent replacement is made. "... appointed provisional governors ..."

14. **sharecropping** the status of working a piece of land in return for a portion of the crop. "... an alternative capital—labor relationship—sharecropping ..."

15. **autonomy** the right and power of self-government. "The president's case for state autonomy ..."

IDENTIFICATION

Briefly identify the meaning and significance of the following terms:

1. Jim Crow _enacted by states to segregate the population_

2. Ten Percent Plan _proposed by Lincoln. Once 10% of voting population is above has taken oath and state has abolished slavery, authorized to set up local govt._

3. Freedmen's Bureau _1865-1872 — Agency established to provide freedmen w/ shelter, food, medicine, schools and help them find employment_

4. Fourteenth Amendment _Granted citizenship regardless of race, previous condition of servitude — Confederate debt repudiated_

5. Radical Republicans _headed by Thaddeus Stevens & Charles Sumner — favored protection of black rights as a precondition of readmission to Union_

6. First Reconstruction Act _passed over Johnson's veto, placed South under military rule — 5 Districts_

7. Black Codes _laws (state, local) limiting the freedoms of ex-slaves. vagrancy, apprenticeship, no testifying, seperate penal code_

8. Compromise of 1877 _Democrats accepted Hayes as president in exchange for withdrawal of federal troops_

9. Ku Klux Klan _started TN 1866 — wanted to disfranchise blacks and stop Reconstruction_

10. "New South" _laissez-faire and white supremacy_

MATCHING

A. Match the following amendments and groups with the appropriate description.

_c_ 1. Thirteenth Amendment

_a_ 2. Fourteenth Amendment

_d_ 3. Fifteenth Amendment

_e_ 4. scalawags

_b_ 5. carpetbaggers

a. guaranteed civil rights regardless of race and penalized former Confederates

b. northern businessmen who sought economic advances in the South

c. prohibited slavery in the United States

d. guaranteed voting rights regardless of race of past condition of servitude

e. southerners who sought commercial and industrial development

f. Southern blacks who controlled some state governments after the Civil War

B. Match the following bills and acts with the appropriate description.

_c_ 1. Wade-Davis Bill

_e_ 2. Black Codes

_a_ 3. Tenure of Office Act

_b_ 4. Force Acts

____ 5. Civil Rights Bill of 1866

a. congressional legislation designed to limit the authority of President Andrew Johnson

b. a series of laws designed to protect black suffrage by authorizing use of the army against the KKK

c. initial congressional plan for Reconstruction vetoed by Lincoln

d. congressional attempt to provide the freedman "full and equal benefit of all laws"

e. southern state laws passed during Reconstruction to impose restrictions on former slaves

f. congressional legislation creating a federal agency to aid the former slaves

COMPLETION

Answer the question or complete the statement by filling in the blanks with the correct word or words.

1. Congressmen such as Thaddeus Stevens and Charles Sumner who insisted on black suffrage and federal protection of civil rights of African Americans were called *Radical Reconstructionists*

2. Slavery was abolished with the ratification of the *13th Amendment*.

3. Lincoln refused to sign the Wade-Davis Bill of 1864 by exercising a *pocket veto*
   _____.

4. The physical destruction of the South would not have been so devastating had there been sufficient *capital* available for rebuilding.

5. The *14th Amendment* Amendment restricted the power of the states to violate the life, liberty, or property of any citizen.

6. By the 1870s, most African Americans were relegated to a system of _____ *sharecropping*, an arrangement whereby they agreed to work a small piece of land in return for a fixed share of the crop.

7. President Johnson faced impeachment for violating the *Tenure of Office Act*

8. The *Ku Klux Klan* was a southern organization bent on restoring white supremacy by intimidating politically active African Americans.

9. The southern Republican party consisted of the following three groups, *businessmen* *N - carpetbaggers* *S - scalawags* _____, *poor, white farmers*, and *freedmen*.

10. From 1876 through the first decade of the twentieth century, southern states imposed a series of restrictions on black civil rights known as *black codes*.

TRUE/FALSE

Mark the following statements either T (True) or F (False).

___T___ 1.   Lincoln favored a lenient plan for Reconstruction in order to shorten the war by attracting southern support.

_____ 2.   The dominant view of the Republican-led Congress toward the Reconstruction process was that strong executive leadership would be required.

_____ 3.   Andrew Johnson abandoned Lincoln's plans for Reconstruction by doing away with the requirement of an oath of allegiance for southern whites.

___T___ 4.   Women's rights leaders Elizabeth Cady Stanton and Susan B. Anthony campaigned against ratification of the Fifteenth Amendment.

___F___ 5.   As a result of his impeachment trial, Andrew Johnson became the first president to be removed from office.

___T___ 6.   Physical reconstruction of the South was difficult because its per capita wealth in 1865 was only about half of what it had been in 1860.

___F___ 7.   Most ex-slaves did not see access to education as vital to equality because their occupations required little formal training.

___T___ 8.   The Fifteenth Amendment to the Constitution prohibited any state from denying any citizen the right to vote because of race, color, or previous condition of servitude.

___T___ 9.   During Grant's first term, the greatest threat to southern Republican governments came from white supremacist societies like the KKK.

_____ 10. The factor that most contributed to Democrat Samuel Tilden's defeat in the presidential election in 1876 was the continued strength of the Republican regimes in the South and his consequent lack of popular support there.

MULTIPLE CHOICE

Circle the one alternative that best completes the statement or answers the question.

1. Which of the following statements reflects Lincoln's view of Reconstruction?
   a. Amnesty for those southerners who had never willingly aided the Confederacy.
   b. Reconstruction would guarantee full political and civil equality for southern blacks.
   c. Congress would determine the terms for readmission of the seceded states.
   d. Pardon would be granted to all southerners taking an oath of allegiance to the Union and acknowledging the legality of emancipation.

2. President Andrew Johnson's plan for Reconstruction called for the southern states to
   a. declare their ordinances of secession illegal.
   b. repay their Confederate war debts.
   c. ratify the Fourteenth Amendment.
   d. prohibit former Confederates from holding government offices.

3. The Fourteenth Amendment to the Constitution
   a. prohibited slavery in the United States.
   b. provided for franchise regardless of race, color, or past servitude.
   c. defined national citizenship and prohibited the states from abridging the constitutional rights of people without due process of law.
   d. restored the former slave states to the union after congressional requirements were met.

4. President Johnson antagonized Republicans in Congress by
   a. calling for an extension of the Freedmen's Bureau.
   b. supporting a civil rights bill meant to guarantee equality for African Americans.
   c. urging confiscation and redistribution of land.
   d. campaigning against Radical Republicans in the elections of 1866.

5. After rejecting Johnson's Reconstruction plan, Congress enacted a program based on
   a. the social and moral regeneration of the South.
   b. the confiscation and redistribution of land.
   c. immediate enfranchisement of both the freedmen and ex-Confederates.
   d. guarantees for the rights of all citizens with the Fourteenth Amendment.

6. The House of Representatives impeached President Johnson on the grounds that he
    a. dismissed officers in the southern military districts.
    b. challenged the Tenure of Office Act by removing Secretary of War Edwin Stanton.
    c. vetoed the Reconstruction Bill.
    d. attempted to abolish the Freedmen's Bureau.

7. "Regeneration before Reconstruction" referred to
    a. restructuring southern state governments before readmission to the union.
    b. funding the rehabilitation of those areas in the South damaged during the war.
    c. transforming southern society, including land reform, before readmission.
    d. repudiating the debts owed by the former Confederate states to the Union.

8. Which of the following contributed LEAST to whites maintaining economic and political dominance over blacks by the end of Reconstruction?
    a. Jim Crow laws
    b. Fifteenth Amendment
    c. sharecropping
    d. Black Codes

9. While in power, Republican governments in the South did all of the following EXCEPT
    a. build healthy state economies.
    b. establish the first adequate systems of public education.
    c. subsidize construction of railroads and other internal improvements.
    d. democratize state and local governments.

10. The main reason[s] for the Ku Klux Klan's success in the South after 1868 would be
    a. popular support from whites of all social classes for white supremacy.
    b. its centralized political organization.
    c. its support from the southern state Republican governments.
    d. the persistent threat of a violent black uprising against the white planter class.

11. Southern blacks tried to make their freedom meaningful during Reconstruction by
    a. legalizing their marriages.
    b. seeking education for themselves and their children.
    c. establishing their own churches, political organizations, and community institutions.
    d. All of the above.

12. The Force acts were designed in response to the activities of what group?
    a. Scalawags
    a. Radical Republicans
    b. Ku Klux Klan
    c. Southern Farmers' Alliance

13. In defending Republican governments in the South, President Grant
    a. was quick to react with the military to any threat of violence.
    b. intervened only to protect the civil rights of African Americans.
    c. was inconsistent and hesitant because of northern political realities.
    d. left these governments on their own to defend themselves.

14. To ensure the election of Rutherford Hayes, Republican leaders agreed to
    a. offer lucrative positions to members of the electoral commission.
    b. end federal support for southern radical regimes.
    c. support fraudulent elections with federal troops.
    d. continue federal support for southern radical regimes.

15. The "Redeemers" in the South favored
    a. egalitarian democracy and continued Republican leadership.
    b. government appropriations for schools and public services and economic diversification.
    c. strengthening the Black Codes and support for white supremacist organizations like the Klan.
    d. political restoration of white supremacy and laissez-faire.

THOUGHT QUESTIONS

To check your understanding of the key issues of this period, solve the following problems:

1. If Lincoln had lived, would the events and outcome of Reconstruction have been substantially different?

2. Was radical Reconstruction policy based more on humanitarian concern for the freedmen or on selfish political and economic interests?

3. Andrew Johnson was the only U.S. president impeached in our history until President William Clinton in 1999. (Richard M. Nixon tendered a timely resignation.) What does it mean to impeach a president? Should Andrew Johnson have been convicted?

4. What factors contributed to the development of segregation in the late nineteenth century?

5. Why did professional historians from the 1890s to the 1940s regard Reconstruction as a "tragic era"? In the eyes of the revisionists, what was the real tragedy of Reconstruction?

6. Would the redistribution of land have changed the outcome of Reconstruction for southern blacks and poor whites? How?

CRITICAL THINKING EXERCISE

Using material in Chapter 16 of the text and the primary sources provided below, please answer the questions that follow the reading selections.

"The Freedman's Agenda for Reconstruction"
Bayley Wyatt, "A Right to the Land"
Henry Blake, "Working on Shares"

"The Freedmen's Agenda for Reconstruction"

1st. *Resolved*, That the rights and interests of the colored citizens of Virginia are more directly, immediately and deeply affected in the restoration of the State to the Federal Union than any other class of citizens; and hence, that we have peculiar claims to be heard in regard to the question of its reconstruction, and that we cannot keep silence without dereliction of duty to ourselves, to our country, and to our God.

2d. *Resolved*, That personal servitude having been abolished in Virginia, it behooves us, and is demanded of us, by every consideration of right and duty, to speak and act as freemen, and as such to claim and insist upon equality before the law, and equal rights of suffrage at the "ballot box."

3d. *Resolved*, That it is a wretched policy and most unwise statesmanship that would withhold from the laboring population of the country any of the rights of citizenship essential to their well-being and to their advancement and improvement as citizens.

4th. *Resolved*, That invidious political or legal distinctions, on account of color merely, if acquiesced in, or voluntarily submitted to, is inconsistent with our own self-respect, or to the respect of others, placing us at great disadvantages, and seriously retards our advancement or progress in improvement, and that the removal of such disabilities and distinctions are alike demanded by sound political economy, by patriotism, humanity and religion.

5th. *Resolved*, That we will prove ourselves worthy of the elective franchise, by insisting upon it as a right, by not tamely submitting to its deprivation, by never abusing it by voting the state out of the Union, and never using it for purposes of rebellion, treason, or oppression.

6th. *Resolved*, That the safety of all loyal men, black or white, in the midst of the recently slaveholding States, requires that all loyal men, black or white, should have equal political and civil rights, and that this is a necessity as a protection against the votes of secessionists and disloyal men.

7th. *Resolved*, That traitors shall not dictate or prescribe to us the terms or conditions of our citizenship, so help us God.

8th. *Resolved*, That as far as in us lies, we will not patronize or hold business relations with those who deny to us our equal rights.

Bayley Wyatt, "A Right to the Land"

We made bricks without straw under old Pharaoh.... We now, as a people desires to be elevated, and we desires to do all we can to be educated, and we hope our friends will aid us all they can....

I may state to all our friends, and to all our enemies, that we has a right to the land where we are located. For why? I tell you. Our wives, our children, our husbands, has been sold over and over again to purchase the lands we now locate upon; for that reason we have a divine right to the land....

And then didn't we clear the land and raise the crops of corn, of cotton, of tobacco, of rice, of sugar, of everything? And then didn't them large cities in the North grow up on the cotton and the sugars and the rice that we made? Yes! I appeal to the South and the North if I hasn't spoken the words of truth.

I say they have grown rich, and my people is poor.

Henry Blake, "Working on Shares"

After freedom, we worked on shares a while. Then we rented. When we worked on shares, we couldn't make nothing—just overalls, and something to eat. Half went to the white man, and you would destroy your half, if you weren't careful. A man that didn't know how to count would always lose. He might lose anyhow. The white folks didn't give no itemized statements. No, you just had to owe so much. No matter how good account you kept, you had to go by their account, and—now, brother, I'm telling you the truth about this—it's been that way for a long time. You had to take the white man's words and notes on everything. Anything you wanted you could get, if you were a good hand. If you didn't make no money, that's all right; they would advance you more. But you better not try to leave and get caught. They'd keep you in debt. They were sharp. Christmas come, you could take up twenty dollars in somethin'-to-eat and as much as you wanted in whiskey. You could buy a gallon of whiskey—anything that kept you a slave. Because he was always right and you were always wrong, if there was a difference. If there was an argument, he would get mad and there would be a shooting take place.

1. After reading the text, explain the labor system that put the freedmen back to work in the planters' fields. How free were the former slaves in the "New South"?

2. Were the resolutions of the "Freedmen's Agenda for Reconstruction" primarily political or economic?

3. Why, in Bayley Wyatt's view, did freedmen have a "divine right" to own land?

4. Describe the operation and effects of sharecropping as Henry Blake explains the system.

5. Given your answer on sharecropping in question 4, which plan would have promoted most effectively the welfare of freed slaves: the one outlined in "The Freedmen's Agenda for Reconstruction" or Wyatt's "A Right to the Land?"

CHAPTER 17

The West: Exploiting an Empire, 1849–1902

SUMMARY
After the Civil War, Americans, who believed expansion was their "manifest destiny," began moving westward across the continent, subduing the Native Americans through various means, and creating a North American empire.

Beyond the Frontier
Prior to the Civil War, the march of white settlement paused at the margin of the semiarid Great Plains, a region seared by hot winds in the summer and buffeted by blizzards and hailstorms in the winter, and presenting a temporary obstacle to further migration.

Crushing the Native Americans
Because they were seen as an additional obstacle to further white migration, Native Americans were pushed from their lands and forced to radically change their cultures by the end of the century. Those who did not peacefully acquiesce were beaten into submission.

Life of the Plains Indians
After they acquired the Spanish horse, the Plains Indians abandoned their former agricultural lifestyle in favor of a strong, unique culture based upon nomadic hunting of the buffalo. Though the Plains Indians generally existed in tribes of thousands people, they lived in smaller bands of several hundred. Within the culture of the Plains Indians, men and women existed in relative egalitarianism as the occupations of both were necessary for group survival.

Searching for an Indian Policy
Earlier in the century, the Great Plains, known as the Great American Desert, was considered by the United States government as unusable for whites and was given to the Native Americans as "one big reservation." But with the discovery of gold in the West, the federal government began a policy of concentration, restricting tribes to specific, limited reservations. This new policy led to conflicts and violence among Native American groups and with whites.

Final Battles on the Plains
From 1867 to 1890, the federal government fought a number of tribes in brutal military campaigns, eliminating any semblance of resistance and culminating in the Massacre at Wounded Knee.

The End of Tribal Life
In the 1870s and 1880s, Congress began a new policy to try to end tribal authority, turn Native Americans into farmers, and educate their children to be more like whites. The Dawes Act of 1887

forced Native Americans to live on individual plots of land and allowed 90 million acres of Indian lands to be sold to white settlers. The crushing blow to traditional tribal ways resulted from the near extermination of the buffalo by white hunters. By 1900, there were only 250,000 Native Americans counted in the census, down from nearly five million in 1492, most of them suffering from extreme poverty and the problems associated with it.

Settlement of the West
In the last three decades of the nineteenth century, whites, along with some blacks, Hispanics, and Asians, moved west seeking adventure, better health and economic opportunity, or religious freedom, in the case of the Mormons.

Men and Women on the Overland Trail
Some one-half million settlers flocked to the West, especially California and Oregon, in the three decades after the Gold Rush of 1849. Traveling the Overland Trail, men and women found the journey both arduous and dangerous. For women in particular, the movement to the West meant separation from friends and family, loneliness, and exhaustive work.

Land for the Taking
Government policy, beginning with the Homestead Act of 1862, provided free or inexpensive land to individual settlers, land speculators, and private corporations like railroads, all of whom were eager to supply the desire of a growing nation for products from the West. Railroads became the West's largest landowners. Often, unscrupulous speculators and companies took advantage of these government land programs.

The Spanish-Speaking Southwest
The Spanish-Mexican heritage of the Southwest also influenced Americans in the West and gave a distinctive shape to that area's politics, language, society, and law.

The Bonanza West
Quests for quick profits led to boom-and-bust cycles in the western economy, wasted resources, and uneven growth.

The Mining Bonanza
Lured by the prospect of mineral wealth throughout the region, many settlers moved west, building hasty and often short-lived communities that reflected primarily materialistic and exploitative interests. Individual prospectors made the first strikes using a process of place mining. As the placers mines gave out, corporations moved in to dig the deep shafts, employing many foreign-born miners, who faced hostility and discrimination. Huge strikes like the Comstock Lode added millions of dollars to the economy, however by the 1890s the mining bonanza was over.

The Cattle Bonanza
Between 1865 and 1885, large profits also were possible for the cattle ranchers who grazed their herds on the prairie grasses. The ranchers used cowboys, many of whom were black or Hispanic, to drive the herds to the railheads. By 1880 more than six million cattle had been driven to northern markets, but the establishment of ranches with barbed wire and the invention of new technologies like the refrigerated railroad car ended the possibility of and need for great drives.

The Farming Bonanza
Like the miners and cattlemen, millions of farmers moved onto the Great Plains seeking economic opportunity as well. Known as *Exodusters*, many of these settlers were blacks fleeing oppression in the South. White or black, Plains farmers encountered enormous hardships, including a lack of accessible water, inadequate lumber for homes and fences, devastatingly hot summer winds, and savage winter storms. Farmers adapted to these conditions through innovations such as barbed wire.

Discontent on the Farm
Bad weather, low prices, and rising railroad rates stirred up many farmers' anger, leading some to form political lobbies and others to adopt more scientific, commercial methods. The Grange and the Farmers' Alliance were organizations that worked for farmers' interests and met important social and economic needs.

The Final Fling
The Oklahoma land rush of 1889 symbolized the closing of the frontier and in many ways reflected the attitude of Anglo-Americans toward Native Americans and their land.

Conclusion: The Meaning of the West
In the 1890s, historian Frederick Jackson Turner theorized that the West and Americans' settlement of it explained American development, by shaping American customs and character, and giving rise to the American ideals of independence and self-reliance, all while fostering invention and adaptation. Later historians challenged Turner's thesis, by pointing out that frontier conservatism, imitativeness, and the importance of family and community on the frontier were more important in shaping Americas development, as opposed to individualism. "New Western Historians" have rejected Turner's ideas altogether, producing a complex view of the West in which racial and ethnic diversity and conflict dominate, and white Americans can be said to have conquered rather than settled the West.

LEARNING OBJECTIVES

After mastering this chapter, you should be able to:

1. Describe the geographic and climatic conditions of the land between Missouri and the Pacific.

2. Distinguish the basic cultural features of the Pueblo, Plains, California, and Northwestern Indian tribes.

3. Analyze the various factors that ended tribal life for Native Americans.

4. Explain the United States's policies toward Native Americans and the results of those policies.

5. Discuss the motives that stimulated migration to the West.

6. Describe the journey along the Overland Trail for men and women.

7. List and explain the land laws passed by the federal government in the latter nineteenth century.

8. Locate the mineral strikes of the West and describe the life that developed in the mining camps.

9. Trace the boom-and-bust development of the open-range cattle industry.

10. Describe the problems faced by early farmers of the Great Plains and the ways with which they addressed their problems.

11. Describe and assess the varying interpretations of the importance of the West in American history.

GLOSSARY

To build your social science vocabulary, familiarize yourself with the following terms:

1. **nomadic** relating to a culture or tribe that moves about in search of food or pasturage. "Nomadic and warlike, the Plains Indians ..."

2. **migratory** roving or wandering from place to place, usually in response to seasonal changes. "Migratory in culture ..."

3. **assimilate** to make similar, alike, or to bring into conformity with. "... urging instead that the nation assimilate them individually into white culture ..."

4. **speculators** buyers or sellers who expect to profit from market fluctuations. "Speculators made ingenious use of the land laws."

5. **placer mining** surface mining in which gravels are picked or dredged from deposits; ore is separated from the wastes by panning or sluicing...." they used a simple process called placer mining."

6. **simple democracy** uncomplicated rules and penalties characteristic of the government of early mining towns. "Mining camps were governed by a simple democracy."

7. **exploitation** using a natural resource or economic condition for one's own profit. "Instead, migration, development, and economic exploitation continued into the twentieth and ..."

8. **Sooner** settler who moved onto government land before it officially opens, hence, a nickname for an Oklahoman. "... 'Sooners' (those who had jumped the gun) reflected the speed of western settlement ..."

IDENTIFICATION

Briefly identify the meaning and significance of the following terms:

1. Chivington massacre _____

_____

3. Wounded Knee _____

_____

4. Dawes Severalty Act _____

_____

5. Overland Trail _____

_____

6. Homestead Act of 1862 _____

_____

7. Comstock Lode _____

_____

8. Chinese Exclusion Act _____

_____

9. The Grange _____

_____

10. Exodusters _____

_____

MATCHING

A. Match the following leaders with the appropriate description:

_____1. Black Kettle

    a. Sioux chief who ambushed Captain William J. Fetterman in response to the government's plans to build the Bozeman Trail

_____2. Red Cloud

    b. leader of the Cheyenne during the massacre by Colonel John M. Chivington at Sand Creek

_____3. Wovoka

    c. Paiute messiah whose visions began the Ghost Dance

_____4. Crazy Horse

    d. war chief of the Sioux who led them in battle against Lieutenant Colonel George A. Custer at Little Big Horn

_____5. Sitting Bull

    e. Sioux medicine man who helped lead the Sioux War

    f. Nez Percè chief who led his tribe on a phenomenal flight to Canada in 1877

B. Match the following individuals with the appropriate description:

_____1. Horace Greeley

    a. early explorer who thought the land west of the Mississippi uninhabitable for whites

_____2. "Buffalo Bill" Cody

    b. historian who wrote that the frontier shaped American character

_____3. "Wild Bill" Hickok

    c. editor who urged unemployed readers to settle western farms

_____4. Oliver Kelley

    d. made a profitable business out of Wild West shows

_____5. Frederick Jackson Turner

    e. western legend who tamed Kansas cow towns and died in Deadwood

    f. government clerk who founded organizations to provide farmers with social, cultural, and educational activities

COMPLETION

Answer the question or complete the statement by filling in the blanks with the correct word or words.

1. Historian Walter Prescott Webb argued that the Great Plains lacked two of the three legs on which eastern civilization had stood. The three legs were _____, _____, and _____.

2. The Paiute messiah Wovoka claimed to have had a vision that Indians would gain a new life if they performed the_____.

3. The Plains Indians developed a nomadic lifestyle following, hunting, and living off every part of the _____.

4. One of the most famous professional buffalo hunters and the producer of a "Wild West" show was _____.

5. Most wagon trains bound for the West began their journey at points along the _____ River.

6. Passed in 1902, the _____ set aside proceeds from the sale of public land in the West to fund irrigation projects.

7. Joseph A. Glidden's invention of _____ in 1874 provided farmers with cheap and effective fencing material.

8. Started in 1867 as a social, cultural, and educational group for isolated farmers, the _____ quickly became a rural political organization.

9. In 1889, Congress forced the Creek and Seminole tribes out of present-day _____, opening it for settlement by whites.

10. African Americans who migrated to the west in 1879 fleeing southern oppression and discrimination were known as _____ .

24

TRUE/FALSE

Mark the following statement either T (True) or F (False):

_____1.   Westerners created subsistence economies that were largely independent of both eastern capital and the federal government.

_____2.   The material culture of the Plains Indians was based on a diversity of animal and plant life.

_____3.   United States policy toward Native Americans was aimed at maintaining tribal life.

_____4.   Red Cloud's victories caused the government to change policy and attempt to "civilize" Native American tribes.

_____5.   Americans settled more land between 1870 and 1900 than in all the years before 1870.

_____6.   Government officials made sure that only legitimate farming families received any of the federal lands.

_____7.   The Spanish-Mexican heritage of the Southwest had an important impact on the development of that region.

_____8.   The mining and cattle industries experienced a slow but steady growth pattern in the decades after the Civil War.

_____9.   The Great Plains area was a problem for Anglo settlers because of Native American tribes, the relative scarcity of trees, and the inadequacy of rainfall.

_____10. The droughts of the 1880s slowed the march of the pioneer Anglo farmers.

MULTIPLE CHOICE

Circle the one alternative that best completes the statement or answers the question.

1. The Ghost Dance
   a. was practiced by the Sioux Indians on the Great Plains.
   b. would bring back buffalo herds and push whites off Indian lands, according to its practitioners.
   c. led to the battle of Wounded Knee.
   d. All of the above.

2. The Plains Indians were
   a. organized into one large and powerful tribal group.
   b. an insignificant proportion of the total Native American population in the United States in 1870.
   c. a complex of tribes, cultures, and bands that assigned most work on the basis of sex.
   d. at a distinct disadvantage when fighting whites because of weapons.

3. Government policy toward Native Americans
   a. ignored or opposed tribal organization.
   b. was consistent but not successful because of tribal organization.
   c. was formulated by humanitarians who wanted to preserve tribal organization.
   d. was a failure because the Indians insisted on being farmers.

4. All of the following were problems for the pioneer farmers of the Great Plains except
   a. lack of rain
   b. declining crop prices
   c. lack of available land
   d. inadequate housing materials

5. By the 1700s, the culture of the Plains Indians had been revolutionized by
   a. reservation life.
   b. new farming techniques.
   c. the Pueblo Indians.
   d. the introduction of the European horse.

6. The Dawes Severalty Act of 1887
   a. gave small plots of reservation lands to individual Native Americans.
   b. succeeded because it respected tribal organization.
   c. placed power in the hands of the Indians' traditional leaders or chiefs.
   d. prevented the alienation of Indian leaders.

7. Between 1870 and 1900, most settlers moved west to
   a. seek freedom from religious persecution.
   b. escape the drab routine of factory life.
   c. escape the diseased conditions of crowded eastern cities.
   d. improve their economic situation.

8. The most difficult leg of the Overland Trail was the
   a. initial journey to Fort Kearney.
   b. pass through the Rocky Mountains.
   c. barren stretch between Fort Laramie and Fort Hall.
   d. final trek through the desert and the Sierra Nevada.

9. One purpose of the Dawes Act was to
   a. separate the civilized from the uncivilized tribes.
   b. enforce all previous treaties between the federal government and the various tribes.
   c. force Native Americans to abandon the communal ownership of land.
   d. support Native American religions, such as the Ghost Dance movement.

10. Between 1862 and 1890, the federal government gave more land to
    a. individual homesteaders.
    b. private corporations.
    c. railroad companies.
    d. state governments.

11. Cities like Abilene and Dodge City owed their population growth and prosperity in the latter nineteenth century to
    a. silver mining.
    b. their location in the farming belt.
    c. shipping or receiving cattle.
    d. the discovery of oil in nearby fields.

12. The Great Plains presented farmers with one problem not faced by farmers of earlier American frontiers which was
    a. hostile Indians.
    b. scarce water and timber.
    c. isolation and loneliness.
    d. inadequate transportation.

13. One of the results of the rapid increase in cultivated acreage during the latter half of the nineteenth century was
    a. higher tariffs on farm products.
    b. lower prices for farm products.
    c. a decrease in demand for farm machinery.
    d. an increase in land values.

14. The farming boom on the Plains lasted until the
    a. Panic of 1893.
    b. bumper crop of 1884.
    c. rise of the bonanza farms in the 1870s.
    d. droughts of 1887–1894.

15. By the Dawes Act of 1887, the Indian Bureau tried to
    a. end the traditional Native American religions and encourage Christianity among the tribes.
    b. increase the power of the tribal councils.
    c. establish Indian-controlled and -funded educational institutions.
    d. seek out urban-industrial employment for young, male Indians.

THOUGHT QUESTIONS

To check your understanding of the key issues of this period, solve the following problems:

1. Was Horace Greeley's 1867 editorial on the agrarian opportunity of the West an overly optimistic view of the conditions and forces at work on the Great Plains?

2. Why did the policy of the government toward Native Americans waver from 1834 to 1934?

3. Theodore Roosevelt once stated that the only alternative to the defeat of the Indian was to "keep the entire continent as a game preserve for squalid savages." Explain the causes and results of such an attitude.

4. What factors propelled and made possible rapid settlement of the American West from 1870 to 1900? What were the economic and political consequences?

5. What influence did the Spanish-Mexican heritage have on the development of the American Southwest?

CRITICAL THINKING QUESTIONS

After reading Black Elk, "Account of the Wounded Knee Massacre," (1890), Benjamin Harrison, "Report on Wounded Knee Massacre and the Decrease in Indian Land Acreage," (1891), and Frederick Jackson Turner, "The Significance of the Frontier in American History," (1893), answer the following questions:

Black Elk, "Account of the Wounded Knee Massacre" (1890)

It was about this time that bad news came to use from the north. We heard that some policemen from Standing Rock had gone to arrest Sitting Bull on Grand River, and that he would not let them take him; so there was a fight, and they killed him.

It was now the end of the Moon of Popping Trees, and I was twenty-seven years old [December 1890]. We heard that Big Foot was coming down from the Badlands with nearly four hundred people. Some of these were from Sitting Bull's band. They had run away when Sitting Bull was killed, and joined Big Foot on Good River. There were only about a hundred warriors in this band, and all the others were women and children and some old men. They were all starving and freezing, and Big Foot was so sick that they had to bring him along in a pony drag. They had all run away to hide in the Badlands, and they were coming now because they were starving and freezing. Soldiers were over there looking for them. The soldiers had everything and were not freezing and starving. Near Porcupine Butte the soldiers came up to the Big Foots, and they surrendered and went along with the soldiers to Wounded Knee Creek.

It was in the evening when we heard that the Big Foots were camped over there with the soldiers, about fifteen miles by the old road from where we were. It was the next morning [December 29, 1890] that something terrible happened.

That evening before it happened, I went into Pine Ridge and heard these things, and while I was there, soldiers started for where the Big Foots were. These made about five hundred soldiers that were there next morning. When I saw them starting I felt that something terrible was going to happen. That night I could hardly sleep at all. I walked around most of the night.

In the morning I went out after my horses, and while I was out I heard shooting off toward the east, and I knew from the sound that it must be wagon-guns [cannon] going off. The sounds went right through my body, and I felt that something terrible would happen … [He donned his ghost shirt, and armed only with a bow, mounted his pony and rode in the direction of the shooting, and was joined on the way by others.]

In a little while we had come to the top of the ridge where, looking to the east, you can see for the first time the monument and the burying ground on the little hill where the church is. That is where the terrible thing started. Just south of the burying ground on the little hill a deep dry gulch runs about east and west, very crooked, and it rises westward to nearly the top of the ridge where we were. It had no name, but the Wasichus [while men] sometimes called Battle Creek now. We stopped on the ridge not far from the head of the dry gulch. Wagon guns were still going off over there on the little hill, and they were going off again where they hit among the gulch. There was much shooting down yonder, and there were many cries, and we could see calvarymen scattered over the hills ahead of us. Calvarymen were riding along the gulch and shooting into it, where the women and children were running away and trying to hide in the gullies and the stunted pines.…

We followed down along the dry gulch, and what we saw was terrible. Dead and wounded women and children and little babies were scattered all along there where they had been trying to run away. The soldiers had followed along the gulch, as they ran, and murdered them in there. Sometimes they were in heaps because they had huddled together, and some were scattered all along. Sometimes bunches of them had been killed and torn to pieces where the wagon guns hit them. I saw a little baby trying to suck its mother, but she was bloody and dead.

There were two little boys at one place in this gulch. They had guns and they had been killing soldiers all by themselves. We could see the soldiers they had killed. The boys were all alone there, and they were not hurt. These were very brave little boys.

When we drove the soldiers back, they dug themselves in, and we were not enough people to drive them out from there. In the evening they marched off up Wounded Knee Creek, and then we saw all that they had one there.

Men and women and children were heaped and scattered all over the flat at the bottom of the little hill where the soldiers had their wagon-guns, and westward up the dry gulch all the way to the high ridge, the dead women and children and babies were scattered.

When I saw this I wished that I had died too, but I was not sorry for the women and children. It was better for them to be happy in the other world, and I wanted to be there too. But before I went there I wanted to have revenge. I thought there might be a day, and we should have revenge.

In the morning the soldiers began to take all the guns away from the Big Foots, who were camped in the flat below the little hill where the monument and burying ground are now. The people had stacked most of their guns, and even their knives, by the teepee where Big Foot was lying sick. Soldiers were on the little hill and all around, and there were soldiers across the dry gulch to the south and over east along Wounded Knee Creek too. The people were nearly surrounded, and the wagon-guns were pointed at them.

It was a good winter day when all this happened. The sun was shining. But after the soldiers marched away from their dirty work, a heavy snow began to fall. The wind came up in the night. There was a big blizzard, and it grew very cold. The snow drifted deep in the crooked gulch, and it was one long grave of butchered women and children and babies, who had never done any harm and were only trying to run away.

Benjamin Harrison, "Report on Wounded Knee Massacre and the Decrease in Indian Land Acreage" (1891)

The outbreak among the Sioux which occurred in December last is as to its causes and incidents fully reported upon by the War Department and the Department of the Interior. That these Indians had some just complaints, especially in the matter of the reduction of the appropriation for rations and in the delays attending the enactment of laws to enable the Department to perform the engagements entered into with them, is probably true; but the Sioux tribes are naturally warlike and turbulent, and their warriors were excited by their medicine men and chiefs, who preached the coming of an Indian messiah who was to give them power to destroy their enemies. In view of the alarm that prevailed among the white settlers near the reservation and of the fatal consequences that would have resulted from an Indian incursion, I placed at the disposal of General Miles, commanding the Division of the Missouri, all such forces as we thought by him to be required. He is entitled to the credit of having given thorough protection to the settlers and of bringing the hostiles into subjection with the least possible loss of life....

Since March 4, 1889, about 23,000,000 acres have been separated from Indian reservations and added to the public domain for the use of those who desired to secure free homes under our beneficent laws. It is difficult to estimate the increase of wealth which will result from the conversion of these waste lands into farms, but it is more difficult to estimate the betterment which will result to the families that have found renewed hope and courage in the ownership of a home and the assurance of a comfortable subsistence under free and healthful conditions. It is also gratifying to be able to feel, as we may, that this work has proceeded upon lines of justice toward the Indian, and that he may now, if he will, secure to himself the good influences of a settled habitation, the fruits of industry, and the security of citizenship.

Frederick Jackson Turner, "The Significance of the Frontier in American History" (1893)

Up to our own day American history has been in a large degree the history of the colonization of the Great West. The existence of an area of free land, continuous recession, and the advance of American settlements westward, explain American development.

Behind institutions, behind constitutional forms and modifications lie the vital forces that call these organs into life and shape them to meet changing conditions. The peculiarity of American institutions is, the fact that they have been compelled to adapt themselves to the changes of an expanding people-to the changes involved in crossing a continent, this winning a wilderness, and in developing at each area of this progress out of the primitive economic and political conditions of the frontier into the complexity of city life....

Thus American development has exhibited not merely advance along a single line, but a return to primitive conditions on a continually advancing frontier line, and a new development for that area. American social development has been continually beginning over again on the frontier. This perennial rebirth, this fluidity of American life, this expansion westward with its new opportunities, its continuous touch with the simplicity of primitive society, furnish the forces dominating American character. The true point of view in the history of this nation is not the Atlantic coast, it is the West....

The frontier is the line of most rapid and effective Americanization. The wilderness masters the colonist. It finds him a European in dress, industries, tools, modes of travel, and thought. It takes him from the railroad car and puts him in the birch canoe. It strips off the garments of civilization and arrays him in the hunting shirt and the moccasin. It puts him in the log cabin of the Cherokee and Iroquois and runs and Indian palisade around him. Before long he has gone to planting Indian corn and plowing with a sharp stick; he shouts the war cry and takes the scalp in orthodox Indian fashion. In short, at the frontier the environment is at first too strong for the man. He must accept the conditions which it furnishes, or perish, and so he fits himself into the Indian clearings and follows the Indian trails. Little by little he transforms the wilderness but the outcome is not the old Europe, not simply the development of Germanic germs, any more than the first phenomenon was a case of reversion to the Germanic mark. The fact is, that here is a new product that is American. At first, the frontier was the Atlantic coast. It was the frontier of Europe in a very real sense. Moving westward, the frontier became more and more American. As successive terminal moraines result from successive glaciations, so each frontier leaves its traces behind it, and when it becomes a settled area the region still partakes of the frontier characteristics. Thus the advance of the frontier has meant a steady movement away from the influence of Europe, a steady growth of independence on American lines. And to study this advance, the men who grew up under these conditions, and the political, economic, and social results of its, is to study the really American part of our history....

Since the days when the fleet of Columbus sailed into the waters of the New World, America has been another name for opportunity, and the people of the United States have taken their tone form the incessant expansion which has not only been open but has been forced upon them. He would be a rash prophet who should assert that the expansive character has now entirely ceased. Movement has been its dominant fact, and unless this training has no effect upon a people, the American energy will continually demand a wider field for its exercise. But never again will such gifts of free land offer themselves. For a moment, at the frontier, the bonds of custom are broken and unrestraint is triumphant. There is not tabula rasa. The stubborn American environment is there with its imperious summons to accept its conditions; the inherited ways of doing things are also there; and yet, in spite of environment, and in spite of custom, each frontier did indeed furnish a new field of opportunity, a gate of escape from the bondage of the past; and freshness and confidence, and scorn of older society, impatience of its restrains and its ideas, and indifference to its lessons, have accompanied the frontier. What the Mediterranean Sea was to the Greeks, breaking the bond of custom, offering new experiences, calling out new institutions and activities, that, and more, the ever retreating frontier has been to the United States directly, and to the nations of Europe more remotely. And now, four centuries from the discovery of America, at the end of a hundred years of life under the Constitution, the frontier has gone, and with its going has closed the first period in American history.

1. What were the immediate causes of the Wounded Knee Massacre?

2. What were the longer term, more fundamental causes of the inability of whites and Indians to avoid such events as the Wounded Knee Massacre?

3. What is the basic thesis of Turner regarding the most important influence on the American character?

4. What are the implications of Turner referring to the "area of free land" and the Wounded Knee Massacre?

5. Looking back at the Puritan ethos expressed by John Winthrop's notion of a "city upon a hill," and at the ideas of Manifest Destiny, compare these ideas with those of Turner.

CHAPTER 18

The Industrial Society, 1850–1901

SUMMARY
By their centennial of 1876, Americans were rapidly developing their society. Most important in this development was an increase in industrialism and the effects industrialism had on American culture and society.

Industrial Development
Several factors contributed to the rapid economic transformation of the era: an abundance of natural resources for materials, an increasing supply of laborers, an expanded consumer marketplace, increases in railroads for transportation, a plethora of confident investors for capital, and new technology and innovations. Federal, state, and local government also fostered economic growth by providing monetary and resource grants to companies, stability, and freedom from regulation.

An Empire on Rails
Revolutionary changes in transportation and communication, especially the growth of railroads, transformed American life.

Advantages of the Railroad
By ending rural isolation, encouraging economic specialization, creating a national market, and capturing the nation's imagination, the railroads transformed production, distribution, and business practices.

Building the Empire
By the end of the century, Americans, with substantial assistance from federal and state governments, had built almost 200,000 miles of track. Despite much waste and corruption, the railroads probably did more good than harm. For example, they saved the federal government $1 billion from 1850 to 1945.

Linking the Nation via Trunk Lines
Before the Civil War, railroad construction served local markets. After 1865, however, the railroads tied much of the nation together through a system of trunk lines over which passengers and freight traveled with relative speed, comfort, and safety. In the South, railroads were not consolidated and integrated into the national railroad system until after Reconstruction.

Rails Across the Continent
Congress voted to allow two companies, Union Pacific, working westward, and Central Pacific, working eastward, to compete in the construction of the first transcontinental railroad. Having

33

begun in 1863, but lagging somewhat during the war, they completed the tracks in May 1869. By 1893, four more railroad lines reached the west coast.

Problems of Growth

Overbuilding generated vigorous rate wars and intense competition for passengers and freight. At first, railroad managers tried and failed to reduce conflict through cooperation. After 1893, financiers like J. P. Morgan refinanced the railroads and took over the industry, constructing regional monopolies that effectively eliminated competition.

An Industrial Empire

The Bessemer process made possible an industrial empire based on steel.

Carnegie and Steel

The process for manufacturing steel required a great deal of capital, access to abundant resources, and sophisticated production techniques. These requirements limited the number of companies able to participate in the industry to the few that could afford it, including most notably Carnegie Steel Company. Steel companies like Carnegie's grew very large and competition among them was fierce until Carnegie led the industry in a movement toward vertical integration as a means of eliminating competition. In 1901, J. P. Morgan acquired Carnegie Steel Company and several others, combining them into the country's first billion-dollar corporation, U.S. Steel.

Rockefeller and Oil

The oil industry also boomed during this era with John D. Rockefeller as its undisputed king. He reorganized the chaotic oil industry through consolidation, pioneering a new kind of business organization—the trust. By the 1890s, Rockefeller had recognized the cumbersome nature of the trust and reorganized Standard Oil into a holding company.

The Business of Invention

The business of invention also boomed—from fewer than 2,000 patents per year during the 1850s to more than 20,000 per year by the 1880s and 1890s. These inventions transformed the communication, clothing, food, lighting, and power industries.

The Sellers

The advent of brand names, print advertising, chain stores, and mail-order houses in what is known as the *science of marketing* brought the new goods to households far and wide and initiated a new and seemingly unified community of consumers.

The Wage Earners

The labor of millions of men and women made the Untied States's emerging economic empire possible. The lives of Americans improved in many respects because of new goods, expanded health and educational opportunities, better wages and working conditions, and increased influence in national affairs.

Working Men, Working Women, Working Children
At the same time, life for workers was hard, especially unskilled laborers. They suffered grueling, often dangerous jobs, for relatively low pay. There were few holidays or vacations and no life or health insurance system. Men, women, and children were often forced to work in order to make ends meet. Women and children along with African Americans, Catholics, Jews, and immigrants carried an additional burden of discrimination.

Culture of Work
All workers found that the new factory system required difficult and often demeaning adaptations to age-old patterns of work. Most noteworthy of these changes was factory discipline. Workers worked indoors according to a clock with a strict hierarchy of supervisors and harsh rules. As industries grew, work became more and more impersonal. Even so, most workers accepted the system because it offered substantial social mobility.

Labor Unions
National unions gradually took shape during the era and approached the problems of labor in different ways. The Knights of Labor, for example, was organized like a fraternal order and sought broad social reforms, while the American Federation of Labor organized craft unions of skilled workers and sought practical, immediate, and tangible improvements for its members. Few labor unions allowed women or African Americans to join.

Labor Unrest
Though workers joined unions for better wages and working conditions, they also found in them and other social and fraternal organizations companionship, insurance, job listings, and even food for the sick. Employees tried to humanize the factory while employers tried to determine wages and conditions on the basis of supply and demand rather than the welfare of the workers. This conflict of purposes often led to violent strikes. An injunction was the most useful tool employers had to end workers' strikes.

Conclusion: Industrialization's Benefits and Costs
To be sure, industrial growth meant progress and power but it also meant rapid change, social instability, exploitation of labor, and a growing gap between rich and poor.

LEARNING OBJECTIVES

After mastering this chapter, you should be able to:

1. Discuss each of the major factors that contributed to the rapid industrialization of the United States from 1870 to 1900.

2. Describe the principal economic and social effects of the railroad from 1865 to 1900 and trace the building of the American railroad network from 1865 to 1900.

3. Detail the rise and consolidation of the steel industry.

4. Detail the rise and consolidation of the oil industry.

5. List and describe the most important inventions of the last third of the nineteenth century, including their major effects.

6. Identify and explain each of the major factors in the development of a national consumer market.

7. Compare and contrast the effects of industrialization on the working lives of native-born white Anglo-Saxon Protestant males and, on the other hand, women, children, Catholics, Jews, and immigrants.

8. Identify the adaptations in the culture of work required by the new factory system, and the response to those changes by working people.

9. Compare and contrast the policies and methods of the Knights of Labor and the American Federation of Labor.

10. Discuss the violence that emerged from employer/employee conflict and assess the role of the U.S. government in restoring order.

GLOSSARY

To build your social science vocabulary, familiarize yourself with the following terms:

1. **entrepreneurs** those who assume the opportunities and risks for business ventures. "In this atmosphere, entrepreneurs flourished."

2. **economic specialization** the production or distribution of a specific good or service. [The railroad] "… encouraged economic specialization."

3. **trunk lines** major routes or channels of transportation. "… four great trunk lines took shape …"

4. **vertical integration** a business combination that included some of each stage of a production process. "Vertically integrated, Standard Oil owned wells, timberlands, barrel and chemical…"

5. **philanthropy** donation of money, time, or property to the needy or to institutions helping the needy. "… he wanted to devote his full time to philanthropy."

6. **trust** a type of combination of businesses to reduce competition. "… the first of the modern trusts were born."

7. **monopoly** a company that controls an economic good or service. "The word *trust* became synonymous with monopoly …"

8. **socialism** an economic system in which society owns the means of production and distribution of goods and services. "… he experimented for a time with socialism and working-class politics."

9. **anarchism** the doctrine that all governments oppress individuals and should be abolished. "Linking labor and anarchism in the public mind …"

IDENTIFICATION

Briefly identify the meaning and significance of the following terms:

1. Centennial Exposition_____

_____

2. Central and Union Pacific Railroad Companies _____

_____

3. J. P. Morgan _____

_____

4. Andrew Carnegie _____

_____

5. John D. Rockefeller_____

_____

6. Thomas Edison_____

_____

7. Knights of Labor_____

_____

8. American Federation of Labor_____

_____

9. Haymarket Riot_____

_____

10. Trunk lines_____

_____

MATCHING

A. Match the following individuals with the appropriate description:

_____1. Cornelius Vanderbilt

_____2. Andrew Carnegie

_____3. J. P. Morgan

_____4. Jay Gould

_____5. Charles Crocker

a. speculator who built railroad lines just to sell them to competitors

b. shipping magnate who put together his own railroad trunk line

c. financier who dominated American railroading

d. construction chief for the Union Pacific

e. construction chief for the Central Pacific

f. brilliant businessperson who dominated the steel industry before selling his company in 1901

B. Match the following individuals with their invention or process:

_____1. Cyrus W. Field

_____2. George Eastman

_____3. Gustavus F. Swift

_____4. Alexander Graham Bell

_____5. Frank J. Sprague

a. photographic process that led to film

b. meat "disassembly" factory

c. telephone

d. electric streetcar system

e. improved transatlantic cable

f. use of high-voltage alternating current

COMPLETION

Answer the question or complete the statement by filling in the blanks with the correct word or words.

1. The exhibit that attracted the most attention at the 1876 Centennial Exposition was the

   _____.

2. _____ became the nation's leading figure in finance by helping to make railroads more efficient and orderly.

3. The_____ first divided the United States into four time zones.

4. _____ immigrants contributed much of the labor to building the transcontinental railroad, but were later excluded from coming to the United States by a 1882 law.

5. Financier J. P. Morgan combined Carnegie's company with others to establish the

   _____.

6. To centralize control of Standard Oil, John D. Rockefeller led in the establishment of the first modern _____ in 1882.

7. Between the 1850s and 1890s, the number of patents issued to inventors increased from fewer than _____ a year to more than _____ a year.

8. Sears, Roebuck and Montgomery Ward started as _____ businesses.

9. _____ is the business process by which a single company owns and controls the entire process from the unearthing of raw materials to the manufacture and sale of the finished product.

10. The violence in Pennsylvania at the _____ in 1892 led many Americans to regret the heavy price of social upheaval that accompanied industrialization.

TRUE/FALSE

Mark the following statements either T (True) or F (False):

_____1.   By 1900, America's manufacturing output exceeded that of Great Britain, France, and Germany combined.

_____2.   Although the railroads tied together the major cities, they left America's villages and rural areas in greater isolation than ever.

_____3.   Because of waste and corruption, government grants for railroad construction probably did more harm than good.

_____4.   Andrew Carnegie favored workers and unions far more than most industrialists of his era.

_____5.   J. P. Morgan and John D. Rockefeller advocated vigorous competition among corporations because it would improve the quality of goods and services and reduce prices.

_____6.   Soon after Rockefeller established his oil trust, other highly competitive industries, including the sugar industry, adopted the monopolistic method.

_____7.   The establishment of the Menlo Park research laboratory may have been as important as any other invention by Thomas Edison.

_____8.   White, native-born Protestants benefited most from early industrial society.

_____9.   In the late nineteenth century, workers often used court injunctions to protect themselves and their unions from corporate strikebreaking activities.

_____10. To increase their numbers, early unions opened membership to both women and African Americans.

MULTIPLE CHOICE

Circle the one alternative that best completes the statement or answers the question.

1. The 1876 Centennial Exposition focused mainly on
   a. American history.
   b. machinery.
   c. popular culture.
   d. art and literature.

2. Which of the following did not contribute significantly to American industrialization of the late nineteenth century?
   a. abundant resources
   b. rapid population growth
   c. international free trade
   d. investor confidence

3. Which of the following lists industrial developments in proper chronological order?
   a. the completion of the first transcontinental railroad, formation of the first trust, formation of U.S. Steel Corporation
   b. the formation of U.S. Steel Corporation, formation of the first trust, completion of the first transcontinental railroad
   c. the formation of the first trust, completion of the first transcontinental railroad, formation of U.S. Steel Corporation
   d. None of the above.

4. Which of the following industries was *not* transformed by a nineteenth-century invention by either Alexander Graham Bell or Thomas Alva Edison?
   a. communications
   b. power
   c. entertainment
   d. textiles

5. Why did trusts form in the late nineteenth century?
   a. to increase efficiency
   b. to reduce costs
   c. to decrease competition
   d. to increase the supply of capital

6. The Bessemer process transformed the steel industry because it
   a. required less capital.
   b. used far less labor.
   c. produced more durable steel.
   d. used cheap ore.

7. John D. Rockefeller's methods for defeating competitors did not include
   a. high quality and low prices.
   b. threats and bribery.
   c. spies and harassment.
   d. financial support from J. P. Morgan.

8. According to Herbert Gutman, industrialization transformed the "culture of work." Which of the following best states his meaning?
   a. Industrialization dramatically increased leisure time.
   b. Workers eagerly adopted the new technology because it made their work much easier.
   c. The new technology often required difficult and demeaning adaptations of work patterns.
   d. Low pay led to frequent worker resistance, especially "sit-down" strikes.

9. Which of these produced NO innovations for marketing or merchandising?
   a. John Wanamaker
   b. Samuel C. T. Dodd
   c. R. H. Macy
   d. Marshall Field

10. It took about $600 per year to have a decent standard of living in the 1890s, while workers earned a yearly average of
    a. $300–$400.
    b. $400–$500.
    c. $500–$600.
    d. $600–$700.

11. When a substantial number of women entered a profession,
    a. they became a majority of its workers.
    b. men took its management positions.
    c. many men left for jobs in other fields.
    d. All of the above.

12. According to social historian Stephan Thernstrom, what was the extent of social mobility in America in the early industrial era?
    a. almost none
    b. some, but not much
    c. substantial, but limited
    d. a great deal

13. Which of the following best describes the early American Federation of Labor?
    a. an alliance of industrial unions that tried to change the economic system.
    b. an alliance of industrial unions that tried to improve wages and working conditions.
    c. an alliance of craft unions that tried to change the economic system.
    d. an alliance of craft unions that tried to improve wages and working conditions.

14. Which of the following best describes the Knights of Labor?
    a. a union of producers aimed at uplifting, utopian reform
    b. a union of producers aimed only at improving wages and working conditions
    c. a federation of industrial unions aimed at making each man his own employer
    d. a federation of craft unions aimed only at improving wages and working conditions

15. The Haymarket riot weakened the labor movement because it
    a. linked labor and anarchism in the minds of many people.
    b. demonstrated the ineffectiveness of unions.
    c. revealed the violent nature of unions.
    d. initiated the use of court injunctions against strikes.

THOUGHT QUESTIONS

To check your understanding of the key issues of this period, solve the following problems:

1. Was the industrial revolution inevitable, or could Americans have maintained a more agricultural economy?

2. Why did so many Americans accept, and even applaud, ruthless methods used to accumulate personal fortunes?

3. Are our early industrialists best described as "captains of industry" or as "robber barons"?

4. What were the costs and the benefits of the development of an American "community of consumers"?

5. American workers could have gained more by adopting the program of the Knights of Labor rather than that of the American Federation of Labor. True or false? Explain your answer.

CRITICAL THINKING QUESTIONS

Although the following three readings do not all fit within the timeframe of this chapter, each gives a different viewpoint on the effects of industrialization. After reading Andrew Carnegie, from "The Gospel of Wealth" (1899), Mother Jones, "The March of the Mill Children" (1903), and Rose Schneiderman, "The Triangle Fire" (1911), answer the following questions:

Andrew Carnegie, from "The Gospel of Wealth" (1889)

The problem of our age is the proper administration of wealth, that the ties of brotherhood may still bind together the rich and poor in harmonious relationship. The conditions of human life have not only been changed, but revolutionized, within the past few hundred years. In former days there was little difference between the dwelling, dress, food, and environment of the chief and those of his retainers.... The contrast between the palace of the millionaire and the cottage of the laborer with us to-day measures the change which has come with civilization. This change, however, is not to be deplored, but welcomed as highly beneficial. It is well, say, essential, for the progress of the race that the houses of some should be homes for all that is highest and best in literature and the arts, and for all the refinements of civilization, rather than that none should be so. Much better this great irregularity than universal squalor. Without wealth there can be no Meccenas.

... to-day the world obtains commodities of excellent quality at prices which even the preceding generation would have deemed incredible. In the commercial world similar causes have produced similar results, and the race is benefited thereby. The poor enjoy what the rich could not before afford. What were the luxuries have become the necessaries of life ...

Objections to the foundations upon which society is based are not in order, because the condition of the race is better with these than it has been with any other which has been tried.... No evil, but good, has come to the race from the accumulation of wealth by those who have had the ability and energy to produce it....

We start, then, with a condition of affairs under which the best interests of the race are promoted, but which inevitably gives wealth to the few.... What is the proper mode of administering wealth after the laws upon which civilization is founded have thrown it into the hands of the few?...

There are but three modes in which surplus wealth can be disposed of. It can be left to the families of the decedents; or it can be bequeathed for public purposes; or, finally, it can be administered by its possessors during their lives....

There remains, then, only one mode of suing great fortunes; but in this we have the true antidote for the temporary unequal distribution of wealth, the reconciliation of the rich and the poor-a reign of harmony, another ideal, differing, indeed, from that of the Communist in requiring only the further evolution of existing conditions, not the total overthrow of our civilization. It is founded upon the most intense Individualism.... Under its sway we shall have an ideal State, in which the surplus wealth of the few will become, in the best sense, property of the many, because administering for the common good; and this wealth, passes through the hands of the few, can be made much more potent force for the elevation of our race than if distributed in small sums to the people themselves. Even the poorest can be made to see this, and to agree that great sums gathered by some of their fellow-citizens-spent for public purposes, from which masses reap the principal benefit, are more valuable to them than if scattered among themselves in trifling amounts through the course of many years.

If we consider the results which flow from the Cooper Institute, for instance ... , and compare these with those who would have ensured for the good of the man form an equal sum distributed by Mr. Cooper in his lifetime in the form of wages, which the highest form of distributing, being work done and not for charity, we can estimate of the possibilities for the improvement of the race which lie embedded in the present law of the accumulation of wealth....

This, then, is held to be the duty of the man of wealth: To set an example of modest, unostentatious living, shunning display or extravagance; to provide moderately for the legitimate wants of those dependent upon him; and, after doing so, to consider all surplus revenues which come to him simply as trust funds, which he is called upon to administer, and strictly bound as a matter of duty to administer in the manner which, in his judgment, is best calculated to produce the most beneficial results for the community-the man of wealth thus becoming the mere trustee and agent for his poorer brethren, bringing to their service his superior wisdom, experience, and ability to administer, doing for them better than they would or could do for them selves....

In bestowing charity, the main consideration should be to help those who will help themselves; to provide part of the means by which those who desire to improve may do so; to give those who desire to rise the aids by which they may rise; to assist, but rarely or never to do all. Neither the individual nor the race is improved by alms giving. Those worthy of assistance, except in rare cases, seldom require assistance....

The rich man is thus almost restricted to following the examples of Peter Cooper, Enoch Pratt of Baltimore, Mr. Pratt of Brooklyn, Senator Stanford, and others, who know that the best means of benefiting the community is to place within its reach the ladders upon which the aspiring can rise-free libraries, parks, and means of recreation, by which men are helped in body and mind; works of art, certain to give pleasure and improve the general condition of the people; in this manner returning their surplus wealth to the mass of their fellows in the forms best calculated to do them lasting good.

Thus is the problem of rich and poor to be solved. The laws of accumulation will be left free, the laws of distribution free. Individualism will continue, but the millionaire will be but a trustee for the poor, intrusted for a season with a great part of the increased wealth of the community, but administering it for the community far better than if could or would have done for itself. The best minds will thus have reached a stage in the development of the race in which it is clearly seen that there is no mode of disposing of surplus wealth creditable to thoughtful and earnest men into whose hands it flows, save by using it year by year for the general good....

Such, in my opinion, is the true gospel concerning wealth, obedience to which is destined some day to solve the problem of the rich and the poor, and to bring "Peace on earth, among men good will."

Mother Jones, "The March of the Mill Children" (1903)

In the spring of 1903 I went to Kensington, Pennsylvania, where seventy-five thousand textile workers were on strike. Of this number at least ten thousand were little children. The workers were striking for more pay and shorter hours. Every day little children came into Union Headquarters, some with their hands off, some with the thumb missing, some with their fingers off at the knuckle. They were stooped little things, round shouldered and skinny. Many of them were not over ten years of age, although the state law prohibited their working before they were twelve years of age.

The law was poorly enforced and the mothers of these children often swore falsely as to their children's age. In a single block in Kensington, fourteen women, mothers of twenty-two children all under twelve, explained it was a question of starvation or perjury. That the fathers had been killed or maimed at the mines.

I asked the newspapermen why they didn't publish the facts about child labor in Pennsylvania. They said they couldn't because the mill owners had stock in the papers.

"Well, I've got stock in these little children," said I, "and I'll arrange a little publicity."

We assembled a number of boys and girls one morning in Independence Park, and from there were arranged to parade with banners to the courthouse where we would hold a meeting.

A great crowd gathered in the public square in front of the city hall. I put the little boys with their fingers off and hands crushed and maimed on a platform. I held up their mutilated hands and showed them to the crowd, and made the statement that Philadelphia's mansions were built on the broken bones, the quivering hearts and drooping heads of these children. That their little lives went out to make wealth for others. That neither state nor city officials paid any attention to these wrongs. That they did not care that these children were to be the future citizens of the nation....

I called upon the millionaire manufacturers to cease their moral murders, and I cried to the officials in the open windows opposite, "Someday the workers will take possession of your city hall, and when we do, no child will be sacrificed on the altar of profit."

The reporters quoted my statement that Philadelphia mansions were built on the broken bones and quivering hearts of children. The Philadelphia papers and the New York papers got into a squabble with each other over the question. The universities discussed it. Preachers began talking. That was what I wanted. Public attention on the subject of child labor.

The matter quieted down for a while and I concluded the people needed stirring up again.... I asked some of the parents if they would let me have their little boys and girls for a week or ten days, promising to bring them back safe and sound. They consented. A man named Sweeny was marshall for our "army." A few men and women went with me to help with the children. They were on strike and I thought they might as well have a little recreation.

The children carried knapsacks on their backs in which was a knife and fork, a tin cup and a plate. We took along a wash boiler in which to cook the food on the road. One little fellow had a drum and another had a fife. That was our band. We carried banners that said, "We want more schools and less hospitals." "We want time to play." "Prosperity is here. Where is ours!"

We started from Philadelphia where we held a great mass meeting. I decided to go with the children to see President Roosevelt to ask him to have Congress pass a law prohibiting the exploitation of childhood. I thought that President Roosevelt might see these mill children and compare them with his own little ones who were spending the summer on the seashore at Oyster Bay....

The children were very happy, having plenty to eat, taking baths in the brooks and rivers every day. I thought when the strike is over and they go back to the mills, they will never have another holiday like this. All along the line of the march the farmers drove out to meet us with wagon loads of fruit and vegetables. Their wives brought the children clothes and money. The interurban trainmen would stop their trains and give us free rides.

We were on the outskirts of New Trenton, New Jersey, cooking our lunch in the wash boiler, when the conductor on the interurban car stopped and told us the police were coming to notify us that we could not enter the town. There were mills in the town and the mill owners didn't like our coming.

I said, "All right, the police will be just in time for lunch."

Sure enough, the police came and we invited them to dine with us. They looked at the little gathering of children with their tin plates and cups around the wash boiler. They just smiled and spoke kindly to the children, and said nothing at all about not going into the city.

We went in, held our meeting, and it was the wives of the police who took the little children and cared for them that night, sending them back in the morning with a nice lunch rolled up in paper napkins.

Everywhere we had meetings, showing up with living children, the horrors of child labor....

I called on the mayor of Princeton and asked for permission to speak opposite the campus of the University. I said I wanted to speak on higher education. The mayor gave me permission. A great crowd gathered, professors and students and the people; and I told them that the rich robbed these little children of any education of the lowest order, that they might send their sons and daughters to places of higher education.... And I showed those professors children in our army who could scarcely read or write because they were working ten hours a day in the silk mills of Pennsylvania.

"Here's a text book on economics," I said, pointing to a little chap, James Ashworth, who was ten years old and who was stooped over like an old man from carrying bundles of yarn that weighed seventy-five pounds. "He gets three dollars a week." ...

I sent a committee over to the New York Chief of Police, Ebstein, asking for permission to march up Fourth Avenue to Madison Square, where I wanted to hold a meeting. The chief refused and forbade our entrance to the city.

I went over myself to New York and saw Mayor Seth Low. The mayor was most courteous but he said he would have to support the police commissioner. I asked him what the reason was for refusing us entrance to the city, and he said that we were not citizens of New York.

"Oh, I think we will clear that up, Mr. Mayor," I said. "Permit me to call your attention to an incident which took place in this nation just a year ago. A piece of rotten royalty came over here from Germany, called Prince Henry. The Congress of the United States voted $45,000 to fill that fellow's stomach for three weeks and to entertain him. His brother was getting $4,000,000 in dividends out of the blood of the workers in this country. Was he a citizen of this land?"

"And it was reported, Mr. Mayor, that you and all the officials of New York and the University Club entertained that chap." And I repeated, "Was he a citizen of New York?"

"No, Mother," said the mayor, "he was not." ...

"Well, Mr. Mayor, these are the little citizens of the nation and they also produce its wealth. Aren't we entitled to enter your city?" ...

We marched to Twentieth Street. I told an immense crowd of the horrors of child labor in the mills around the anthracite region, and I showed them some of the children. I showed them Eddie Dunphy, a little fellow of twelve, whose job it was to sit all day on a high stool, handing in the right thread to another worker. Eleven hours a day he sat on the high stool with dangerous machinery all about him. All day long, winter and summer, spring and fall, for three dollars a week.

And then I showed them Gussie Rangnew, a little girl from whom all the childhood had gone. Her face was like an old woman's. Gussie packed stockings in a factory, eleven hours a day for a few cents a day.

We raised a lot of money for the strikers, and hundreds of friends offered their homes to the little ones while we were in the city.

The next day we went to Coney Island at the invitation of Mr. Bostick, who owned the wild animal show. The children had a wonderful time such as they never had in all their lives. After the exhibition of the trained animals, Mr. Bostick let me speak to the audience.... Right in front were the empty iron cages of the animals. I put my little children in the cages and they clung to the iron bars while I talked....

"Fifty years ago there was a cry against slavery, and men gave up their lives to stop the selling of black children on the block. Today the white child is sold for two dollars a week to the manufacturers. Fifty years ago the black babies were sold C.O.D. Today the white baby is sold on the installment plan....

"The trouble is that no one in Washington cares. I saw our legislators in one hour pass three bills for the relief of the railways, but when labor cries for aid for the children they will not listen.

"I asked a man in prison once how he happened to be there, and he said he had stolen a pair of shoes. I told him if he had stolen a railroad he would be a United States Senator.

"We are told that every American boy has the chance of being president. I tell you that these little boys in the iron cages would sell their chance any day for good square meals and a chance to play."

The next day we left Coney Island for Manhattan Beach to visit Senator Platt, who had made an appointment to see me at nine o'clock in the morning. The children got stuck in the sandbanks and I had a time cleaning the sand off the littlest ones. So we started to walk on the railroad track. I was told it was private property and we had to get off. Finally a saloon keeper showed us a shortcut into the sacred grounds of the hotel, and suddenly the army appeared in the lobby. The little fellows played "Hail, hail, the gang's all here" on their fifes and drums, and Senator Platt, when he saw the little army, ran away through the back door to New York.

I asked the manager if he would give the children breakfast, and charge it up to the Senator, as we had an invitation to breakfast that morning with him. He gave us a private room and he gave those children a breakfast as they had never had in all their lives. I had breakfast too, and a reporter from one of the Hearst papers and I charged it all up to Senator Platt.

We marched down to Oyster Bay, but the President refused to see us and he would not answer my letters. But our march had done its work. We had drawn the attention of the nation to the crime of child labor. And while the strike of the textile workers in Kensington was lost and the children driven back to work, not long afterward the Pennsylvania legislature passed a child labor law that sent thousands of children home from the mills, and kept thousands of others from entering the factory until they were fourteen years of age.

Rose Schneiderman, "The Triangle Fire" (1911)

I would be traitor to these poor burned bodies if I came here to talk good fellowship. We have tried you good people of the public, and we have found you wanting. The old Inquisition had its rack and its thumbscrews and its instruments of torture with iron teeth. We know what these things are today: the iron teeth are our necessities, the thumbscrews the high-powered and swift machinery close to which we must work, and the rack is here in the "fireproof" structures that will destroy us the minute they catch on fire.

This is not the first time girls have been burned alive in the city. Each week I must learn of the untimely death of one of my sister workers. Every year thousands of us are maimed. The life of men and women is so cheap and property is so sacred. There are so many of us for one job it matters little if 143 of us are burned to death.

We tried you, citizens; we are trying you now, and you have a couple of dollars for the sorrowing mothers and daughters and sisters by way of a charity gift. But every time the workers come out in the only way they know to protest against conditions which are unbearable, the strong hand of the law is allowed to press down heavily upon us. Public officials have only words of warning to us—warning that we must be intensely orderly and must be intensely peaceable, and they have the workhouse just back of all their warnings. The strong hand of the law beats us back when we rise into the conditions that make life bearable.

I can't talk fellowship to you who are gathered here. Too much blood has been spilled. I know from my experience it is up to the working people to save themselves. The only way they can save themselves is by a strong working-class movement.

1. Compare the ideas of Andrew Carnegie in "The Gospel of Wealth" with the Puritan ideas of John Winthrop and the theories of social Darwinism.

2. According to Mother Jones, who caused the mill children to suffer?

3. What are the key differences between the ideas of Andrew Carnegie and Mother Jones?

4. What action does Rose Schneiderman suggest is justified?

5. According to Mother Jones, how free was the press? Why were the newspapers silent regarding the exploitation of children?

CHAPTER 19

Toward an Urban Society, 1877–1900

SUMMARY
The development of American cities radically altered the nation's social environment and problems.

The Lure of the City
In the late nineteenth century, the city became a symbol of American life and people flocked to it, drawn by the hope of economic opportunity and the promise of a more exciting life. By 1900, the United States had three cities with over one-half million and three more with more than one million people.

Skyscrapers and Suburbs
Between 1870 and 1900, cities expanded upward and outward on a base of new technologies including metal-frame skyscrapers, electric elevators, streetcar systems, and outlying green suburbs. Cities were no longer "walking cities." As the middle class moved out, immigrants and working-class people poured in, creating urban slums through overcrowding. The city produced what was an increasingly stratified and fragmented society

Tenements and the Problems of Overcrowding
Immigrants from abroad joined rural Americans in search of jobs in the nation's cities. These newcomers to the city were often forced to live in hastily constructed and overcrowded tenement houses with primitive, if any, sanitation facilities. The "dumbbell tenement" was the most infamous housing of this type.

Strangers in a New Land
The "new" immigrants, mostly poor, unskilled, non-Protestant laborers between the ages of 15 and 40, clung to their native languages, religions, and cultural traditions to endure the economic and social stresses of industrial capitalism. Between 1877 and 1890, 6.3 million people immigrated to the United States, most from southern and eastern Europe. Much of mainstream society found these new immigrants troubling, resulting in a rise in anti-immigrant feeling and activity.

Immigrants and the City
Immigrant families were mostly close-knit nuclear families, and they tended to marry within their own ethnic groups. They depended on immigrant associations for their social safety net, native language newspapers for their news and political views, and community-based churches and schools.

The Tweed Ring

Political machines provided some needed services for these immigrants while also enriching themselves by exploiting the dependency of the cities' new residents. William "Boss" Tweed and his Tammany Hall in New York was the most infamous of the political machines.

Social and Cultural Change, 1877–1900

The rapid development of an urban society transformed America. How people lived, what and how they ate, and how they took care of their health all changed.

Manners and Mores

Victorian morality, epitomized by strict rules of dress, manners, and sexual behavior, set the tone for the era, but adherence to such prescriptions often declined in the face of rapid social change brought on by industrialization and urbanization. There were vast differences in the manners and mores adhered to by the middle and upper classes and the lower socioeconomic classes. These differences often caused social tension as the former tried to control the behavior of the latter.

Leisure and Entertainment

This period saw the rise of organized spectator sports, which supplemented traditional leisure activities such as concerts, fairs, the circus, and even croquet. Technology brought a variety of new forms of leisure and entertainment, and the use of gas and electric street lights ensured that fewer people stayed home at night.

Changes in Family Life

Economic changes also produced new roles for women and the family. Working-class families rarely toiled together, but did maintain the strong ties needed to survive the urban industrial struggle. Middle-class women and children became more isolated, and homemakers attempted to construct a sphere of domesticity as a haven from rampaging materialism. Families, especially white families, became smaller as the birthrate fell dramatically.

Changing Views: A Growing Assertiveness Among Women

Americans also began to change their views about women, demonstrating a limited but growing acceptance of the "new woman." Important changes included a rise in working and career women, more liberalized divorce laws, an increasingly frank discussion of sexuality, and a growing women's rights movement.

Educating the Masses

With the development of childhood as a distinct time of life, Americans placed greater emphasis on education as the means by which individuals were prepared for life and work in an industrial world. Schools instituted a structured curriculum, a longer school day, and new educational techniques that varied according to the gender of the student. The South lagged behind in such educational changes primarily because of its Jim Crow laws.

Higher Education

Colleges grew in number, expanded in size, broadened their curriculum, developed the first American graduate schools, and provided more educational opportunities for women. They provided few prospects for African Americans and other minorities, however, forcing men like W.E.B. Du Bois and Booker T. Washington, who differed in their methods, to develop independent schools to train black students.

The Stirrings of Reform

In spite of the period's adherence to the beliefs of social Darwinism, increasing numbers of Americans in fields that varied from religion and economics to politics, literature, and the law proposed the need for reforms.

Progress and Poverty

Henry George launched critical studies of the new urban America with his book *Progress and Poverty*. While his reforms were not adopted, many began to ask the same questions and recognize, as George did, the need for reform.

New Currents in Social Thought

Social thinkers challenged the tenets of social Darwinism, arguing the importance of environmental influences on people's behavior, the exploitation of labor by a predatory business class that was allowed by laissez-faire economic policies, and the societal value of cooperation over competition. Churches established missions in the inner-cities and began to preach the Social Gospel to encourage those with means to help those in need.

The Settlement Houses

New professional social workers, many of them middle-class women, established settlement houses in inner cities allowing them to experience the slum conditions of lower-class life firsthand. As residents they could then provide education, training, and other social services within their neighborhoods. Settlement house workers also tried to abolish child labor. The settlement house movement had its limits, mostly racial and ethnic. Best known among the settlement movement workers is Jane Addams of Hull House in Chicago.

A Crisis in Social Welfare

In responding to the depression of 1893, professional social workers introduced new methods of providing assistance that would also allow them to study the poor in order to alleviate their condition. Such efforts approached poverty as a social problem rather than an individual shortcoming.

Conclusion: The Pluralistic Society

By 1920, most Americans lived in cities rather than rural areas. Almost half of the population were descended from immigrants that arrived after the conclusion of the American Revolution, creating a society that was a jumble of ethnic and racial groups of varying class standing. Social changes wrought by industrialization and urbanization created tension and often open conflict, initiating the beginning efforts at reform.

LEARNING OBJECTIVES

After mastering this chapter, you should be able to

1. Trace the journeys of the new immigrants from their places of origin to America and explain their adaptation to urban stresses and their effect on American cities.

2. Specify the role of skyscrapers, suburbs and tenements in the rise of the city.

3. Identify and describe the major problems of American central cities in the Victorian era.

4. Explain and evaluate the operation of the early political machines.

5. Describe the most common form of food, housing, and medical care in 1877 and trace the changes through 1900.

6. Identify and describe the principal moral values and issues of Victorian America.

7. Describe the most popular pastimes and forms of entertainment in Victorian America.

8. Delineate the changing roles of both women and the family in America from 1877 to 1900.

9. Describe the changes taking place in public education from 1877 to 1890.

10. Describe the major changes taking place in American higher education from 1877 to 1900.

11. Compare and contrast the educational and civil rights policies of Booker T. Washington and W.E.B. Du Bois.

12. Describe the principal tenets of social Darwinism and the opposing reform theory, including some of the specific arguments of major proponents of each view.

13. Trace the rise of professional social workers in the settlement houses and in the depression of 1893.

GLOSSARY

To build your social science vocabulary, familiarize yourself with the following terms:

1. **philanthropy** charitable donation or action. "Private philanthropy ... spurred growth in higher education."

2. **land-grant institutions** colleges and universities established with large tracts of land granted to states by the federal government under the Morrill Land Grant Act of 1862. "The act fostered 69 'land grant' institutions."

3. **nuclear family** the immediate family of father, mother, and children. "... most immigrant families were nuclear in structure...."

4. **nativists** those who support the interests of the native born as opposed to those of immigrants. "... a fact that worried nativists opposed to immigration."

5. **wards** administrative and political districts of a city. "... one of whose wards had a population density of 334,000 people per square mile."

6. **boss** one who controls a political organization. "... they were headed by a strong, influential leader—the 'boss' ...."

7. **precinct captain** a political leader of the ward, precinct, or neighborhood level, subordinate to the boss. "... a network of ward and precinct captains, each of whom looked after his local constituents."

8. **mores** customs of a group or society that are considered so important that they usually have legal sanction. "Manners and Mores"

9. **mortality** the death rate, usually expressed as a ratio of the number of deaths to the total population. "Infant mortality declined...."

10. **behavioral** a school of social or psychological studies founded on facts of human behavior. "William James ... laid the foundations of modern behavioral psychology...."

11. **census** an official counting of the population and its constituent groups. "By 1920, the census showed that...most Americans lived in cities."

12. **common law** law based on court decision and custom, as opposed to written, statutory law. "One important change occurred in ... common law doctrine...."

13. **chattel** movable, personal property. "Under that doctrine, wives were chattel of their husbands...."

IDENTIFICATION

Briefly identify the meaning and significance of the following terms.

1. "new immigrants" _____

   _____

2. Mugwumps _____

   _____

3. tenements _____

   _____

4. political machines _____

   _____

5. The "new woman" _____

   _____

6. Booker T. Washington _____

   _____

7. social Darwinism _____

   _____

8. *Plessy* v. *Ferguson* _____

   _____

9. Social Gospel _____

   _____

10. settlement houses _____

_____

MATCHING

A. Match the following authors with the appropriate titles and themes.

_____ 1. William Graham Sumner

_____ 2. Henry George

_____ 3. Edward Bellamy

_____ 4. William T. Stead

_____ 5. W.E.B. Du Bois

a. *If Christ Came to Chicago*; called for civic revival

b. *What Social Classes Owe to Each Other*; held that government aid to the poor interferes with evolution

c. *Looking Backward, 2000–1887*; described a socialist utopia of the future

d. *Progress and Poverty*; urged a tax on land to equalize wealth

e. *Progress and Poverty*; proposed a "single tax" on unearned increment from land ownership

f. *The Souls of Black Folk*; urged blacks to get an education, demand civil rights, and aspire to professional careers

B. Match the following reformers with the appropriate description.

_____ 1. Stanton Coit

_____ 2. Jane Addams

_____ 3. W.E.B. Du Bois

_____ 4. Lillian Wald

_____ 5. Harriet Vittum

a. study on urban life suggesting that crime in a black ward a result of environment, not inborn degeneracy

b. founded Hull House in Chicago's slums

c. established Henry Street Settlement in New York

d. borrowed the settlement house idea from England

e. described tenements in *How the Other Half Lives*

f. known as "the police lady in brown," she headed a Chicago settlement house with strict rules that were often resented by immigrants

COMPLETION

Answer the question or complete the statement by filling in the blanks with the correct word or words.

1. A Chicago architect, _____ moved from giant masonry buildings to skyscrapers.

2. Educated upper-class individuals who worked to end political corruption were called _____.

3. Eight-story apartment complexes in New York called_____ crammed multiple families onto single floors that were unsanitary.

4. The discovery that germs cause infection and disease by _____ led to breakthroughs in vaccines and other preventative measures.

5. Critics of the turn of the century denounced as "vulgar, filthy, and suggestive" a new form of music called _____.

6. In 1869, Princeton and Rutgers played the first intercollegiate _____ game.

7. By 1890, the number of Americans who were foreign-born had reached _____ percent of the total population.

8. Booker T. Washington's _____ called for slow progress though self-improvement for blacks to achieve civil rights.

9. The leader of Tammany Hall who provided a model of the political machine was _____.

10. In 1890 Susan B. Anthony helped to form the _____ to work for the enfranchisement of American women.

TRUE/FALSE

Mark the following statements either T (True) or F (False).

_____ 1. By 1877, technological change had produced a set of sharply defined political issues.

_____ 2. Because of their rather sedate taste in entertainment, nineteenth-century Americans opposed such frivolities as circuses and melodramas.

_____ 3. Between 1877 and 1890, the American family was declining in its economic function but increasing in emotional significance.

_____ 4. In the late nineteenth century, American colleges and universities moved away from the traditional classical curriculum toward "reality and practicality."

_____ 5. By 1890 many states had substantially revised their laws regarding *femme couverte*.

_____ 6. The South's Jim Crow system was the primary reason it lagged behind the rest of the nation in educational progress between 1877 and 1900.

_____ 7. Immigrant associations helped newly arrived immigrants get a start in their adopted country.

_____ 8. Anti-Catholicism and anti-Semitism became prominent again in the 1890s with the arrival of immigrants from eastern and southern Europe.

_____ 9. Clarence Darrow argued that the "unjust condition of human life" produced criminals.

_____ 10. The new social workers of the late nineteenth century produced theoretical and utopian studies that neglected specifics and details.

MULTIPLE CHOICE

Circle the one alternative that best completes the statement or answers the question.

1. The term "walking cities" refers to
    a. suburbs that sprang up during the late 1800s.
    b. commercial districts with an abundance of department stores.
    c. an exercise and sports craze of the 1880s.
    d. the size cities were confined to based on how far people could walk.

2. What was the average life expectancy of Americans in 1900?
    a. thirty-seven years, but only thirty-five years for African Americans
    b. forty-seven years, but only forty-five years for African Americans
    c. forty-seven years, but only thirty-three years for African Americans
    d. fifty-seven years, but only fifty-three years for African Americans

3. Late nineteenth-century reforms benefiting women included
    a. increased status for housewives.
    b. laws granting women control of their earnings.
    c. the right to vote.
    d. laws granting women equal pay for equal work.

4. Educational changes in the years 1877 to 1900 did not include
    a. a decrease in illiteracy.
    b. "practical" courses in manual training and homemaking for older children.
    c. development of the kindergarten.
    d. compulsory school attendance in all states.

5. In response to Booker T. Washington's policies of political passivity and vocational training for blacks, W.E.B. Du Bois proposed
    a. a trained, black, intellectual elite to lead the fight for civil rights.
    b. segregated schools.
    c. limited college education.
    d. All of the above.

6. Which of the following places events in the correct chronological order?
    a. Morrill Land Grant Act, *Plessy* v. *Ferguson*, establishment of Tuskegee Institute
    b. *Plessy* v. *Ferguson*, Morrill Land Grant Act, establishment of Tuskegee Institute
    c. Establishment of Tuskegee Institute, Morrill Land Grant Act, *Plessy* v. *Ferguson*
    d. Morrill Land Grant Act, establishment of Tuskegee Institute, *Plessy* v. *Ferguson*

7. During the late nineteenth century, American women did not
   a. move into the work force in greater numbers.
   b. cease to be chattel of their husbands in the law of many states.
   c. espouse fewer reforms than earlier generations of American women.
   d. All of the above.

8. As a solution to the poverty in modern society, Henry George proposed
   a. to let nature take its evolutionary course.
   b. to replace all taxes with a "single tax" on land.
   c. a socialist utopia in which the government owns the means of production.
   d. to establish worker and farmer "cooperatives" to own the means of production.

9. Herbert Spencer's social Darwinism held that
   a. humans advanced civilization with social cooperation.
   b. society should help the rich and powerful to encourage "survival of the fittest."
   c. government should help the poor to overcome the "struggle to survive."
   d. society evolved by adapting to the environment through social selection.

10. Leaders of the "settlement house" movement tried to
    a. help immigrants to learn American history and language while preserving their own ethnic heritage.
    b. reduce school dropouts and regulate child labor.
    c. create for the city small-town values and community.
    d. All of the above.

11. Which of the following authors argued that the American ideal of women's "innocence" really meant their ignorance?
    a. Charlotte Perkins Gilman in *Women and Economics*
    b. Edward Bliss Foote in *Plain Home Talk of Love, Marriage, and Parentage*
    c. Bessie and Marie Von Vorst in *The Woman Who Toils*
    d. Helen Campbell in *Women Wage Earners*

12. Changes in higher education included all of the following *except*
    a. an increased number of colleges and universities.
    b. the first separate graduate schools.
    c. an increased emphasis on a classical curriculum.
    d. more educational opportunities for women.

13. According to George Washington Plunkitt, political machines survived because they
    a. offered good, honest government.
    b. offered needed services for the poor.
    c. bought votes with "honest graft."
    d. All of the above.

14. Significant medical developments in Victorian America included all of the following EXCEPT
   a. prevention of tuberculosis, typhoid, and diphtheria.
   b. discovery that germs cause infection and disease.
   c. relatively safe and painless surgery.
   d. more antiseptic practices in childbirth.

15. Which approach to poverty was used by professional social workers but not by church and charity volunteers?
   a. reform of individual families
   b. alleviation of underlying conditions of poverty
   c. help in alleviating the suffering caused by economic depression
   d. All of the above.

THOUGHT QUESTIONS

To check your understanding of the key issues of this period, solve the following problems:

1. Many historians have emphasized the role of the western frontier in shaping American society. Should we place greater emphasis on the significance of the city? Why or why not?

2. What factors led to the rapid development of the city in the late nineteenth century?

3. Why have urban Americans been more tolerant of individual social and cultural differences?

4. The social workers tried to alleviate the conditions of poverty that the political machines exploited. To what extent have they succeeded? Have they simply transformed the dependency of the urban poor?

5. On the whole, has our society gained more than it lost in the transition from rural to urban?

6. In what ways did ethnic pluralism shape the American city? American society?

CRITICAL THINKING EXERCISE

Using material in Chapter 19 of the text and the Primary Sources provided below, please answer the questions that follow the documents.

Charles Lorin Brace, "The Life of the Street Rats"
The Secret Oath of the American Protective Society (1893)

Charles Loring Brace, "The Life of the Street Rats" (1872)

... The intensity of the American temperament is felt in every fibre of these children of poverty and vice. Their crimes have the unrestrained and sanguinary character of a race accustomed to overcome all obstacles. They rifle a bank, where English thieves pick a pocket; they murder, where European proletaires cudgel or fight with fists; in a riot, they begin what seems about to be the sacking of a city, where English rioters would merely batter policemen, or smash lamps. The "dangerous classes" of New York are mainly American-born, but the children of Irish and German immigrants....

There are thousands on thousands in New York who have no assignable home, and "flirt" from attic to attic, and cellar to cellar; there are other thousands more or less connected with criminal enterprises; and still other tens of thousands, poor, hard pressed, and depending for daily bread on the day's earnings, swarming in tenement-houses, who behold the gilded rewards of toil all about them, but are never permitted to touch them.

All these great masses of destitute, miserable, and criminal persons believe that for ages the rich have had all the good things of life, while to them have been left the evil things. Capital to them is the tyrant.

Let but Law lift its hand from them for a season, or let the civilizing influences of American life fail to reach them, and, if the opportunity offered, we should see an explosion from this class which might leave this city in ashes and blood.

Seventeen years ago, my attention had been called to the extraordinarily degraded condition of the children in a district lying on the west side of the city, between Seventeenth and Nineteenth Streets, and the Seventh and Tenth Avenues. A certain block, called "Misery Row," in Tenth Avenue, was the main seed-bed of crime and poverty in the quarter, and was also invariably a "fever-nest." Here the poor obtained wretched rooms at a comparatively low rent; these they sub-let, and thus, in little, crowded, close tenements, were herded men, women and children of all ages. The parents were invariably given to hard drinking, and the children were sent out to beg or to steal. Besides them, other children, who were orphans, or who had run away from drunkards' homes, or had been working on the canal-boats that discharged on the docks near by, drifted into the quarter, as if attracted by the atmosphere of crime and laziness that prevailed in the neighborhood. These slept around the breweries of the ward, or on the
hay-barges, or in the old sheds of Eighteenth and Nineteenth Streets. They were mere children, and kept life together by all sorts of street-jobs-helping the brewery laborers, blackening boots, sweeping sidewalks, "smashing baggages" (as they called it), and the like. Herding together, they soon began to form an unconscious society for vagrancy and idleness. Finding that work brought but poor pay, they tried shorter roads to getting money by petty [sic] thefts, in which they were very adroit. Even if they earned a considerable sum by a lucky day's job, they quickly spent it in gambling, or for some folly.

The police soon knew them as "street-rats"; but, like the rats, they were too quick and cunning to be often caught in their petty plunderings, so they gnawed away at the foundations of society undisturbed.

The Secret Oath of the American Protective Association (1893)

I do most solemnly promise and swear that I will always, to the utmost of my ability, labor, plead, and wage a continuous warfare against ignorance and fanaticism; that I will use my utmost power to strike the shackles and chains of blind obedience to the Roman Catholic Church from the hampered and bound consciences of a priest-ridden and church-oppressed people; that I will never allow anyone, a member of the Roman Catholic Church, to become a member of this order, I knowing him to be such; that I will use my influence to promote the interest of all Protestants everywhere in the world that I may be; that I will not employ a Roman Catholic in any capacity, if I can procure the services of a Protestant.

I furthermore promise and swear that I will not aid in building or maintaining, by my resources, any Roman Catholic church or institution of their sect or creed whatsoever, but will do all in my power to retard and break down the power of the Pope, in this country or any other; that I will not enter into any controversy with a Roman Catholic upon the subject of this order, nor will I enter into any agreement with a Roman Catholic to strike or create a disturbance whereby the Catholic employees may

61

undermine and substitute their Protestant co-workers; that in all grievances I will seek only Protestants, and counsel with them to the exclusion of all Roman Catholics, and will not make known to them anything of any nature matured at such conferences.

I furthermore promise and swear that I will not countenance the nomination, in any caucus or convention, of a Roman Catholic for any office in the gift of the American people, and that I will not vote for, or counsel others to vote for, any Roman Catholic, but will vote only for a Protestant, so far as may lie in my power (should there be two Roman Catholics in opposite tickets, I will erase the name on the ticket I vote); that I will at all times endeavor to place the political positions of this government in the hands of Protestants, to the entire exclusion of the Roman Catholic Church, of the members thereof, and the mandate of the Pope.

To all of which I do most solemnly promise and swear, so help me God.

Amen.

1. After reading the text, describe each of the following: changes in the roles of women and the family; the operation of political machines; the competing educational and civil rights strategies of Washington and Du Bois.

2. After reading the text, describe the principal tenets of both social Darwinism and reform theory.

3. Does Brace's explanation of the life of the "street rat" reflect the views of social Darwinism, reform theory, or both? If both, which of the two views does it emphasize most?

4. Contrast the American Protective Society's attitude toward immigrants with Brace's treatment of the "street role."

5. Do today's social and immigration debates reflect the issues raised by your answer to question 4? If so, which provides the best general approach to those issues, social Darwinism, or reform theory?

CHAPTER 20

Political Realignments, 1876–1901

SUMMARY
Economic depression dominated the 1890s and reshaped political alignments and attitudes.

Politics of Stalemate
America's white male voters of the 1870s and 1880s displayed a keen interest in partisan politics. Southern states increasingly disfranchised black men.

The Party Deadlock
While Democrats emphasized decentralized power located in the states, the Republicans favored a more active national government. Voters generally adhered to their pre-Civil War loyalties, basically stalemating national government. The New England and many northern states went Republican and southern states went Democratic, leaving elections dependent upon a few key "swing" states—New York, New Jersey, Connecticut, Ohio, Indiana, and Illinois—and national politics at a cautious standstill.

Reestablishing Presidential Power
Between 1880 and 1900, American presidents succeeded in reasserting the authority of their office, which had been weakened considerably by the Johnson impeachment, the Grant scandals, and the electoral controversy of 1876. By the late 1890s, they had laid the basis for the modern powerful presidency.

Republicans in Power: The Billion-Dollar Congress
In 1888, the Republicans broke the electoral stalemate by winning control of the presidency and both houses of Congress. Despite Democratic efforts to stall Congressional votes, the Republicans enacted the Reed rules and adopted their party's program.

Tariffs, Trusts, and Silver
In the following two years, the Republicans enacted a significant legislative program including the McKinley Tariff, the Sherman Antitrust Act and the Sherman Silver Purchase Acts.

The 1890 Elections
Americans rejected the Republican's activism by crushing them in the elections of 1890, allowing the Democrats to gain new power, especially in the Midwest.

The Rise of the Populist Movement
By the summer of 1890, Farmers' Alliance organizers were recruiting huge numbers of unhappy farmers, sometimes at the rate of 1,000 a week, leading to a political movement known as *populism*.

The Farm Problem
Populism surged as a response to an agrarian sense of social and economic loss based on what they perceived as low farm prices, high railroad rates, and burdensome mortgages. Though their complaints were in some ways justified, they were not altogether valid. What is important, however, is that they believed they were oppressed, and that angered them.

The Fast-Growing Farmers' Alliance
Farmers organized the Grange and the Farmers' Alliance, which sponsored social and economic programs, but also tried to influence politics, adopting the Ocala Demands in 1890. In the South, the Alliance enjoyed considerable success within the Democratic party; in the North and West, it successfully ran many of its own candidates.

The People's Party
In 1892, the Alliance led in the formation of the Populist party, which collected over one million votes for its 1892 presidential candidate. The party began to lose strength thereafter. In the South, racism played a major role in the decline of Populism. While it existed, Populism was one of the most powerful reform movements in American history.

The Crisis of the Depression
Grover Cleveland and the Democratic party swept the election of 1892, but then faced a severe depression brought on by the too rapid expansion of the American economy.

The Panic of 1893
The depression of the 1890s started with the Panic of 1893. As the economy slumped into a crisis, banks failed at record rates, factories and mines shut down, and millions were put out of work. The next year was worse, and the economic crisis lingered into the latter days of the 1890s.

The Pullman Strike
The depression led to numerous protests demanding relief for workers. Disaffected workers at the Pullman Palace Car Company went on strike, spurring other railroad workers in the American Railway Union to do the same. The Pullman Strike shut down the railroads of the West and produced the Socialist leader Eugene Debs.

A Beleaguered President
President Cleveland blamed the depression entirely on the Sherman Silver Purchase Act and the free coinage of silver. He pushed for its repeal in 1893, splitting, and, in combination with the depression, wrecking the Democratic party.

Breaking the Party Deadlock
The depression led to a new Republican supremacy and made the Democratic party little more than a southern, sectional party.

Changing Attitudes
The depression also changed the country's traditional social views. Many Americans now saw poverty as a failure of the economy rather than the individual, so they demanded reforms to help the poor and unemployed, an important step toward national authority and activism.

Women and Children in the Labor Force
The entrance of women and children in to the labor force accelerated during the depression because employers made jobs available to them because they were paid less than men. Men still dominated in business offices, but more clerks, telegraph and telephone operators, and teachers were women during and after the 1890s. Children's increasing presence in the workforce led to more calls for protective laws.

Changing Themes in Literature
Rejecting the romanticism that had dominated before, during and immediately after the Civil War, realistic and naturalistic writers portrayed everyday life as it was. They wrote regional stories and emphasized true relationships between people. Notable authors include Joel Chandler Harris, Mark Twain, Stephen Crane, and Theodore Dreiser.

The Presidential Election of 1896
The Republican dominance initiated in 1894 was solidified with the victory of William McKinley over the Democrat and Populist William Jennings Bryan. The election, known as the "battle of the standards," focused primarily on the debate over the gold or silver monetary standard.

The Mystique of Silver
People wanted a solution to the depression, and many, believing that the more money in circulation the better, favored the free coinage of silver. It also became a patriotic and moral symbol. For some it represented independence because the rest of the world was abandoning the coinage of silver. For others it embodied the interests of the common people, especially farmers in the West, against the industrial elites of the Northeast.

The Republicans and Gold
Opposing the silverite argument, McKinley and the Republicans promised a return to the gold standard, which they claimed would end the depression.

The Democrats and Silver

Although somewhat divided over the silver issue, the silver Democrats controlled the party, endorsing its free coinage and nominating William Jennings Bryan after he captured the convention with the oratory of his "Cross of Gold" speech.

Campaign and Election

McKinley won the election handily over Bryan, the Democratic and Populist candidate. The People's party vanished after 1896, but major parts of its presidential platform were later incorporated into law.

The McKinley Administration

McKinley's government took over as the economy began to recover and prosper, allowing them to raise the protective tariff, demonetize silver with the Gold Standard Act, and shift from promoting to regulating industrialism. By the time of McKinley's assassination and Theodore Roosevelt's ascent to the presidency, the Republican party had clearly emerged as the dominant party associated with progress and prosperity, as Americans rallied to reform the system that had produced the depression of the 1890s.

Conclusion: A Decade's Dramatic Changes

The 1890s was a decade of change. They influenced and shaped nearly everything—society, culture, politics, and the economy—that came after them, making them as much a part of the twentieth century as of the nineteenth.

LEARNING OBJECTIVES

After mastering this chapter, you should be able to

1. Discuss the stalemate of partisan politics in the 1870s and 1880s.

2. Trace the reassertion of presidential power from 1876 to 1888.

3. Identify and describe the legislation passed by the Republican party in 1890 and the voters' response to that "billion-dollar Congress."

4. Describe and evaluate the grievances of American farmers in the late nineteenth century.

5. Trace the growth of the farmers' protest from the Grange through the Farmers' Alliance.

6. Detail the establishment of the People's (Populist) party, its platform, and its first presidential election.

7. Discuss the "great" Pullman strike of 1894 and its importance in the 1890s.

8. Describe the changes in American attitudes toward poverty brought on by the depression of the 1890s.

9. Describe the changes in the American work force brought on by the depression of the 1890s.

10. Trace the rise of the new realist and naturalist movements in American literature and explain why they emerged.

11. Explain how the silver issue served as a symbol for a social and political movement.

12. Compare and contrast the Democratic and Republican presidential campaigns of 1896.

13. Evaluate the role of the election and administration of William McKinley in the emergence of modern urban, industrial government and politics.

GLOSSARY

To build your social science vocabulary, familiarize yourself with the following terms:

1. **poll tax** a tax charged against each person, often for the right to vote. "In 1877, Georgia adopted the poll tax ..."

2. **literacy test** a test of reading ability used to prevent African Americans and others from registering to vote. "... the famous 'grandfather clause,' which used a literacy test ..."

3. **injunction** a court order prohibiting a certain act to prevent irreparable damage. "...the Supreme Court endorsed the use of the injunction in labor disputes..."

4. **bipartisan** supported by or consisting of members of two political parties. "... the act created a bipartisan Civil Service Commission ..."

5. **trust** a combination of businesses to eliminate competition and control prices. "It declared illegal "... 'every ... combination in the form of trust ... in restraint of trade...'"

6. **lien** a claim against property as security for satisfaction of an obligation. "...Colored Farmers' National Alliance and Cooperative Union enlisted..."

7. **cooperative** jointly owned and operated for mutual benefit. "... between 1886 and 1892, cooperative enterprises blossomed in the South."

8. **platform** a statement of the public principles and policies of a political party or group. "... the Alliance adopted the Ocala Demands, the platform [it] pushed for as long as it existed."

9. **special session** an unscheduled legislative session called by an executive for specific purposes. "... Cleveland summoned Congress into special session ..."

10. **romanticism** a style of art and literature emphasizing emotion, imagination and freedom of form. "In the years after the Civil War, literature often reflected the mood of romanticism ..."

11. **realism** a style of art and literature emphasizing realistic depiction of everyday life. "... a number of talented authors began to reject ... escapism, turning instead to realism ..."

12. **naturalism** a style of art and literature emphasizing a detailed, clinical, deterministic view of life. "The depression also gave point to a growing movement in literature toward ... naturalism."

13. **imperialism** the policy of achieving economic or political power over other nations. "Bryan stressed the issues of imperialism and the trusts ..."

IDENTIFICATION

Briefly identify the meaning and significance of the following terms.

1. *Minor* v. *Happersett*_____

_____

2. Pendleton Act _____

_____

3. Populism _____

_____

4. Sherman Silver Purchase Act_____

_____

5. Pullman strike_____

_____

6. The Alliance Movement_____

_____

7. realism_____

_____

8. naturalism _____

_____

9. free coinage of silver_____

_____

10. William McKinley_____

_____

MATCHING

A. Match the following politician with the appropriate description.

_____ 1. James Weaver

_____ 2. William Jennings Bryan

_____ 3. James A. Garfield

_____ 4. Grover Cleveland

_____ 5. Thomas B. Reed

a. nominated for president in 1896 by both Democrats and People's party

b. Speaker of the House who glorified the United States as a "Billion-Dollar country"

c. elected president in 1888

d. ran for president with the People's party in 1892

e. president assassinated by Charles Guiteau in 1881

f. first Democratic president since 1861

B. Match the following authors with the appropriate description.

_____ 1. Mark Twain

_____ 2. Louisa May Alcott

_____ 3. Stephen Crane

_____ 4. Joel Chandler Harris

_____ 5. Theodore Dreiser

a. regional writer who depicted the South

b. portrayed a grim world of the exhausted factory worker in *Sister Carrie*

c. changed American prose style by replacing literary language with common speech and dialect

d. portrayed wise youth explaining currency to famous people

e. described the daily life of four New England girls in *Little Women*

f. depicted the impact of poverty in *Maggie: A Girl of the Streets*

COMPLETION

Answer the question or complete the statement by filling in the blanks with the correct word or words.

1.   The _____ of 1878 called for partial coinage of silver over the veto of President Hayes.

2.   In 1883, Congress legislated the establishment of a Civil Service Commission with the _____ Act.

3.   Foremost in the Ocala Demands of the Farmers' Alliance was the _____.

4.   The _____ allowed men who had failed the literacy test to vote, provided their fathers or grandfathers had before 1867.

5.   In the presidential elections of 1876 through 1896, an average percentage of about _____ of the electorate voted.

6.   American Railway Union leader _____ was jailed after the Pullman Strike.

7.   In 1892, the Populist party nominated _____ for the presidency.

8.   The _____ represented the Alliance political platform.

9.   The _____ of 1894 did little to uphold the Democrats' campaign pledge to reduce the tariff.

10. Concerned about child labor and lack of schooling, middle-class women in 1896 formed the _____ demanding compulsory education.

TRUE/FALSE

Mark the following statements either T (True) or F (False).

_____ 1. In 1892, some southern Populists tried to unite black and white farmers.

_____ 2. In 1891 the Colored Farmers' National Alliance led a successful cotton pickers strike.

_____ 3. While the Republican party of the 1870s and 1880s supported increased power and activity at the national level of government, the Democrats emphasized decentralized government with more power and activity at the state and local level.

_____ 4. In the election of 1894, Democrats won the greatest victory in congressional history.

_____ 5. The Panic of 1893 was a small downturn in Wall Street investments that had little effect on the general American population.

_____ 6. Between the years 1877 and 1888, the American presidency lost power as Congress reasserted much power and authority that it had lost during the period of the Civil War and Reconstruction.

_____ 7. Southern Democrats Thomas Watson and Leonidas Polk used fraud and manipulation to defeat Populist candidates in 1892.

_____ 8. Between 1877 and 1900, southern states disfranchised African Americans with laws establishing poll taxes, literacy tests, and "grandfather" clauses.

_____ 9. As a result of the Pullman Strike the Supreme Court endorsed the use of injunctions in labor disputes.

_____ 10. The central belief of silverites was a quantity theory of money.

MULTIPLE CHOICE

Circle the one alternative that best completes the statement or answers the question.

1. The Dingley Tariff
   a. was a major victory for Democrats.
   b. was passed during McKinley's second term.
   c. was a major defeat for protectionism.
   d. raised average tariff duties to record levels.

2. The Colored Farmers' National Alliance ended when
   a. a posse lynched fifteen strikers.
   b. prices on cotton increased significantly.
   c. southern planters used strike breakers in the cotton fields.
   d. the Farmers' Alliance leadership expelled all African Americans from the organization.

3. In 1890, the American electorate rejected
   a. Democratic legislative activism by crushing the party in the congressional elections.
   b. Republican legislative activism by crushing the party in the congressional elections.
   c. the legislative passiveness of both major parties by electing many third-party and especially Populist candidates to Congress.
   d. Republican passiveness by crushing the party in the congressional elections.

4. During the 1890s, writers who rejected romanticism often wrote
   a. regional stories depicting everyday life.
   b. grand epic stories in which the hero always defeated the villain.
   c. disparaging tales about ethnic groups that perpetuated anti-immigrant feelings.
   d. political pamphlets championing their candidate.

5. Which of the following is NOT true of American farmers in the 1865–1890 period?
   a. Prices for their crops declined.
   b. Their purchasing power declined.
   c. Farm mortgages were common.
   d. Their productivity increased.

6. Which best describes the source of agrarian anger and protest in the late nineteenth century?
   a. Farm prices fell far more than did prices for other commodities.
   b. Railroad rates increased dramatically between 1870 and 1900.
   c. Farmers perceived their social and economic position as declining period.
   d. All of the above.

7. The Pendleton Act
   a. created a bipartisan Civil Service Commission.
   b. made poll taxes illegal.
   c. allowed for the partial coinage of silver.
   d. was used to crush unions.

8. Leaders of the Southern Farmers' Alliance
   a. formed the first major People's party.
   b. tried to capture the Democratic party.
   c. eschewed politics for more radical methods.
   d. often crossed over to the Republican party.

9. In the Pullman Strike of 1894, Cleveland's intervention
   a. gave business the court injunction as a new weapon against labor.
   b. ensured the success of the strike.
   c. failed to end the strike.
   d. gave workers the protection of a court injunction.

10. A 1901 study revealed that among working-class families
    a. child labor had virtually ceased.
    b. the number of working women decreased.
    c. over 50% of the principal breadwinners were out of work.
    d. children were attending school in record numbers.

11. Which of the following lists events in the correct chronological order?
    a. Republican policy to regulate industry, Panic of 1893, Republican policy to promote industry
    b. Republican policy to promote industry, Republican policy to regulate industry, Panic of 1893
    c. Republican policy to promote industry, Panic of 1893, Republican policy to regulate industry
    d. None of the above.

12. Support for free silver coinage grew rapidly from 1894 to 1896 because
    a. the issue offered a simple, compelling answer for economic crisis.
    b. workers joined farmers in support of coinage.
    c. Cleveland Democrats joined workers in support of coinage.
    d. All of the above.

13. Which best describes the decision that shattered the Populist party in 1896?
    a. the endorsement for the presidency of the Democratic candidate William Jennings Bryan
    b. the admission of African Americans to the party's ranks
    c. the nomination of their own candidate, James Weaver, for the presidency
    d. the expulsion of all African-American members in an attempt to attract more southern support

14. McKinley's first term in office was characterized by
    a. increased economic prosperity.
    b. gold discoveries that inflated the currency.
    c. presidential activism.
    d. All of the above.

15. By 1900 McKinley had begun prodding the Republican party toward a new policy of
    a. monetary inflation through silver coinage.
    b. promoting economic growth with subsidies and tariffs.
    c. regulating and controlling industry.
    d. another increase in tariff rates.

THOUGHT QUESTIONS

To check your understanding of the key issues of this period, solve the following problems:

1. Why were the presidential elections of the "Gilded Age" so very close?

2. The Populists' political rebellion defined the American response to industrialism. True or false? Explain your answer.

3. What was the basic difference in the approaches of the Republican and Democratic parties to the problems of the 1890s? Why did Americans choose the Republican approach?

4. Was the silver issue a symbol of class differences? Of sectional differences? Explain your answers.

5. What determined the outcome of the Populist-Democratic contest in the South? Did class differences play a significant role? Did race play a significant role?

CRITICAL THINKING EXERCISE

Using material in Chapter 20 of the text and the Primary Sources provided below, please answer the questions that follow the documents: Susan B. Anthony, *Bread Not Ballots (1867)*, Mary Elizabeth Lease, *Populist Crusader (1892)*

Susan B. Anthony, *Bread Not Ballots* (c. 1867)

It is said women do not need the ballot for their protection because they are supported by men. Statistics show that there are 3,000,000 women in this nation supporting themselves. In the crowded cities of the East they are compelled to work in shops, stores and factories for the merest pittance. In New York alone, there are over 50,000 of these women receiving less than fifty cents a day. Women wage-earners in different occupations have organized themselves into trades unions, from time to time, and made their strikes to get justice at the hands of their employers just as men had done, but I have yet to learn of a successful strike of any body of women. The best organized one I ever knew was that of the collar laundry women of the city of Troy, N.Y., the great emporium for the manufacture of shirts, collars and cuffs. They formed a trades union of several hundred members and demanded an increase of wages. It was refused. So one May morning in 1867, each woman threw down her scissors and her needle, her starch-pan and flat-iron, and for three long months not one returned to the factories. At the end of that time they were literally starved out, and majority of them were compelled to go back, but not at their old wages, for their employers cut them down to even a lower figure.

In the winter following I met the president of this union, a bright young Irish girl, and asked her, "Do you not think if you had been 500 carpenters or 500 masons, you would have succeeded?" "Certainly," she said, and then she told me of 200 bricklayers who had the year before been on strike and gained every point with their employers. "What could have made the difference? Their 200 were but a fraction of that trade, while your 500 absolutely controlled yours." Finally she said, "It was because the editors ridiculed and denounced us." "Did they ridicule and denounce the bricklayers?" "No." "What did they say about you?" "Why, that our wages were good enough now, better than those of any other workingwoman except teachers; and if we weren't satisfied, we had better go and get married.... It must have been because our employers bribed the editors." ... In the case of the bricklayers, no editor, either Democrat or Republican, would have accepted the proffer of a bribe, because he would have known that if he denounced or ridiculed those men, not only they but all the trades union men of the city at the next election would vote solidly against the nominees advocated by the editor. If those collar laundrywomen had been voters, they would have held, in that little city of Troy, the "balance of political power." ...

There are many women equally well qualified with men for principals and superintendents of schools, and yet, while three-fourths of the teachers are women, nearly all of them are relegated to subordinate positions on half or at most two-thirds the salaries paid to me ... sex alone settles the question....

And then again you say, "Capital, not the vote, regulates labor." Granted, for the sake of argument, that capital does control the labor of women ... but no one with eyes to see and ears to hear, will concede for a moment that capital absolutely dominates the work and wages of the free and enfranchised men of this republic. It is in order to lift the millions of our wage earning women into a position of as much power over their own labor as men possess, that they should be invested with the franchise. This ought to be done not only for the sake of justice to the women, but to the men with whom they compete; for, just so long as there is a degraded class of labor in the market, it always will be used by the capitalists to checkmate and undermine the superior classes.

Now that as a result of the agitation for equality of chances, and through the invention of machinery, there has come a great revolution in the world of economics, so that wherever a man may go to earn an honest dollar, a woman may go also, there is no escape from the conclusion that she must be clothed with equal power to protect herself. That power is the ballot, the symbol of freedom and equality, without which no citizen is sure of keeping even that which he hath, much less of getting that which he hath not.

Mary Elizabeth Lease, *Populist Crusader* (1892)

Yet, after all our years of toil and privation, dangers and hardships upon the Western frontier, monopoly is taking our homes from us by an infamous system of mortgage foreclosure, the most infamous that has ever disgraced the statutes of a civilized nation. It takes from us at the rate of five hundred a month the homes that represent the best years of our life, our toil, our hopes, our happiness. How did it happen? The government, at the bid of Wall Street, repudiated its contracts with the people; the circulating medium was contracted in the interest of Shylock from $54 per capita to less than $8 per capita; or, as Senator Plumb tells us, "Our debts were increased, while the means to pay them was decreased;" or as grand Senator Steward puts it, "For twenty years the market value of the dollar has gone up and the market value of labor has gone down, till today the American laborer, in bitterness and wrath, asks which is the worst—the black slavery that has gone or the white slavery that has come?"

Do you wonder the women are joining the Alliance? I wonder if there is a woman in this broad land who can afford to stay out of the Alliance. Our loyal, white-ribbon women should be heart and hand in this Farmers' Alliance movement, for the men whom we have sent to represent us are the only men in the councils of this nation who have not been elected on a liquor platform; and I want to say here, with exultant pride, that the five farmer Congressmen and the United States Senator we have sent up from Kansas—the liquor traffic, Wall Street, "nor the gates of hell shall not prevail against them."

It would sound boastful were I to detail to you the active, earnest part the Kansas women took in the recent campaign. A Republican majority of 82,000 was reduced to less than 8,000, when we elected 97 representatives, 5 out of 7 Congressmen, and a United States Senator, for to the women of Kansas belongs the credit of defeating John J. Ingalls. He is feeling badly about it yet, too, for he said today that "women and Indians were the only class that would scalp a dead man." I rejoice that he realizes that he is politically dead.

I might weary you to tell you in detail how the Alliance women found time from cares of home and children to prepare the tempting, generous viands for the Alliance picnic dinners; where hungry thousands and tens of thousands gathered in the forests and groves to listen to the words of impassioned oratory, oftentimes from woman's lips, that nerved the men of Kansas to forget their party prejudice and vote for "Mollie and the babies." And not only did they find their way to the voters' hearts, through their stomachs, but they sang their way as well. I hold here a book of Alliance songs, composed and set to music by an Alliance woman, Mrs. Florence Olmstead of Bulter County, Kan., that did much toward molding public sentiment. Alliance Glee Clubs composed of women, gave us such stirring melodies as the nation has not heard since the Tippecanoe and Tyler campaign of 1840. And while I am individualizing, let me call your attention to a book written also by an Alliance woman. I wish a copy of it could be placed in the hands of every woman in this land. "The Fate of a Fool" is written by Mrs. Emma G. Curtis of Colorado. This book in the hands of women would teach them to be just and generous toward women, and help them to forgive and condemn in each other the sins so sweetly forgiven when committed by men.

Let no one for a moment believe that this uprising and federation of the people is but a passing episode in politics. It is a religious as well as a political movement, for we seek to put into practical operation the teachings and precepts of Jesus of Nazareth. We seek to enact justice and equity between man and man. We seek to bring the nation back to the constitutional liberties guaranteed us by our forefathers. The voice that is coming up today from the mystic chords of the American heart is the same voice that Lincoln heard blending with the guns of Fort Sumter and the Wilderness, and it is breaking into a clarion cry today that will be heard around the world.

Crowns will fall, thrones will tremble, kingdoms will disappear, the divine right of kings and the divine right of capital will fade away like the mists of the morning, when the Angel of Liberty shall kindle the fires of justice in the hearts of men. "Exact justice to all, special privileges to none." No more millionaires, and no more paupers; no more gold kings, silver kings and oil kings, and no more little waifs of humanity starving for a crust of bread. No more gaunt faced, hollow-eyed girls in the factories, and no more little boys reared in poverty and crime for the penitentiaries and the gallows. But we shall have the golden age of which Isaiah sang and the prophets have so long foretold; when the farmers shall be prosperous and happy, dwelling under their own vine and fig tree; when the laborer shall have that for which he toils; when occupancy and use shall be the only title to land, and everyone shall obey the divine injunction, "In the sweat of thy face shalt thou eat bread." When men shall be just and generous, little less than gods, and women shall be just and charitable toward each other, little less than angels; when we shall have not a government of the people by capitalists, but a government of the people, by the people.

1. After reading the text, describe the social and economic complaints of both urban   and industrial workers.

2. Describe the change in popular attitudes toward the impoverished during the economic depression of 1893.

3. Were the political and economic orientations of either the Republicans or Democrats adequate to the needs of workers and farmers?

4. Evaluate Susan B. Anthony's speech as a response to the problems of working women. Were her proposals adequate to meet their needs?

5. Define Mary Elizabeth Lease's protest against capitalist exploitation of workers and farmers and her feminist emphasis on women's suffrage. Would her emphasis on protest better serve the working people than Anthony's promotion of voting?

CHAPTER 21

Toward Empire, 1865–1902

SUMMARY
As the American frontier "closed," many in America pushed for new frontiers of an empire for exploration, settlement, and new markets.

America Looks Outward
In contrast to prior expansion into contiguous territories intended for settlement and equal annexation, the United States in the 1890s acquired island colonies intended as naval bases and commercial outposts for the expansion and protection of American markets.

Catching the Spirit of Empire
Immediately after the Civil War, Americans were concerned almost exclusively with domestic concerns leading to a sense of isolationism. After the 1870s, however, Americans, linked to the world through new communication technologies, began to take a greater interest in international affairs, and even expansion. Still, few Americans were interested in imperialism.

Reasons for Expansion
Stimulated by a closing frontier and an expanding economy at home, the United States became increasingly interested in the worldwide scramble for colonies in the latter nineteenth century. Advocates of Anglo-Saxon racial superiority exhorted expansion of American trade and dominion as both our duty and destiny in "civilizing" the less advanced regions of the world.

Foreign Policy Approaches, 1867–1900
During this era, American policymakers were rarely consistent, but basically sought to avoid entanglements in Europe while expanding American trade, and perhaps territory, in Latin American and Asia. The United States reasserted the Monroe Doctrine and promoted Pan-American interests.

The Lure of Hawaii
The Hawaiian Islands attracted Americans primarily as stepping stones to the valuable trade of the Far East and as strategic locations for South Pacific naval bases. American residents in Hawaii instigated a revolution and the creation of a republican government in 1893, but the United States resisted annexation of the islands until 1898.

The New Navy
Captain Alfred Thayer Mahan, naval strategist and historian, convinced many Americans of the need for an expanded navy to guarantee the nation's wealth and power in international affairs. Benjamin F. Tracy, secretary of the navy under President Benjamin Harrison, pushed Congress

to begin a build-up program that would move the United States from twelfth among world navies in 1889 to third by 1900.

War with Spain

The brief war with Spain increased American confidence, strengthened the office of the presidency, dramatically enlarged the empire of the United States, and made the United States the dominant force in the twentieth century.

A War for Principle

In 1895, economic depression and discontent with Spanish rule led to revolution in Cuba. Spain responded with a policy of brutal repression. Exaggerated accounts of Spanish atrocities by America's "yellow press," the publication of a letter written by the Spanish ambassador in Washington insulting President McKinley, and the sinking of the American battleship *Maine* in Havana harbor all contributed to a growing clamor for United States intervention in the war on behalf of Cuban independence. Dissatisfied with Spain's response to Cuban and American demands, President McKinley called for war in April 1898. The passage of the Teller Amendment assured Americans that the war was not a war for the acquisition of Cuba.

The Spanish-American War

Congress and the American public responded enthusiastically to war. More soldiers volunteered to fight than could be trained, fed, or equipped. The war lasted only ten weeks and resulted in relatively few American deaths—more to tropical diseases than battle—prompting the soon-to-be secretary of state John Hay's famous observation of the conflict as "a splendid little war." Many of the units that fought in the war were National Guard units, and they mirrored many of the changes in American society.

African American Soldiers in the War

Certain that African-American men could resist tropical diseases, United States military officials recruited them as soldiers. Although subjected to segregation and discrimination, these "smoked Yankees" (as the Spanish troops referred to them) responded bravely and played a crucial role in the American invasion and takeover of Cuba.

The Course of the War

American military operations began with a stunning naval victory directed by Commodore George Dewey over the Spanish fleet in Manila Bay, resulting in the U.S. occupation of the Philippine Islands. In the Caribbean, the United States invaded Cuba, captured Santiago, occupied Puerto Rico, and destroyed Spain's only remaining battle fleet, forcing Spain's surrender in August 1898. Only 379 Americans died in battle, but more than 5,200 died of disease or accidents.

Acquisition of Empire

The treaty ending the Spanish-American War called for Spanish recognition of Cuban independence; Spanish cession of Puerto Rico, Guam, and the Philippine Islands to the United States; and U.S. payment of $20 million to Spain.

The Treaty of Paris Debate

Promptly submitted to the Senate for ratification, the Treaty of Paris set off a storm of debate throughout the country. Members of an Anti-Imperialistic League argued that American acquisition of colonies would prove to be undemocratic, costly, and potentially harmful to the interests of labor and racial harmony. Proponents of imperialism repeated the economic, strategic, and intellectual arguments justifying American expansionism. The Senate ratified the treaty in February 1899, with only two votes to spare.

Guerrilla Warfare in the Philippines

Demanding independence, Filipino insurgents led by Emilio Aguinaldo fought a guerrilla war against American takeover of the islands. Proving much more difficult and costly than the war against Spain, the Philippine-American War (1899–1902) convinced American leaders of the need to prepare the island archipelago for eventual self-government.

The Open Door

By the end of the nineteenth century, outside powers had carved China into spheres of influence, threatening to reduce or even eliminate American economic interests there. Through a series of diplomatic notes written in 1899–1900, Secretary of State John Hay urged an "Open Door" policy in China that preserved for China some semblance of national authority over its territory and trade. The "Open Door" policy would allow the United States access to commercial opportunities equal to the other foreign powers.

Conclusion: Outcome of the War with Spain

The war with Spain propelled McKinley and the Republicans to new heights of popularity and solidified American confidence. From 1867 to 1900, the United States had transformed itself from a relatively small, isolationist nation to a bona fide world power.

LEARNING OBJECTIVES

After mastering this chapter, you should be able to:

1. Analyze how and why United States territorial expansion in the 1890s differed from the nation's earlier expansionist moves.

2. Explain the economic, strategic, and intellectual factors sparking American interest in overseas expansion in the latter nineteenth century.

3. Illustrate how the United States reasserted the Monroe Doctrine and promoted Pan-American interests during this era.

4. List the territories acquired by the United States during this era and explain the various processes of acquisition.

5. Describe the causes, major events, and consequences of the Spanish-American War.

6. List and explain the factors contributing to the growth of American newspapers in the 1890s, noting especially the popularity of "yellow journalism."

7. Evaluate the performance of President McKinley in resolving international problems.

8. Discuss the treatment and performance of African-American soldiers during the Spanish-American War.

9. Contrast the arguments offered for and against ratification of the treaty ending the Spanish-American War and providing for American colonies.

10. Describe the causes, course, and consequences of the Philippine-American War (1899–1902).

11. Explain the origin and purpose of the Open Door policy in China.

GLOSSARY

To build your social science vocabulary, familiarize yourself with the following terms:

1. **contiguous** touching; adjoining. "Most of these lands were contiguous with existing territories ..."

2. **aberration** departure from a moral standard or a normal state. "Historian Samuel F. Bemis described the overseas expansion of the 1890s as 'the great aberration ...'"

3. **impregnable** incapable of being taken; unconquerable. "they could enunciate bold policies ... while remaining virtually impregnable to foreign attack."

4. **imperialistic** marked by a policy of extending control of one nation or another. "The idea of imperialistic expansion was in the air ..."

5. **Pan-American** involving all of the nations on the American continents in unified activities. "... they based policy on ... Pan-American unity against the nations of the Old World."

6. **protectorate** relationship of superior authority assumed by one nation over another; the dependent nation in such a relationship. "its political clauses effectively made Hawaii an American protectorate ..."

7. **insular** relating to an island; isolated; detached. "The war with Spain ... altered older, more insular patterns of thought ..."

8. **junta** a committee for political purposes, especially the planning or controlling of a revolutionary action. "Cuban insurgents established a junta in New York City ..."

9. **yellow journalism** a technique of newspapers or journals featuring sensationalism as a way to stir attention and increase sales. "...engaged in blatant sensationalization of the news, which became known as 'yellow journalism'"

10. **autonomy** the quality or state of self-government. "The new government ... agreed to offer the Cubans some form of autonomy."

11. **archipelago** a group of islands. "the president can see but one plain path of duty—the acceptance of the archipelago ..."

12. **assimilation** absorption into the cultural tradition of a population or group. "... anti-imperialists argued against assimilation of different races ..."

13. **guerrilla** irregular warfare by independent bands; especially harassment and sabotage. "...a guerilla war between American troops and the newly freed Filipinos..."

IDENTIFICATION

Briefly identify the meaning and significance of the following terms:

1. Theodore Roosevelt_____

_____

2. James G. Blaine_____

_____

3. Queen Liliuokalani_____

_____

4. yellow journalism_____

_____

5. Alfred Thayer Mahan_____

_____

6. The *Maine*_____

_____

7. Anti-Imperialist League_____

_____

8. Emilio Aguinaldo_____

_____

9. Teller Amendment_____

_____

10. Open Door Policy_____

_____

MATCHING

A. Match the following nations with the appropriate description:

_____1. Philippine Islands

    a. joined with the United States and Germany to end the Boxer Rebellion

_____2. China

    b. concluded a treaty with Secretary of State Seward for the sale of Alaska to the U.S.

_____3. Russia

    c. erupted in guerrilla warfare after U.S. refused to recognize its independence

_____4. Venezuela

    d. forced to accept a constitutional provision allowing future United States intervention

_____5. Britain

    e. accepted United States arbitration in a border dispute with British Guiana

    f. subject of America's open door policy

B. Match the following policy statements with the appropriate description:

_____1. Monroe Doctrine

    a. 1867 treaty with Russia that permitted the United States to purchase Alaska

_____2. Teller Amendment

    b. denied European nations the right to meddle in the affairs of the western hemisphere

_____3. Treaty of Paris

    c. preserved for China some semblance of national authority in matters of trade

_____4. Open Door

    d. provided for the organization of civil government in the Philippines

_____5. "Seward's Folly"

    e. ended the Spanish-American War

    f. pledged that the United States had no intention of annexing Cuba

COMPLETION

Answer the question or complete the statement by filling in the blanks with the correct word or words.

1. In 1898, Theodore Roosevelt recruited an intriguing mixture of college athletes and western frontiersmen for his volunteer cavalry unit known as the

    _____.

2. The biological theories of _____, when applied by various writers to human and social development, seemed to call for the triumph of the fit and the elimination of the unfit.

3. Congregational minister and fervent expansionist _____ argued that Americans were members of a God-favored race destined to lead the world.

4. The Hawaiian Islands were known as the _____ because the trading ships of many nations stopped there.

5. American Minister John L. Stevens ordered the marines to assist American rebels in their 1893 revolt against the native government in _____.

6. In his influential book, *The Influence of Sea Power upon History*, _____ argued for the creation of a larger navy to ensure national security and economic growth.

7. One of the foremost champions of an expanded American navy was President Harrison's secretary of the navy from 1889 to 1893, _____.

8. On May 1, 1898, the American fleet under Commodore _____ easily crushed the Spanish fleet in Manila Bay.

9. Prominent anti-imperialist and labor leader _____ feared an influx of cheap labor from Pacific colonies.

10. Sensationalist newspaper reporting called _____ contributed to public opinion backing the Spanish-American War.

TRUE/FALSE

Mark the following statements either T (True) or F (False).

_____ 1. Theodore Roosevelt felt than an occasional war was necessary for the United States to prove its power and test the national spirit.

_____ 2. American business people generally opposed United States acquisition of overseas colonies for fear that foreign products would undercut American prices.

_____ 3. Secretary of State James G. Blaine negotiated reciprocity treaties with Latin American countries in hopes of diverting their trade from Europe to the United States.

_____ 4. As president, Grover Cleveland consistently opposed an imperialistic policy for the United States.

_____ 5. President McKinley in 1897 urged Congress to help the Cuban rebels against Spain.

_____ 6. McKinley's goal in declaring war against Spain was to acquire Cuba as an American colony.

_____ 7. The Spanish American War was inevitable, given Spain's intransigence in refusing to consider any negotiation of the Cuban issue.

_____ 8. Racial theories of the latter nineteenth century contributed to racial harmony and understanding within the United States, easing the burdens of discrimination and segregation suffered by African Americans.

_____ 9. The Spanish-American War established the United States as a dominant force for the twentieth century.

_____ 10. American proclamation, and lack of military enforcement, of the Open Door policy in China would lead to later controversy between the United States and Japan.

MULTIPLE CHOICE

1. During the early nineteenth century, some Americans urged abolition of the foreign service because
   a. our friendship with powerful Britain rendered the service unnecessary.
   b. there existed a shortage of candidates willing to enter the diplomatic field.
   c. the profession itself stirred dangers of entanglement in world struggles.
   d. American policy was too vulnerable to the whims of an uninformed electorate.

2. Proponents in favor of overseas expansion by the United States in the latter nineteenth century argued that
   a. increasing American production necessitated the acquisition of additional markets.
   b. a worldwide scramble for empire might eliminate American opportunities for growth.
   c. it was our duty to extend civilization and Christianity to less privileged peoples.
   d. All of the above.

3. Evangelical Protestants in the latter nineteenth century
   a. believed that the Bible was subject to multiple interpretations.
   b. emphasized the here-and-now as well as the hereafter.
   c. often favored expansionism as a way to reach the lost souls of foreign "heathens."
   d. argued that religion was best discussed in small, private settings.

4. The Inter-American Conference held in 1889 provided for the
   a. automatic arbitration of disputes in the Western Hemisphere.
   b. union of the United States and Latin America in a customs-free trade partnership.
   c. exchange of political, scientific, and cultural information among member nations.
   d. All of the above.

5. The United States reasserted the Monroe Doctrine as a foreign policy by
   a. negotiating reciprocity treaties with the nations of Latin America.
   b. insisting that Britain submit its dispute with Venezuela over the boundary of British Guiana to the United States for arbitration.
   c. insisting that Britain pay the United States for damages caused by Confederate raiders built and outfitted in British shipyards during the Civil War.
   d. entering the Spanish-American War on behalf of Cuban independence.

6. Hawaii was annexed to the United States when
   a. a treaty was negotiated with the islands in 1875.
   b. American residents revolted in 1893 and formed a republic.
   c. President Cleveland served his second term as president.
   d. a joint resolution was passed by Congress during the Spanish-American War.

7. Military strategist and historian Alfred Thayer Mahan advocated an American policy of
   a. increasing imports of agricultural and manufactured goods.
   b. constructing railroads in Central and South America.
   c. expanding the nation's merchant marine and navy.
   d. All of the above.

8. President Grover Cleveland responded to Cuba's war against Spain by
   a. supporting U.S. annexation of Cuba.
   b. offering to mediate the struggle.
   c. urging U.S. intervention in the war on Cuba's behalf.
   d. favoring recognition of Cuban independence.

9. In 1898, the American battleship *Maine* was
   a. sent to Manila as a gesture of strength and good will.
   b. captured by Spanish authorities in Havana.
   c. probably sunk as a result of an accidental internal explosion.
   d. sabotaged by Cuban revolutionaries.

10. In leading the country toward war, McKinley might properly be labeled a
    a. weak and indecisive president.
    b. victim of the war hysteria sweeping the country.
    c. wily manipulator for imperial gains.
    d. moderate in weighing both American interests and international considerations.

11. During the Spanish-American War, African-American soldiers
    a. played a major role in the Cuban campaign.
    b. were utilized only in back-up and support positions.
    c. encountered little or no discrimination during training at home.
    d. refused to volunteer for military actions.

12. The Spanish-American War resulted in a
    a. long and costly military effort for the United States.
    b. sharp sense among Americans of deception and betrayal by their government.
    c. series of particularly embarrassing American naval defeats.
    d. greater loss of American lives to tropical diseases than battle.

13. Many anti-imperialists opposed American annexation of the Philippines because they feared that
    a. too many uneducated Filipinos would vote.
    b. it violated the very principles of independence and self-determination.
    c. too many Americans would move to the islands.
    d. expanded trade in the Philippines would hurt our trade with China.

14. The Filipinos
    a. cooperated with Americans to drive the Spanish from their islands.
    b. willingly accepted American rule upon defeat of the Spanish.
    c. were granted independence by the United States in 1901.
    d. rejected suggested improvements offered by the Taft Commission for the Philippines.

15. United States Secretary of State John Hay's Open Door policy
    a. provoked the Boxer Rebellion of Chinese nationalists intent on ridding their country of foreign influences.
    b. called for China to grant the United States a sphere of influence with exclusive mining concessions.
    c. demanded the elimination of excessive Chinese tariffs and trade restrictions.
    d. guarded against the partition of China into foreign colonies and the consequent loss of American trading opportunities.

THOUGHT QUESTIONS

To check your understanding of the key issues of this period, solve the following problems:

1. What factors of the latter nineteenth century contributed to an increasing interest by Americans in events abroad, preparing them for a larger role in the world?

2. Discuss the underlying as well as the immediate causes of the Spanish-American War. Why did Secretary of State Hay refer to the conflict as "a splendid little war"?

3. Detail the arguments presented by American anti-imperialists against ratification of the Treaty of Paris in 1898-1899. Why did they fail?

4. The author notes that "historians rarely write of the Philippine-American War." Speculate on why this is so. Does the Philippine-American War seem similar to any other American war? Explain.

5. Why is the debate over whether or not the United States Constitution "follows the flag" into American territories important? How does Cuba's winning of her independence following the Spanish-American War reflect on the debate?

6. Explain the concept of the Open Door policy in China. Would it prove to be a successful policy for the United States?

CRITICAL THINKING EXERCISE

Read the following selections: "The March of the Flag" (1898) by Albert Beveridge and "On Empire and the Philippines" (1898) by William Graham Sumner. Answer the questions following the reading selections.

Albert Beveridge, "The March of the Flag" (1898)

It is a noble land that God has given us; a land that can feed and clothe the world; a land whose coastlines would enclose half the countries of Europe; a land set like a sentinel between the two imperial oceans of the globe, a greater England with a nobler destiny.

It is a mighty people that He has planted on this soil; a people sprung from the most masterful blood of history; a people perpetually revitalized by the virile, man-producing working folk of all the earth; a people imperial by virtue of their power, by right of their institutions, by authority of their Heaven-directed purposes-the propagandists and not the misers of liberty.

It is a glorious history our God has bestowed upon His chosen people; a history heroic with faith in our mission and our future; a history of statesmen who flung the boundaries of the Republic out into unexplored lands and savage wilderness; a history of soldiers who carried the flag across blazing deserts and through the ranks of hostile mountains, even to the gates of sunset; a history of a multiplying people who overran a continent in half a century; a history of prophets who saw the consequences of evils inherited from the past and of martyrs who died to save us from them; a history divinely logical, in the process of whose tremendous seasoning we find ourselves to-day.

Therefore, in this campaign, the question is larger than a party question. It is an American question. It is a world question. Shall the American people continue their march toward the commercial supremacy of the world? Shall free institutions broaden their blessed reign as the children of liberty wax in strength, until the empire of our principles is established over the hearts of all mankind?

Have we no mission to perform, no duty to discharge to our fellowman? Has God endowed us with gifts beyond our deserts and marked us as the people of His peculiar favor, merely to rot in our own selfishness, as men and nations must, who take cowardice for their companion and self for their deity-as China has, as India has, as Egypt has?

Shall we be as the man who had one talent and hid it, or as he who had ten talents and use them until they grew to riches? And shall we reap the reward that waits on our discharge of our high duty; shall we occupy new markets for what our farmers raise, our factories make, our merchants sell-aye, and, please God, new markets for what our ships shall carry?

Hawaii is ours, Puerto Rico is to be ours; at the prayer of her people Cuba finally will be ours; in the islands of the East, even to the gates of Asia, coaling stations are to be ours at the very least; the flag of a liberal government is to float over the Philippines, and may it be the banner that Taylor unfurled in Texas and Frémont carried to the coast.

The Opposition tells us that we ought not to govern a people without their consent. I answer, The rule of liberty that all just government derives its authority from the consent of the governed, applies only to those who are capable of self-government. We govern the Indians without their consent, we govern our territories without their consent, we govern our children without their consent. How do they know that our government would be without their consent? Would not the people of the Philippines prefer the just, human, civilizing government of this Republic to the savage, bloody rule of pillage and extortion from which we have rescued them?

And, regardless of this formula of words made only for enlightened, self-governing people, do we owe no duty to the world? Shall we turn these peoples back to the reeking hands from which we have taken them? Shall we abandon them, with Germany, England, Japan, hungering for them? Shall we save them from those nations, to give them a self-rule of tragedy? ... Then, like men and not like children, let us on to our tasks, our mission, and our destiny.

Wonderfully has God guided us. Yonder at Bunker Hill and Yorktown His providence was above us. At New Orleans and on ensanguined seas His hand sustained us. Abraham Lincoln was His minister and His was the altar of freedom the Nation's soldiers set up on a hundred battle-fields. His power directed Dewey in the East and delivered the Spanish fleet into our hands, as He delivered the elder Armada into the hands of our English sires two centuries ago. The American people can not use a dishonest medium of exchange; it is ours to set the world its example of right and honor. We can not fly from our world duties; it is ours to execute the purpose of a fate that has driven us to be greater than our small intentions. we can not retreat from any soil where Providence has unfurled our banner; it is ours to save that soil for liberty and civilization.

William Graham Sumner, from "On Empire and the Philippines" (1898)

There is not a civilized nation that does not talk about its civilizing mission just as grandly as we do. The English, who really have more to boast of it in this respect than anybody else, talk least about it, but the Phariseeism with which they correct and instruct other people has made them hated all over the globe. The French believe themselves the guardians of the highest and purest culture, and that the eyes of all mankind are fixed on Paris, whence they expect oracles of thought and taste. The Germans regard themselves as charged with a mission, especially to us Americans, to save us from egoism and materialism. The Russians, in their books and newspapers, talk about the civilizing mission of Russian in language that might be translated from some of the finest paragraphs of our imperialistic newspapers.

The first principle of Mohammedanism is that we Christians are dogs and infidels, fit only to be enslaved or butchered by Moslems. It is a corollary that wherever Mohammedanism extends it carries, in the belief of its votaries, the highest blessings, and that the whole human race would be enormously elevated if Mohammedanism should supplant Christianity everywhere.

To come, last, to Spain, the Spaniards have, for centuries, considered themselves the most zealous and self-sacrificing Christians, especially charged by the Almighty, on this account, to spread the true religion and civilization over the globe. They think themselves free and noble, leaders in refinement and the sentiments of personal honor, and they despise us as sordid money-grabbers and heretics. I could bring you passages from peninsular authors of the first rank about the grand role of Spain and Portugal in spreading freedom and truth.

Now each nation laughs at all the others when it observes these manifestations of national vanity. You may rely upon it that they are all ridiculous by virtue of these pretensions, including ourselves. The point is that each of them repudiates the standards of the others, and the outlying nations, which are to be civilized, hate all the standards of civilized men.

We assume that what we like and practice, and what we think better, must come as a welcome blessing to Spanish-Americans and Filipinos. This is grossly and obviously untrue. They hate our ways. They are hostile to our ideas. Our religion, language, institutions, and manners offend them. They like their own ways, and if we appear amongst them as rulers, there will be social discord in all the great departments of social interest. The most important thing which we shall inherit from the Spaniards will be the task of suppressing rebellions.

If the United States takes out of the hands of Spain her mission, on the ground that Spain is not executing it well, and if this nation in its turn attempts to be schoolmistress to others, it will shrivel up into the same vanity and self-conceit of which Spain now presents an example. To read our current literature one would think that we were already well on the way to it.

Now, the great reason why all these enterprises which begin by saying to somebody else, "We know what is good for you better than you know yourself and we are going to make you do it," are false and wrong is that they violate liberty; or, to turn the same statement into other words, the reason why liberty, of which we Americans talk so much, is a good thing is that it means leaving people to live out their own lives in their own way, while we do the same.

If we believe in liberty, as an American principle, why do we not stand by it? Why are we going to throw it away to enter upon a Spanish policy of dominion and regulation?

1. What arguments does Beveridge use to support an American policy of imperialism?

2. How does Beveridge respond to the anti-imperialist argument that "we ought not to govern a people without their consent?"

3. Does Sumner seem to think Americans are better or worse than other peoples?

4. How does Sumner respond to the ideas of Beveridge and other imperialists?

5. Why do you think so many Americans of 1898 tended to agree with Beveridge's rather than Sumner's views on the issue of colonial expansion? Faced with a similar issue today, how do you think current Americans would respond?

CHAPTER 22

The Progressive Era, 1895–1917

SUMMARY

In late 1902, writers for *McClure's Magazine* introduced a new type of journalism, investigating and exposing the problems caused by rapid industrialization and urbanization. These journalists, dubbed "muckrakers" by Theodore Roosevelt, contributed to a broad reform movement called *progressivism*. From the mid-1890s through World War I, progressives challenged the status quo and sought changes in the nation's society, politics, economy, culture, and environment.

The Changing Face of Industrialism

In spite of persistent problems of poverty, disease, and racism, a new century and generally improved economic conditions brought a sense of optimism to Americans. The emergence of mammoth business enterprises from 1895 to 1915 led to inevitable changes in managerial attitudes, business organization, and worker roles.

The Innovative Model T

In 1913, Henry Ford established a moving assembly line to mass produce his standard automobile, the Model T. By dramatically reducing the time and costs of production, Ford managed to lower prices and expand sales and profits.

The Burgeoning Trusts

Standard Oil began a national trend among American big businesses toward oligopoly by swallowing up smaller competitors. By 1909, nearly one-third of the nation's manufactured goods were produced by only one percent of the industrial companies. Massive business mergers and reorganizations touched off a national debate over what the national government could and/or should do about the trusts. Many progressives as well as business leaders generally favored moderate reforms that would promote economic progress while protecting private property.

Managing the Machines

Assembly line production caused management to focus on speed and product rather than on the worker. Following Frederick Winslow Taylor's principles of "scientific management," managers tried to extract maximum efficiency from their workers. Factories ran round the clock; jobs became increasingly monotonous and dangerous; and workers lost control of the work pace as well as the "folkways" of the workplace. A 1911 fire at the Triangle Shirtwaist Company in New York City killed 146 people and focused national attention on unsafe working conditions.

Society's Masses

The mass production of goods in America allowed for greater consumption and required a larger work force. Women, African Americans, Mexican Americans, and immigrants played significant roles in the nation's economic expansion and sought to improve their individual as well as group conditions. For many of these people life was incredibly hard, characterized by long hours, low wages, and inadequate housing.

Better Times on the Farm

As many Americans continued to migrate to the cities, those who remained on the nation's farms experienced some prosperity, benefiting from greater production and expanding urban markets. Improved roads and mail services diminished rural isolation and brought farmers into the larger society. Progressive reforms, including efforts to eliminate "farm-bred" diseases and irrigation projects, also contributed to a "better life" on the farm. At the same time, however, land prices rose with improved crop prices, causing rates of farm tenancy to increase, especially in the South.

Women and Children at Work

In 1900, one-fifth of all adult women worked, but most earned only meager wages in industrial or service-oriented jobs. Women of color had even fewer job opportunities or protections, and most found themselves restricted to domestic service. The increase in the number of white women working did not go unnoticed, provoking the criticism that working women threatened the home. Continuing use of child labor also aroused public indignation, and led women reformers to lobby for federal protection of maternal and infant health.

The Niagara Movement and the NAACP

Progressive reforms seemed barely to touch the lives of African Americans. Most continued to live in rural areas, many in the Jim Crow South, laboring in the cotton fields or in unskilled jobs. Few belonged to unions, obtained adequate education, or earned pay equal to that of white workers in the same jobs. African-American leader W.E.B. Du Bois rejected the gradualist approach urged by Booker T. Washington and began the Niagara Movement for racial justice and equality, resulting in the creation of the National Association for the Advancement of Colored People (NAACP) in 1910. Despite limited gains, African Americans continued to experience violence, segregation, and discrimination.

Immigrants in the Labor Force

The "new" immigration of southern and eastern Europeans continued in the early twentieth century. Not all immigrants were permanent. Among some groups, up to fifty percent returned to their homelands. For those who stayed, employers used "Americanization" programs to fashion dutiful habits among foreign workers. Such programs were often resisted by labor unions. After 1910, large numbers of Mexicans fled to the United States, transforming society in the Southwest. Though fewer Chinese immigrants arrived, many Japanese came and settled along the Pacific Coast. The increasing numbers of immigrants intensified nativist sentiments.

Conflict in the Workplace

Long hours, low pay, and the impersonal and unsafe conditions of factory jobs led to an increase of worker strikes, absenteeism, and union membership. Mindful of workers' problems and fearful of potential violence, progressives urged labor reforms.

Organizing Labor

The most successful union, the American Federation of Labor (AFL), restricted membership to skilled male workers and limited its agenda to issues of wages and working conditions. The Women's Trade Union League (WTUL) led the effort to organize women workers and promote their interests. The militant International Workers of the World (IWW) welcomed anyone regardless of gender or race, urging labor solidarity and calling for social revolution.

A New Urban Culture

The first two decades of the twentieth century saw a general improvement in the quality of life for many Americans. Jobs were plentiful, the professions increased, the middle class grew, and new entertainments and inventions emerged.

Production and Consumption

Consumer advertising increased tremendously between 1900 and 1920, informing the new consumer generation about new products and improvements on old ones. Although most Americans' income increased, so did prices, eating up most workers' available spending money. And despite the growth of the middle class, the rich above all, grew richer.

Living and Dying in an Urban Nation

Due to medical advances and improved living conditions, average life expectancies for Americans increased dramatically. Infant mortality remained high, however. Cities grew by leaps and bounds, and by 1920 fewer than one-half of all Americans lived in rural areas. Rising urban affluence led to outlying suburbs, and major cities used zoning as a technique to shape growth and, often, extend racial and ethnic segregation.

Popular Pastimes

Changing work rules and increasing mechanization from 1890 to 1920 gradually allowed American workers greater leisure time for play and enjoyment of the arts. Mass entertainment consisted of sporting events, vaudeville, and later, movies, while phonograph records brought new types of music—ragtime, blues, and jazz—into people's homes. Even popular fiction became mass produced. As audiences grew, entertainment became big business.

Experimentation in the Arts

In the fine arts, Americans sought new forms and styles of expression, reflecting the period's pervading call for change and progress. The nation's urban centers, especially New York City and Chicago, attracted painters, writers, poets, dancers, and musicians interested in artistic experimentation. These artists joined with a generation of people in the fields of politics, journalism, science, education, and a host of others in hopes of progressive change.

Conclusion: *A Ferment of Discovery and Reform*

The first two decades of the twentieth century were a time of sweeping change that affected American society, culture, politics, and the economy. Progressive reform reshaped the landscape of the country, restructured taxes, regulated business, changed the political system, and altered the lives of Americans, especially the working and middle classes, in an attempt to make a difference and fulfill the promise of the nation.

LEARNING OBJECTIVES

After mastering this chapter, you should be able to:

1. Relate the purposes and results of muckraking to the broader movement of progressivism.

2. Discuss the factors that contributed to a progressive movement of reform from 1890 to 1920.

3. Describe what Henry Ford meant when he said he was "going to democratize the automobile" and Ford's contribution to industrialization.

4. Explain the changes in American industrialism during the early twentieth century regarding management and organization.

5. Explain why farmers experienced better times during the early twentieth century.

6. Discuss the contributions made and benefits derived by women, African Americans, Mexican Americans, and immigrants to the nation's economic expansion during the Progressive Era.

7. Explain the origins and purposes of the Niagara Movement and the National Association for the Advancement of Colored People (NAACP).

8. Examine the causes for and results of conflict in the industrial workplace.

9. Analyze the successes and failures of union activities during this era.

10. Discuss the new methods employed by industrialists to increase productivity, job safety, and worker satisfaction.

11. Explain how the effects of mass production and mass entertainment altered the lifestyles and tastes of Americans.

12. Describe the various types of experimentation in the fine arts in America during this era.

GLOSSARY

To build your social science vocabulary, familiarize yourself with the following terms:

1. **muckrakers** those who search out and expose publicly real or apparent misconduct of prominent figures. "Readers were enthralled, … by other muckrakers ... spread swiftly."

2. **burgeoning** expanding; flourishing. "Americans took pride in teeming cities, burgeoning corporations, and other marks of the mass society."

3. **oligopoly** control of an industry or service by a few powerful companies. "… oligopoly— control of a commodity or service by a small number of large, powerful companies."

4. **finance capitalists** investors or business people who subsidize capitalist endeavors. "finance capitalists like J. P. Morgan tended to replace the industrial capitalists of an earlier era."

5. **hallmark** a conspicuous indication of the character or quality of something. "Their efforts ... became another important hallmark of the Progressive Era."

6. **tenancy** the occupancy of lands by paying rent to the owner. "Tenancy grew from one-quarter of all farms in 1880 to more than one-third in 1910."

7. **stereotypes** common or standard impressions usually representing an oversimplified opinion, feeling, or judgment. "Immigrant patterns often departed from traditional stereotypes."

8. **barrios** ethnic grouping in a certain part of a town or city by Latin Americans. "…these *barrios* became cultural islands of family life…."

9. **productivity** a measure of the efficiency of production, usually expressed in terms of output per man-hours. "labor productivity dropped 10 percent between 1915 and 1918 …"

10. **arbitration** process by which the parties to a dispute submit their differences to the judgment of an impartial third party. "the important Hart, Schaffner agreement, which created an arbitration committee ..."

11. **utopian** characterized by impossibly ideal or perfect conditions. "At first scornful of the 'utopian' plan, business leaders across the country soon copied it ..."

12. **zoning** to set aside areas of a city by legal restriction for purposes of business, residential, or entertainment needs. "Zoning ordered city development ..."

13. **avant-garde** characterized by the creation or application of new or experimental ideas, especially in the arts. "Defiantly avant-garde, they shook off convention and experimented with new forms."

IDENTIFICATION

Briefly identify the meaning and significance of the following terms:

1. muckrakers_____

_____

2. progressivism_____

_____

3. Henry Ford_____

_____

4. Triangle Shirtwaist Company Fire_____

_____

5. National Association for the Advancement of Colored People (NAACP)_____

_____

6. Ashcan School_____

_____

7. *Birth of a Nation*_____

_____

8. Women's Trade Union League (WTUL) _____

_____

9. Frederick Winslow Taylor _____

_____

10. International Workers of the World (IWW) _____

_____

MATCHING

A. Match the following with the appropriate description:

_____ 1. Ida Tarbell

a. social worker that headed the Children's Bureau within the Bureau of Labor

_____ 2. Margaret Sanger

b. muckraking author of the "History of the Standard Oil Company"

_____ 3. Grace Abbott

c. fiery young radical who joined the International Workers of the World (IWW) as a teenager

_____ 4. Elizabeth Gurley Flynn

d. outspoken social reformer and head of the birth control movement

_____ 5. Margaret Dreier Robins

e. one of the founding members of the National Association for the Advancement of Colored People (NAACP)

f. organizer of the influential Women's Trade Union League (WTUL)

B. Match the following entertainers with the appropriate description:

_____ 1. D. W. Griffith

a. "Empress of the Blues," she made over eighty records that sold nearly ten million copies

_____ 2. Victor Herbert

b. talented and creative director, he produced the nation's first movie spectacular, *The Birth of a Nation* in 1915

_____ 3. Louis Armstrong

c. classical dancer, she rejected traditional ballet steps to stress improvisation, emotion, and the human form

_____ 4. Bessie Smith

d. composer who helped found ASCAP in 1914

_____ 5. Isadora Duncan

e. played improvisational music that became known as jazz

f. daughter of minstrels who sang in black Vaudeville for over 35 years

100

COMPLETION

Answer the question or complete the statement by filling in the blanks with the correct word or words.

1. The term *muckraker* was coined by _____ in 1906 to describe the practice of exposing the corruption of public and prominent figures.

2. In 1908, Henry Ford introduced the Model T, or _____, in an effort to produce affordable cars for the masses.

3. An industrial research laboratory where scientists and engineers developed new products was first established by _____ in 1900.

4. The Rockefeller Sanitary Commission began a campaign in 1909 that eventually wiped out the _____ disease in rural America.

5. Rejecting the gradualist approach toward civil rights for African Americans, _____ provided inspiration for the Niagara Movement.

6. Begun in 1896, _____ helped diminish farmers' sense of isolation and exposed them to urban thinking, national advertising, and political events.

7. Designed to curtail immigration from southern and eastern Europe, Congress passed a _____ requirement over President Wilson's veto in 1917.

8. A militant labor union, the _____, attracted the support of immigrant factory workers, migrant farm laborers, loggers, and miners.

9. New Orleans musicians Charles "Buddy" Bolden, Ferdinand "Jelly Roll" Morton, and Louis Armstrong helped popularize the new improvisational musical form called _____.

10. During the Progressive Era, a new group of realistic artists in America, known to their critics as the _____, painted scenes of American slums and tenements.

TRUE/FALSE

Mark the following statements either T (True) or F (False).

_____ 1. In responding to the disorder created by industrialization and urbanization, progressives remained hopeful of positive change.

_____ 2. Henry Ford applied the vital economic lesson that a larger unit profit on a smaller number of sales meant greater profits.

_____ 3. Progressive reformers unanimously agreed that business trusts should be broken up to restore individual opportunity and prevent price manipulations.

_____ 4. From 1900 to 1920 in the United States, the divorce rate dropped and the birth rate soared.

_____ 5. To discuss their campaign for civil rights in 1905, African American leaders had to meet on the Canadian side of Niagara Falls because no hotel on the American side would take them.

_____ 6. Mexican Americans significantly contributed to the economic development of the American Southwest.

_____ 7. Industrial psychologists argued that "time and motion" efficiency studies had to be complemented with consideration of worker satisfaction to improve productivity.

_____ 8. The Women's Trade Union League attracted substantial numbers of members but exerted relatively little influence in the promotion of women's rights.

_____ 9. The introduction of zoning laws tended to enforce racial and ethnic segregation in American cities.

_____ 10. The 1913 art show of European Post-Impressionists at the New York Armory was hailed by critics for the realistic presentations of ordinary people and familiar scenes.

MULTIPLE CHOICE

Circle the one alternative that best completes the statement or answers the question.

1. Which of the following authors is NOT associated with muckraking journalism?
   a. Ida Tarbell
   b. Ezra Pound
   c. Lincoln Steffens
   d. Upton Sinclair

2. According to Henry Ford, the key to "democratizing" the automobile was
   a. applying the principles of scientific management.
   b. mass production through a continuous assembly-line process.
   c. increasing workers' wages to $5 per day.
   d. granting workers' demands for an eight-hour workday.

3. The debate between progressives and business leaders over trusts
   a. represented a simple contest between high-minded reformers and greedy businesspeople.
   b. involved all progressives in a national attempt to break up big business.
   c. led businesspeople to oppose virtually all government attempts to regulate the economy.
   d. often found both groups in agreement on fundamental principles.

4. Frederick W. Taylor believed that
   a. machines would end the domination of well-paid craftspeople.
   b. the assembly line would dehumanize workers and damage productivity.
   c. workers should have the unrestricted right to organize.
   d. management should take responsibility for job-related knowledge and enforce its control of the workplace.

5. The Triangle Shirtwaist Company disaster in 1911 called national attention to
   a. militant labor strikes, which seemed to threaten a national revolution.
   b. inadequate regulation of railroads and public transportation.
   c. unsafe and oppressive working conditions in New York factories.
   d. overcrowded residential conditions in New York's Lower East Side.

6. In comparison to 1890, American farmers by 1920
   a. lived in greater isolation from urban society.
   b. had increased in terms of numbers and percentage of the total population.
   c. benefited from greater production and expanded markets.
   d. suffered from greater incidence of "farm-bred" diseases.

7. Most women workers of the early twentieth century
    a. earned minimum standards of wages in unskilled jobs.
    b. possessed the same education and job skills as their male counterparts.
    c. attained managerial or professional positions.
    d. tended to be married rather than single.

8. "Birds of passage" refers to
    a. the journal of the NAACP.
    b. temporary migrants who returned to their homeland.
    c. a group of post-impressionist poets.
    d. an innovative singing technique.

9. Chinese Americans differed from other immigrant groups coming to America during the Progressive Era in that they
    a. intended to remain and establish permanent homes.
    b. declined rather than increased in numbers due to exclusionary laws.
    c. were more likely to be female rather than male.
    d. worked hard to adopt American rather than maintain traditional Chinese customs.

10. Immigrants from Mexico to the United States
    a. arrived in increasing numbers after revolution there in 1910 forced many to flee.
    b. typically came from the lower classes, eager to escape poverty and violence at home.
    c. contributed significantly to the building of highways and railroads in the Southwest.
    d. All of the above.

11. The key to success for the American Federation of Labor (AFL) in the early twentieth century was the union's
    a. acceptance for membership of all industrial workers.
    b. refusal to engage in strikes at the local levels.
    c. limited membership and a concentration on basic issues.
    d. ideological support for labor solidarity and ultimate social revolution.

12. The primary objective of the International Workers of the World (IWW) was to
    a. provide education and "Americanization" for foreign workers.
    b. overthrow the capitalist system.
    c. increase workers' wages and reduce their hours.
    d. convince politicians of the need for protective legislation.

13. In the important Hart, Schaffner agreement, the Women's Trade Union League (WTUL) gained for striking women workers
    a. substantial wage increases.
    b. drastic reduction in work hours.
    c. the right of collective bargaining.
    d. All of the above.

104

14. From 1900 to 1920 in the United States, the
    a. life expectancy for most Americans increased.
    b. farm population significantly increased.
    c. incidence of heart disease and cancer declined.
    d. zoning of American cities reduced patterns of racial segregation.

15. Concerning the fine arts, which of the following trends marked the Progressive Era in America?
    a. Classical ballet steps were emphasized in dance.
    b. Traditional meter and rhyme were rejected as artificial constraints in poetry.
    c. Painting was romanticized and impressionistic.
    d. Americans rejected such crass musical forms as ragtime, blues, and jazz.

THOUGHT QUESTIONS

To check your understanding of the key issues of this period, solve the following problems:

1. What factors combined to create the Progressive Movement for reform during the late nineteenth and early twentieth centuries?

2. Discuss the changes in managerial attitudes, business organization, and industrial worker roles during the early twentieth century.

3. Explain the conditions that prompted formation of the National Association for the Advancement of Colored People (NAACP). Evaluate its success during the Progressive Era.

4. Examine the causes for conflict in the industrial workplace from 1900 to 1920. How did workers and managers respond?

5. Was life in America "better" in 1920 than it had been in 1900? Explain.

CRITICAL THINKING QUESTIONS

Read the following selections: "Atlanta Exposition Address" (1895) by Booker T. Washington, "Of Mr. Booker T. Washington and Others" (1903) by W.E.B. Du Bois, and "A Red Record," (1895) by Ida B. Wells-Barnett. Answer the questions following the reading selections.

Booker T. Washington, "Atlanta Exposition Address" (1895)

… Ignorant and inexperienced, it is not strange that in the first years of our new life we began at the top instead of at the bottom; that a seat in Congress or the state legislature was more sought than real estate or industrial skill; that the political convention or stump speaking had more attractions than starting a dairy farm or truck garden.

A ship lost at sea for many days suddenly sighted a friendly vessel. From the mast of the unfortunate vessel was seen a signal, "Water, water; we die of thirst!" The answer from the friendly vessel at once came back, "Cast down your bucket where you are." … The captain of the distressed vessel, at last heeding the injunction, cast down his bucket, and it came up full of fresh, sparkling water…. To those of my race who underestimate the importance of cultivating friendly relations with the southern white man, who is their next-door neighbor, I would say: "Cast down your bucket where you are"—cast it down in making friends in every manly way of the people of all races by whom we are surrounded.

Cast it down in agriculture, mechanics, in commerce, in domestic service, and in the professions…. Our greatest danger is that in the great leap from slavery to freedom we may overlook the fact that the masses of us are to live by the productions of our hands, and fail to keep in mind that we shall prosper in proportion as we learn to dignify and glorify common labour, and put brains and skill into the common occupations of life….

No race can prosper till it learns that there is as much dignity in tilling a field as in writing a poem. It is at the bottom of life we must begin, and not at the top.

To those of the white race who look to the incoming of those of foreign birth and strange tongue and habits for the prosperity of the South, were I permitted I would repeat what I say to my own race, "Cast down your bucket where you are." Cast it down among the eight millions of Negroes whose habits you know, whose fidelity and love you have tested in days when to have proved treacherous meant the ruin of your firesides. Cast down your bucket among these people who have, without strikes and labour wars, tilled your fields, cleared your forests, built your railroads and cities, and brought forth treasures from the bowels of the earth…. Casting down your bucket among my people … you will find that they will buy your surplus land, make blossom the waste places in your fields, and run your factories. While doing this, you can be sure in the future, as in the past, that you and your families will be surrounded by the most patient, faithful, law-abiding, and unresentful people that the world has seen…. In all things that are purely social we can be as separate as the finders, yet one as the hand in all things essential to mutual progress….

The wisest among my race understand that the agitation of questions of social equality is the extremest folly, and that progress in the enjoyment of all the privileges that will come to us must be the result of severe and constant struggle rather than of artificial forcing. No race that has anything to contribute to the markets of the world is long in any degree ostracized. It is important and right that all privileges of the law be ours, but it is vastly more important that we be prepared for the exercise of these privileges. The opportunity to earn a dollar in a factory just now is worth infinitely more than the opportunity to spend a dollar in an opera-house.

W.E.B. Du Bois, from "Of Mr. Booker T. Washington and Others" (1903)

Easily the most striking thing in the history of the American Negro since 1876 is the ascendancy of Mr. Booker T. Washington…. His programme of industrial education, conciliation of the South, and submission and silence as to civil and political rights was not wholly original…. But Mr. Washington first indissolubly linked these things; he … changed it from a by-path into a veritable Way of Life….

Mr. Washington represents in Negro thought the old attitude of adjustment and submission; but adjustment at such a peculiar time as to make his programme unique. This is an age of unusual economic development, and Mr. Washington's programme naturally takes an economic cast, becoming a gospel of Work and Money to such an extent as apparently almost completely to overshadow the higher aims of life…. Mr. Washington's programme practically accepts the alleged inferiority of the Negro races…. In the history of nearly all other races and peoples the doctrine preached at such crises has been that manly self-respect is worth more than lands and houses, and that a people who voluntarily surrender such respect, or cease striving for it, are not worth civilizing.

… Mr. Washington distinctly asks that black people give up, at least for the present, three things,—
First, political power.

Second, insistence on civil rights.

Third, higher education of Negro youth,

… The question then comes: Is it possible, and probable, that nine millions of men can make effective progress in economic lines if they are deprived of political rights, made a servile caste, and allowed only the most meagre chance for developing their exceptional men? If history and reason give any distinct answer to these questions, it is an emphatic No....

… while it is a great truth to say that the Negro must strive and strive mightily to help himself, it is equally true that unless his striving be not simply seconded, but rather aroused and encouraged, by the initiative of the richer and wiser environing group, he cannot hope for great success.

… So far as Mr. Washington preaches Thrift, Patience, and Industrial Training for the masses, we must hold up his hands and strive with him, rejoicing in his honors and glorying in the strength of this Joshua called of God and of man to lead the headless host. But so far as Mr. Washington apologizes for injustice, North or South, does not rightly value the privilege and duty of voting, belittles the emasculating effects of caste distinctions, and opposes the higher training and ambition of our brighter minds,—so far as he, the South, or the Nation, does this, we must unceasingly and firmly oppose them.

Ida Wells Barnett, *A Red Record* (1895)

A word as to the charge itself. In considering the third reason assigned by the Southern white people for the butchery of blacks, the question must be asked, what the white man means when he charges the black man with rape. Does he mean the crime which the statutes of the states describe as such? Not by any means. With the Southern white man, any misalliance existing between a white woman and a colored man is a sufficient foundation for the charge of rape. The Southern white man says that it is impossible for a voluntary alliance to exist between a white woman and a colored man, and therefore, the fact of an alliance is a proof of force. In numerous instances where colored men have been lynched on the charge of rape, it was positively known at the time of lynching, and indisputably proven after the victim's death, that the relationship sustained between the man and the woman was voluntary and clandestine, and that in no court of law could even the charge of assault have been successfully maintained.

It was for the assertion of this fact, in the defense of her own race, that the writer hereof became an exile; her property destroyed and her return to her home forbidden under penalty of death, for writing the following editorial which was printed in her paper, the *Free Speech*, in Memphis, Tenn., May 21, 1892:

"Eight Negroes lynched since last issue of the *Free Speech*: one at Little Rock, Ark., last Saturday morning where the citizens broke (?) into the penitentiary and got their man; three near Anniston, Ala., one near New Orleans; and three at Clarksville, Ga.; the last three for killing a white man, and five on the same old racket—the new alarm about raping white women. The same programme of hanging, then shooting bullets into the lifeless bodies was carried out to the letter. Nobody in this section of the country believes in the old threadbare lie that Negro men rape white women. If Southern white men are not careful, they will overreach themselves and public sentiment will have a reaction; a conclusion will then be reached which will be very damaging to the moral reputation of their women."

But threats cannot suppress the truth, and while the Negro suffers the soul deformity, resultant from two and a half centuries of slavery, he is no more guilty of this vilest of all vile charges than the white man who would blacken his name.

During all the years of slavery, no such charge was ever made, not even during the dark days of the rebellion.... While the master was away fighting to forge the fetters upon the slave, he left his wife and children with no protectors save the Negroes themselves....

Likewise during the period of alleged "insurrection," and alarming "race riots," it never occurred to the white man that his wife and children were in danger of assault. Nor in the Reconstruction era, when the hue and cry was against "Negro Domination," was there ever a thought that the domination would ever contaminate a fireside or strike toward the virtue of womanhood....

It is not the purpose of this defense to say one word against the white women of the South. Such need not be said, but it is their misfortune that the … white men of that section … to justify their own barbarism … assume a chivalry which they do not possess. True chivalry respects all womanhood, and no one who reads the record, as it is written in the faces of the million mulattos in the South, will for a minute conceive that the southern white man had a very chivalrous regard for the honor due the women of his race, or respect for the womanhood which circumstances placed in his power.... Virtue knows no color line, and the chivalry which depends on complexion of skin and texture of hair can command no honest respect.

When emancipation came to the Negroes ... from every nook and corner of the North, brave young white women ... left their cultured homes, their happy associations and their lives of ease, and with heroic determination went to the South to carry light and truth to the benighted blacks.... They became the social outlaws in the South. The peculiar sensitiveness of the southern white men for women, never shed its protecting influence about them. No friendly word from their own race cheered them in their work; no hospitable doors gave them the companionship like that from which they had come. No chivalrous white man doffed his hat in honor or respect. They were "Nigger teachers"—unpardonable offenders in the social ethics of the South, and were insulted, persecuted and ostracized, not by Negroes, but by the white manhood which boasts of its chivalry toward women.

And yet these northern women worked on, year after year.... Threading their way through dense forests, working in schoolhouses, in the cabin and in the church, thrown at all times and in all places among the unfortunate and lowly Negroes, whom they had come to find and to serve, these northern women, thousands and thousands of them, have spent more than a quarter of a century in giving the colored people their splendid lessons for home and heart and soul. Without protection, save that which innocence gives to every good woman, they went about their work, fearing no assault and suffering none. Their chivalrous protectors were hundreds of miles away in their northern homes, and yet they never feared any "great dark-faced mobs." ... They never complained of assaults, and no mob was ever called into existence to avenge crimes against them. Before the world adjudges the Negro a moral monster, a vicious assailant of womanhood and a menace to the sacred precincts of home, the colored people ask the consideration of the silent record of gratitude, respect, protection and devotion of the millions of the race in the South, to the thousands of northern white women who have served as teachers and missionaries since the war....

These pages are written in no spirit of vindictiveness.... We plead not for the colored people alone, but for all victims of the terrible injustice which puts men and women to death without form of law. During the year 1894, there were 132 persons executed in the United States by due form of law, while in the same year, 197 persons were put to death by mobs, who gave the victims no opportunity to make a lawful defense. No comment need be made upon a condition of public sentiment responsible for such alarming results.

1. Which of the authors would most whites of the day have found most acceptable, Washington, Du Bois, or Wells-Barnett? Explain.

2. What was the meaning of Washington's admonition to "Cast down your bucket where you are?" To whom was he addressing this phrase?

3. Does Du Bois agree with Washington in any way? In what ways does Du Bois find Washington's message unacceptable?

4. According to Wells-Barnett, what was the purported cause of most lynchings of southern black men? What evidence does she offer to prove such charges false?

5. Who are the real "moral monsters" in the view of Wells-Barnett?

CHAPTER 23

From Roosevelt to Wilson in the Age of Progressivism, 1900–1920

SUMMARY

Presidents Roosevelt, Taft, and Wilson all espoused the progressive spirit of reform in the legislation that they championed and in their view of the federal government's role in the life of the nation. Despite trying to continue with Roosevelt's basic policies and directions, Taft's presidency was far from smooth, and a bitter rift developed between the two men and within their party opening the door for Democrat Woodrow Wilson.

The Spirit of Progressivism

Despite philosophical differences and divergent concerns, progressives held to several basic tenets. They were optimistic about human nature as they sought to humanize and regulate big business and politics. They believed in the necessity of direct intervention in people's lives. They wanted the government at all levels to take an active role in manifesting reform. They were driven by their Protestant morals to reform the nation using the techniques of science. And finally, Progressivism touched the entire nation in one way or another.

The Rise of the Professions

Between 1890 and 1920, national societies and associations emerged among accountants, architects, teachers, ministers, doctors, lawyers, social workers, and others. These professionals were part of a new middle class that was educated, active, and assertive, dedicated not only to improving their respective professions, but also to bettering living conditions on all levels of society. They provided the leadership for much of the progressive reform that occurred during the period.

The Social-Justice Movement

Groups of concerned professionals put pressure on cities and businesses to dramatically improve housing, recreational, and health conditions in urban areas. These social-justice reformers were interested in social cures, not individual charity. They collected data on urban conditions, wrote books and pamphlets, and sought recognition of social work as a distinct field within the social sciences.

The Purity Crusade

Many reform-conscious women dedicated themselves to the crusade to abolish alcohol and its evils from American life. Promoted by superb organizational efforts under the Women's Christian Temperance Union and the Anti-Saloon League, these reformers succeeded in winning passage of the Prohibition Amendment to the U.S. Constitution which they thought was a major step in eliminating social instability, poverty, and moral wrong. Many prohibitionists also worked to eliminate prostitution in society.

Woman Suffrage, Woman Rights

With more women now college-educated and becoming reform-conscious, numerous organizations and groups were started to promote the rights and welfare of American women. Women progressives also worked to regulate child and female labor. African-American women, who were often excluded from mainstream groups, formed their own associations to address their concerns. Driven by the need to influence public officials, many women in the social-justice movement dedicated themselves to winning the vote. After long delays, the suffragists succeeded in gaining passage of the Nineteenth Amendment.

A Ferment of Ideas: Challenging the Status Quo

Stressing the role of the environment in shaping human behavior and a more pragmatic approach to knowledge, a new generation of thinkers demanded reform. John Dewey pioneered a pragmatic revolution in education, decrying rote learning and simple memorization. Louis Brandeis pioneered a movement of "sociological jurisprudence" which recognized the motivations behind crime and the role of the environment in shaping those motivations. Socialists, led by Eugene Debs, attacked the abuses of capitalism and formed the Socialist party of America, which doubled in membership between 1904 and 1908 and elected many local officials.

Reform in the Cities and States

Progressive reformers wanted to utilize the government at every level to effect change. To do so, they tried to limit the influence of special interest groups by supporting political reforms like the direct primary and direct elections of senators to make government more accountable to the people. They also believed that reform should be in the hands of experts rather than politicians who could be easily influenced. Through their efforts, a multitude of special commissions and agencies staffed by experts emerged to regulate everything from railroad rates to public health.

Interest Groups and the Decline of Popular Politics

Due to various factors, voter turnout dropped sharply in the quarter century after 1900. Many people turned to interest groups and professional and trade associations to promote their respective concerns.

Reform in the Cities

Stressing efficiency and results, substantial reform movements within city governments spread across the nation. Using new corps of experts, city officials constructed model governments, relatively independent from the state legislature's control, that pushed through scientifically-based policies that reformed everything from the tax code to municipal ownership of public utilities to the regulation of corrupt electoral practices.

Action in the States

Finding that many problems were greater than the cities, progressive reformers looked to state governments for action. States across the nation formed commissions to regulate businesses, especially the utilities, insurance, and transportation. Through these commissions, progressives hoped to eradicate corrupt alliances between politicians and business leaders. They also pushed for political reforms like the initiative, recall, and referendum to make politicians more accountable to the people and less allied with business leaders. Progressives also pushed state legislatures to pass laws to improve and regulate labor conditions, especially for women and children, and to dedicate more state money to the improvement of mental and penal institutions and universities. The most famous reform governor of the Progressive Era was Robert LaFollette of Wisconsin. Under the "Wisconsin Idea," LaFollette improved education and workers' compensation, lowered railroad rates, and brought forth the first state income tax.

The Republican Roosevelt

As McKinley's successor, Roosevelt brought a new spirit of enthusiasm and aggressiveness to the presidency. He believed that the presidency was a "bully pulpit" for reform. Early in his administration, Roosevelt appeared to support racial progress but later retreated in the face of growing criticism and his own belief in African-American inferiority.

Busting the Trusts

Distinguishing between "good" and "bad" trusts, Roosevelt sought to protect the former and regulate the latter. To regulate corporations, Congress created the Department of Commerce and Labor and the Bureau of Corporations. Roosevelt also pursued regulation through antitrust suits, most notably against J. P. Morgan's Northern Securities Company and the American Tobacco Company. Roosevelt was not a trustbuster, however. For the most part, he used antitrust threats to control and regulate business.

"Square Deal" in the Coalfields

Viewing the federal government as an impartial broker between labor and management, Roosevelt pressured the coal companies to settle their differences with the United Mine Workers, even bringing both sides to the White House for a conference. When the coal companies failed to compromise, Roosevelt threatened to use the army to seize control of the mines, forcing them to settle. Roosevelt was neither pro-labor or pro-business; he pursued a middle-of-the-road approach to curb abuse and enlarge individual opportunity.

Roosevelt Progressivism at Its Height

Easily winning in his bid for reelection in 1904 with 57 percent of the vote, Roosevelt readied himself for more reform.

Regulating the Railroads

Roosevelt moved into other areas of reform in his second term including railroad regulation, employers' liability for federal employees, greater federal control over corporations, and laws regulating child labor and factory inspections. Winning a major victory in the regulation of railroads, the powers of the Interstate Commerce Commission were strengthened by passage of the Hepburn Act.

Cleaning up Food and Drugs
The Meat Inspection Act and the Pure Food and Drug Act that answered the public demand for regulation of the food and drug industry was inspired by Sinclair's *The Jungle*. These laws significantly increased the safety of the nation's food and drug supply.

Conserving the Land
Roosevelt significantly broadened the concept and policy of conservation of natural resources. He increased the amount of land in preserves from 45 million acres to almost 195 million acres and pushed for national parks and forests.

The Ordeal of William Howard Taft
William Howard Taft, who unlike his predecessor disdained the limelight, succeeded Roosevelt as president in 1908. Though initially supported by Roosevelt, he lacked Roosevelt's zest for politics and his faith in the power of the federal government to intercede in the public arena. Facing tension within his own party and a number of troublesome problems, Taft's years in the White House were not happy, and he suffered by comparison to both his predecessor, Roosevelt, and his successor, Woodrow Wilson.

Party Insurgency
Republicans were divided over many issues, tariffs being one of the most important. An attempt to lower tariffs that was stalled in the house by protectionists put Taft in the middle between progressives and protectionists. Taft tried to compromise, eventually supporting the Payne-Aldrich Act, which angered progressives. Discredited in their eyes, he leaned more on party conservatives. Among progressive Republicans there was a growing desire for a Roosevelt revival.

The Ballinger-Pinchot Affair
The conservation issue caused more problems for Taft when he supported the attempt by Secretary of Interior Ballinger to sell a million acres of public land that Gifford Pinchot, the chief forester, had withdrawn from sale. When Pinchot protested and leaked information to the press, Ballinger was fired from the Forest Service, and conservationists were furious.

Taft Alienates the Progressives
Though progressives were interested in increased railroad regulation, they found some elements of Taft's Mann-Elkins Act, intended to further strengthen the Interstate Commerce Commission, problematic. When Taft made support of the bill a test of party loyalty, the progressives resisted, leading Taft to openly oppose them in the midterm elections of 1910. With progressive and democratic gains in those elections, Taft lost ground. Despite his difficulties, he successfully supported several important pieces of legislation, including the Sixteenth Amendment authorizing income taxes, the creation of a Children's Bureau in the federal government, and laws mandating employer liability and an eight-hour work day. Taft was also active in initiating antitrust suits, supporting the court's use of the "rule of reason" against unfair trade practices by

corporations. As his presidency continued, Taft further alienated himself from his former mentor Roosevelt, and the former president decided to seek the presidency in 1912.

Differing Philosophies in the Election of 1912
Taft controlled the party machinery and captured the Republican nomination. Roosevelt, promoting his program of New Nationalism organized progressive Republicans into the Progressive Party. The Democrats, in nominating the scholarly Woodrow Wilson and his program of New Freedom, took advantage of the wounded Republican party and won the presidency. Wilson's New Freedom emphasized business competition and small government while still supporting the social-justice movement. Though both Roosevelt and Wilson saw the nation's economic growth and its effects on individuals and society as the main problem for the nation, they disagreed as to the solution. Where Roosevelt welcomed the centralization of federal power, Wilson distrusted it.

Woodrow Wilson's New Freedom
Wilson announced his New Freedom program and called for a return to business competition and an end to special privilege. Often a moralist, Wilson was able to inspire Americans with his ideas, his graceful oratory, and his passionate belief in his causes.

The New Freedom in Action
Despite his lack of political experience, Wilson seized the progressive initiative and pushed landmark legislation through Congress. Days after his inauguration, Wilson called Congress into special session and successfully pushed through the Underwood Tariff, substantially reducing rates and levying a modest income tax to make up for the lower tariff. Taking advantage of a new unity in the Democratic party, Wilson also successfully supported the Federal Reserve Act, which centralized banking and created the Federal Reserve Board to regulate interest rates and the money supply; the Clayton Antitrust Act, which brought about much needed improvements in regulating trusts; and outlawed interlocking directorates. Wilson saw these laws as the completion of his New Freedom program, which angered some progressives.

Wilson Moves Toward the New Nationalism
Despite measured successes during 1914 and 1915 in labor, child labor, banking, business, and farming reforms, Wilson's New Freedom was a disappointment to women and African Americans. In 1916, partially motivated by the upcoming election, Wilson began pushing for a multitude of reforms. After 1916, Wilson accepted much of Roosevelt's New Nationalism, supporting greater federal power and regulation. But as America neared military intervention in the war in Europe, the reform experiment came to an end.

Conclusion: The Fruits of Progressivism

Though the progressives were extremely successful in some respects—regulatory commissions, child labor laws, direct primaries, and city improvements—there were many social problems they did not solve. Some problems like race, they failed even to address. Despite this, the actions of Roosevelt and Wilson significantly expanded the powers of the presidency, and government at all levels began to accept the responsibility for the welfare of society. The onset of World War I, however, cut short the progressive spirit of reform.

LEARNING OBJECTIVES

After mastering this chapter, you should be able to:

1. Determine specifically what progressivism meant at the city and state level (especially the reform efforts under Robert La Follette).

2. Explain what Roosevelt meant by the "bully pulpit" and how he applied this to his administration.

3. Analyze Roosevelt's attitude toward the trusts and the role of the federal government in trade issues and labor disputes.

4. Summarize the progressive measures of the Roosevelt presidency, emphasizing railroad regulation, food and drug regulation, and conservation.

5. Contrast Taft's approach to executive leadership with Roosevelt's, specifying their different attitudes toward reform.

6. Determine the issues that adversely affected Taft's relationship with progressives and influenced his downfall in 1912.

7. Determine the political effects of Taft's handling of the Ballinger-Pinchot affair and his support for the Payne-Aldrich Tariff.

8. Reveal the specific disappointments of African Americans, farmers, and women to Wilson's first-term policies.

9. List and briefly explain the major reforms of Wilson's second term.

10. Discuss the six or so major characteristics that defined and shaped progressivism.

11. Examine the participation of women in the social-justice movement and in the efforts to bring about prohibition and women's suffrage.

11. Summarize the impact of new ideas such as pragmatism, socialism, and environmentalism on progressive reform.

13. Discuss the issues involved and the reasons for Wilson's success in the 1912 election.

14. Define the basic theory and attitude behind Wilson's New Freedom.

15. Outline the major components of the Underwood Tariff, the Federal Reserve Act, and the Clayton Antitrust Act.

GLOSSARY

To build your social science vocabulary, familiarize yourself with the following terms:

1. **protectionist** one who believes in high protective tariffs to shield domestic manufacturing. "... passed a bill providing for lower rates, but in the Senate, protectionists raised them."

2. **rule of reason** discretionary standard applied by the courts to determine whether a corporation is in violation of antitrust laws. "... established the 'rule of reason' which allowed the Court to determine whether a business was a 'reasonable' restraint on trade."

3. **interlocking directorates** companies that are united by common directors or trustees. "...the Sherman Antitrust Act of 1890, this law outlawed interlocking directorates..."

4. **antitrust** of or relating to laws protecting industry and commerce from unfair or illegal business practices. "Taft thought the decisions gave the Court too much discretion, and he pushed ahead with the antitrust effort ..."

5. **suffragist** one who advocates the right of women to vote. "After three generations of suffragist efforts, the Nineteenth Amendment ..."

6. **workers compensation** state laws that guarantee monetary compensation to workers injured on the job, paid in part or full by the employer. "He improved education, workers' compensation…"

7. **referendum** a device (usually implemented at the state level) that allows voters to accept or reject an existing statute at the ballot box "Oregon adopted the initiative and referendum…"

8. **conservationist** one who believes in preserving natural resources such as forests and wildlife. "He established the first comprehensive national conservation policy."

9. **insurgency** an aggressive or rebellious attitude. "There was growing party insurgency against high rates."

10. **pragmatism** the belief in that which is practical, measurable, or useful. "A new doctrine called pragmatism emerged in this ferment of ideas."

11. **progressivism** the movement for political, economic, and social reforms. "Finally, progressivism was distinctive because it touched virtually the whole nation."

12. **methodology** a set of methods or procedures for regulating a discipline. "social workers discovered each other's efforts, shared methodology."

116

IDENTIFICATION

Briefly identify the meaning and significance of the following terms:

1. Northern Securities Company _____

_____

2. social-justice movement_____

_____

3. Ben Lindsey _____

_____

4. General Federation of Women's Clubs_____

_____

5. Square Deal _____

_____

6. pragmatism _____

_____

7. New Freedom_____

_____

8. "rise of the professions" _____

_____

9. Women's Christian Temperance Union (WCTU)_____

_____

10. Adamson Act _____

_____

MATCHING

A. Match the following public figures with the appropriate description:

_____1. Gifford Pinchot

    a. reform governor of Wisconsin who campaigned for federal control of railroads

_____2. Upton Sinclair

    b. leader of the NAACP who proposed a National Race Commission

_____3. Oswald Garrison Villard

    c. conservation activist and head of the Forest Service under Roosevelt

_____4. Richard Ballinger

    d. writer who exposed "hideous" conditions and practices within the meatpacking industry

_____5. Robert La Follette

    e. Taft's secretary of the interior who offered for sale a million acres of land to private concerns

    f. progressive and first Jewish justice of the Supreme Court, appointed by Wilson

B. Match the following federal laws with the appropriate description:

_____1. Hepburn Act

    a. established a sound, flexible currency system

_____2. Payne-Aldrich Act

    b. outlawed interlocking directorates and unfair pricing policies

_____3. Underwood Act

    c. lowered tariff rates an average of 15 percent and authorized the first graduated income tax

_____4. Clayton Act

    d. placed telephone and telegraph companies under ICC supervision

_____5. Mann-Elkins Act

    e. empowered the ICC to fix reasonable maximum railroad rates

    f. conservative tariff law that discredited Taft and split the Republican party

COMPLETION

Answer the question or complete the statement by filling in the blanks with the correct word or words.

1. Because he believed that the presidency should be the primary institution for leadership and activity, Roosevelt called it the _____.

2. The executive department created by Roosevelt to investigate corporate and business practices was the Department of _____.

3. The direct primary, the direct election of Senators and three measures that made politicians responsive to popular will—the _____, the _____, and the _____—were among the political reforms achieved by the progressives.

4. Republican progressives and conservatives split after 1909, mainly because of congressional passage of the _____.

5. In the 1912 presidential campaign, Roosevelt called for a national approach to U.S. problems and called his program the _____.

6. The _____ was influential in the enactment of the Eighteenth Amendment to the Constitution, which prohibited the manufacture, sale, and transportation of intoxicating liquors.

7. Upton Sinclair's novel *The Jungle* caused Roosevelt to demand an investigation of the meat-packing industry and led to the passage of the _____.

8. Robert La Follette's _____ was one of the most important reform programs in the history of state government.

9. For Woodrow Wilson, the most important issue of the 1912 campaign was an economy that was not planned, but was _____.

10. In pursuing reform objectives, the progressives displayed _____ about human nature.

119

TRUE/FALSE

Mark the following statements either T (True) or F (False):

_____1. "A crime equal to treason," as one newspaper put it, was Roosevelt's invitation to Booker T. Washington to lunch at the White House.

_____2. Roosevelt's intervention in the Anthracite Coal Strike revealed his solid and consistent pro-labor stance in disputes against ownership.

_____3. Roosevelt believed that all trusts, whether good or bad, should be broken up.

_____4. Progressives tended to emphasize reforming the individual more so than reforming the environment.

_____5. Women in the social-justice movement cared more about their moral influence than in influencing legislation.

_____6. Roosevelt brought suit against the Northern Securities Company because he felt it violated the Sherman Antitrust Act.

_____7. The number of Americans voting socialist increased almost tenfold from 1900 to 1912.

_____8. The Payne-Aldrich Tariff was a victory for the free trade advocates.

_____9. The Federal Reserve Act was designed to blend public and private control of the banking system.

_____10. In contrast to the New Nationalism, the New Freedom emphasized less government regulatory control over the economy.

MULTIPLE CHOICE

Circle the one alternative that *best* completes the statement or answers the question.

1. According to Roosevelt, the role of the federal government in labor issues should be to
   a. pursue a middle ground to curb corporate or labor abuses.
   b. side with labor in practically all matters.
   c. support ownership unless it is in violation of the Sherman Act.
   d. remain completely outside or above the issue.

2. The most accurate statement revealing Roosevelt's attitude toward the trusts would be that
   a. some controls were necessary, but large-scale industrial growth and production were natural and beneficial.
   b. trusts represented the corporate abuses and worker exploitation by the "malefactors of great wealth."
   c. a return to smaller scale corporate development and increased competition among more producers was necessary.
   d. large trusts were desirable as long as the owners recognized the unqualified right of unions to organize and represent their workers.

3. The Hepburn Act
   a. created the Interstate Commerce Commission.
   b. required the burden of proof of railroad company abuses upon the courts.
   c. established the Department of Commerce and the Bureau of Corporations.
   d. broadened the jurisdiction and increased the powers of the ICC, allowing it to establish maximum railroad rates.

4. Concerning reform, Taft differed from Roosevelt in that he
   a. believed the federal government should take responsibility for all social and economic reforms.
   b. saw the principal responsibility as lying with the states.
   c. distrusted the government's ability to impose reforms or improve individual behavior.
   d. thought the president should be a stern, aggressive executive and take charge when improvements were needed.

5. The result of the Payne-Aldrich Act in terms of political fallout was that
   a. the Republican party was perceived for the first time to oppose wholesale tariff reduction.
   b. the progressive Republicans were alienated from Taft and increasingly turned to Roosevelt for leadership.
   c. the power of "Uncle Joe" Cannon as Speaker of the House was strengthened, stifling further reform impetus.
   d. most congressional Democrats supported the act, improving the position and image of that party in future elections.

6. The New Nationalism supported
   a. stronger antitrust legislation to prevent large concentrations of labor and capital.
   b. a retreat from progressive reforms—a new conservatism in other words.
   c. a stronger president, efficiency in government and society, and additional reforms to protect workers, women, and children.
   d. significant tariff reduction and establishment of sound, flexible currency.

7. The two groups that were conspicuously ignored by Wilson's progressive reforms in his first term were
   a. labor and farmers.
   b. Jews and bankers.
   c. women and African Americans.
   d. income-tax supporters and downward tariff revision advocates.

8. The "Wisconsin Idea" under La Follette consisted of
   a. industrial commissions, improved education, public utility controls, and lowered railroad rates.
   b. the first statewide use of property taxes to fund new programs.
   c. the "busting" of large corporations that violated the public trust.
   d. lower taxes of all kinds.

9. Judge Ben Lindsey
   a. worked for playgrounds, slum clearance, public baths, and technical schools.
   b. argued that criminals were made by their environment.
   c. sentenced youthful offenders to education and good care rather than jail.
   d. All of the above.

10. Wilson's position regarding the labor movement was that he supported
    a. retreat from the previous two administrations' policies of consideration for labor reforms.
    b. business over labor categorically.
    c. balance between business and labor, union recognition, and collective bargaining.
    d. the use of military force to quell labor disturbances rather than negotiations.

11. As the leading educational progressive, John Dewey stressed
    a. children's individual needs and capabilities and the changed social situation.
    b. rote memorization and authoritarian teaching methods.
    c. that education was directly related to inherited and racial factors.
    d. strict common standards that all students should meet.

12. The rise of the professions resulted in
    a. leadership for the progressive movement.
    b. a transformed middle-class.
    c. new guidelines for entering professions.
    d. All of the above.

13. Progressives were united in the faith that
    a. the rights of women and minorities were more important than other concerns.
    b. legislative reforms were usually inadequate in meeting the prominent needs for social change.
    c. humans possessed the capacity to achieve a better world.
    d. most reforms should be addressed at local and regional levels rather than national.

14. Wilson could be best described personally as
    a. slow and amiable.
    b. moralistic and prone to self-righteousness.
    c. practical and down-to-earth.
    d. personable and compromising.

15. In the 1910 congressional elections,
    a. Republicans lost control of the House and Senate.
    b. most Republicans were reelected, indicating popular support for Taft's policies.
    c. most progressive candidates were defeated by conservatives.
    d. there was very little change in either Republican or Democratic membership.

THOUGHT QUESTIONS

To check your understanding of the key issues of this period, solve the following problems:

1. How would you explain Roosevelt's attitude toward trusts, the labor movement, and conservation?

2. Despite his good intentions and prior success as an administrator, Taft in his administration was plagued by problems and, as the public perceived, numerous failures. How do you account for this?

3. Wilson's administration revolutionized the role of the federal government in regulating banking, business, and trade. To what extent were the reforms of the New Freedom permanent, and to what extent do they affect American society today?

4. What problems were left unsolved or even unaddressed by progressive reformers and progressive presidents?

5. What new view of government and its roles and responsibilities did most progressives have?

6. What basic views united progressives? Were progressives accurate in their appraisal of human nature?

123

7. How would you describe the conditions from which women suffered in the early twentieth century?

8. Roosevelt believed that the president should exhibit strong, active executive leadership as well as initiate reforms. How do you think his administration measured up to those standards?

CRITICAL THINKING EXERCISE

Using material in Chapter 23 of the text and the primary sources provided below, please answer the questions that follow the documents, Booker T. Washington, *The "Atlanta Compromise,"* W.E.B. Du Bois, *Organizing for Protest* and Anna Garlin Spencer, *Women Citizens*

Booker T. Washington, The *"Atlanta Compromise"*

Mr. President and Gentlemen of the Board of Directors and Citizens:

One-third of the population of the South is of the Negro race. No enterprise seeking the material, civil, or moral welfare of this section can disregard this element of our population and reach the highest success. I but convey to you, Mr. President and Directors, the sentiment of the masses of my race when I say that in no way have the value and manhood of the American Negro been more fittingly and generously recognized than by the managers of this magnificent Exposition at every stage of its progress. It is a recognition that will do more to cement the friendship of the two races than any occurrence since the dawn of our freedom.

Not only this, but the opportunity here afforded will awaken among us a new era of industrial progress. Ignorant and inexperienced, it is not strange that in the first years of our new life we began at the top instead of at the bottom; that a seat in Congress or the state legislature was more sought than real estate or industrial skill; that the political convention or stump speaking had more attractions than starting a dairy farm or truck garden.

A ship lost at sea for many days suddenly sighted a friendly vessel. From the mast of the unfortunate vessel was seen a signal, "Water, water; we die of thirst!" The answer from the friendly vessel at once came back, "Cast down your bucket where you are." A second time the signal, "Water, water; send us water!" ran up from the distressed vessel, and was answered, "Cast down your bucket where you are." And a third and fourth signal for water was answered, "Cast down your bucket where you are." The captain of the distressed vessel, at last heeding the injunction, cast down his bucket, and it came up full of fresh, sparkling water from the mouth of the Amazon River. To those of my race who depend on bettering their condition in a foreign land or who underestimate the importance of cultivating friendly relations with the Southern white man, who is their next-door neighbor, I would say: "Cast down your bucket where you are"—cast it down in making friends in every manly way of the people of all races by whom we are surrounded.

Cast it down in agriculture, mechanics, in commerce, in domestic service, and in the professions. And in this connection, it is well to bear in mind that whatever other sins the South may be called to bear, when it comes to business, pure and simple, it is in the South that the Negro is given a man's chance in the commercial world, and in nothing is this Exposition more eloquent than in emphasizing this chance. Our greatest danger is that in the great leap from slavery to freedom we may overlook the fact that the masses of us are to live by the productions of our hands, and fail to keep in mind that we shall prosper in proportion as we learn to dignify and glorify common labour, and put brains and skill into the common occupations of life; shall prosper in proportion as we learn to draw the line between the superficial and the substantial, the ornamental gewgaws of life and the useful. No race can prosper till it learns that there is as much dignity in tilling a field as in writing a poem. It is at the bottom of life we must begin, and not at the top. Nor should we permit our grievances to overshadow our opportunities.

To those of the white race who look to the incoming of those of foreign birth and strange tongue and habits for the prosperity of the South, were I permitted I would repeat what I say to my own race, "Cast down your bucket where you are." Cast it down among the eight millions of Negroes whose habits you know, whose fidelity and love you have tested in days when to have proved treacherous meant the ruin of your firesides. Cast down your bucket among these people who have, without strikes and labour wars, tilled your fields, cleared your forests, builded your railroads and cities, and brought forth treasures from the bowels of the earth, and helped make possible this magnificent representation of the progress of the South. Casting down your bucket among my people, helping and encouraging them as you are doing on these grounds, and to education of head, hand, and heart, you will find that they will buy your surplus land, make blossom the waste places in your fields, and run your factories. While doing this, you can be sure in the future, as in the past, that you and your families will be surrounded by the most patient, faithful, law-abiding, and unresentful people that the world has seen. As we have proved our loyalty to you in the past, in nursing your children, watching by the sick-bed of your mothers and fathers, and often following them with tear-dimmed eyes to their graves, so in the future, in our humble way, we shall stand by you with a devotion that no foreigner can approach, ready to lay down our lives, if need be, in defense of yours, interlacing our industrial, commercial, civil, and religious life with yours in a way that shall make the interests of both races one. In all things that are purely social we can be as separate as the fingers, yet one as the hand in all things essential to mutual progress.

There is no defense or security for any of us except in the highest intelligence and development of all. If anywhere there are efforts tending to curtail the fullest growth of the Negro, let these efforts be turned into stimulating, encouraging, and making him the most useful and intelligent citizen. Effort or means so invested will pay a thousand per cent interest. These efforts will be twice blessed—"blessing him that gives and him that takes."

There is no escape through law of man or God from the inevitable:
"The laws of changeless justice bind
Oppressor with oppressed;
And close as sin and suffering joined
We march to fate abreast."

Nearly sixteen millions of hands will aid you in pulling the load upward, or they will pull against you the load downward. We shall constitute one-third and more of the ignorance and crime of the South, or one-third [of] its intelligence and progress; we shall contribute one-third to the business and industrial prosperity of the South, or we shall prove a veritable body of death, stagnating, depressing, retarding every effort to advance the body politic.

Gentlemen of the Exposition, as we present to you our humble effort at an exhibition of our progress, you must not expect overmuch. Starting thirty years ago with ownership here and there in a few quilts and pumpkins and chickens (gathered from miscellaneous sources), remember the path that has led from these to the inventions and production of agricultural implements, buggies, steam-engines, newspapers, books, statuary, carving, paintings, the management of drug stores and banks, has not been trodden without contact with thorns and thistles. While we take pride in what we exhibit as a result of our independent efforts, we do not for a moment forget that our part in this exhibition would fall far short of your expectations but for the constant help that has come to our educational life, not only from the Southern states, but especially from Northern philanthropists, who have made their gifts a constant stream of blessing and encouragement.

The wisest among my race understand that the agitation of questions of social equality is the extremest folly, and that progress in the enjoyment of all privileges that will come to us must be the result of severe and constant struggle rather than of artificial forcing. No race that has anything to contribute to the markets of the world is long in any degree ostracized. It is important and right that all privileges of the law be ours, but it is vastly more important that we be prepared for the exercise of these privileges. The opportunity to earn a dollar in a factory just now is worth infinitely more than the opportunity to spend a dollar in an opera-house.

In conclusion, may I repeat that nothing in thirty years has given us more hope and encouragement, and drawn us so near to you of the white race, as this opportunity offered by the Exposition; and here bending, as it were, over the altar that represents the results of the struggles of your race and mine, both starting practically empty-handed three decades ago, I pledge that in your effort to work out the great and intricate problem which God has laid at the doors of the South, you shall have at all times the patient, sympathetic help of my race; only let this be constantly in mind, that, while from representations in these buildings of the product of field, of forest, of mine, of factory, letters, and art, much good will come, yet far above and beyond material benefits will be that higher good, that, let us pray God, will come, in a blotting out of sectional differences and racial animosities and suspicions in a determination to administer absolute justice, in a willing obedience among all classes to the mandates of law. This, coupled with our material prosperity, will bring into our beloved South a new heaven and a new earth.

W.E.B. Du Bois, "Organizing for Protest"

The men of the Niagara Movement coming from the toil of the year's hard work and pausing a moment from the earning of their daily bread turn toward the nation and again ask in the name of ten million the privilege of a hearing. In the past year the work of the Negro hater has flourished in the land. Step by step the defenders of the rights of American citizens have retreated. The work of stealing the black man's ballot has progressed and the fifty and more representatives of stolen votes still sit in the nation's capital. Discrimination in travel and public accommodation has so spread that some of our weaker brethren are actually afraid to thunder against color discrimination as such and are simply whispering for ordinary decencies.

Against this the Niagara Movement eternally protests. We will not be satisfied to take one jot or tittle less than our full manhood rights. W[ith] nastiness the new American creed says: Fear to let black men even try to claim for ourselves every single right that belongs to a freeborn American, political, civil, and social; and until we get these rights we will never cease to protest and assail the ears of America. The battle we wage is not for ourselves alone but for all true Americans. It is a fight for ideals, lest this, our common fatherland, false to its founding, become in truth the land of the thief and the home of the Slave—a by-word and a hissing among the nations for its sounding pretensions and pitiful accomplishments.

125

Never before in the modern age has a great and civilized folk threatened to adopt so cowardly a creed in the treatment of its fellow-citizens born and bred on its soil. Stripped of verbiage and subterfuge and in its naked [form] rise lest they become the equals of the white. And this is the land that professes to follow Jesus Christ. The blasphemy of such a course is only matched by its cowardice.

In detail our demands are clear and unequivocal. First. We would vote; with the right to vote goes everything: Freedom, manhood, the honor of your wives, the chastity of your daughters, the right to work, and the chance to rise, and let no man listen to those who deny this.

We want full manhood suffrage, and we want it now, henceforth and forever.

Second. We want discrimination in public accommodation to cease. Separation in railway and street cars, based simply on race and color, is un-American, undemocratic, and silly. We protest against all such discrimination.

Third. We claim the right of freemen to walk, talk, and be with them that wish to be with us. No man has a right to choose another man's friends, and to attempt to do so is an impudent interference with the most fundamental human privilege.

Fourth. We want the laws enforced against rich as well as poor; against Capitalist as well as Laborer; against white as well as black. We are not more lawless than the white race; we are more often arrested, convicted and mobbed. We want justice even for criminals and outlaws. We want the Constitution of the country enforced. We want Congress to take charge of Congressional elections. We want the Fourteenth Amendment carried out to the letter and every State disfranchised in Congress which attempts to disenfranchise its rightful voters. We want the Fifteenth Amendment enforced and no State allowed to base its franchise simply on color.

The failure of the Republican Party in Congress at the session just closed to redeem its pledge of 1904 with reference to suffrage conditions [in] the South seems a plain, deliberate, and premeditated breach of promise, and stamps that party as guilty of obtaining votes under false pretense.

Fifth. We want our children educated. The school system in the country districts of the South is a disgrace and in few towns and cities are the Negro schools what they ought to be. We want the national government to step in and wipe out illiteracy in the South. Either the United States will destroy ignorance or ignorance will destroy the United States.

And when we call for education we mean real education. We believe in work. We ourselves are workers, but work is not necessarily education. Education is the development of power and ideal. We want our children trained as intelligent human beings should be, and we will fight for all time against any proposal to educate black boys and girls simply as servants and underlings, or simply for the use of other people. They have a right to know, to think, to aspire.

These are some of the chief things which we want. How shall we get them? By voting where we may vote, by persistent, unceasing agitation, by hammering at the truth, by sacrifice and work.

We do not believe in violence, neither in the despised violence of the raid nor the lauded violence of the soldier, nor the barbarous violence of the mob, but we do believe in John Brown, in that incarnate spirit of justice, that hatred of a lie, that willingness to sacrifice money, reputation, and life itself on the altar of right. And here on the scene of John Brown's martyrdom we reconsecrate ourselves, our honor, our property to the final emancipation of the race which John Brown died to make free.

Our enemies, triumphant for the present, are fighting the stars in their courses. Justice and humanity must prevail. We live to tell these dark brothers of ours—scattered in counsel, wavering and weak—that no bribe of money or notoriety, no promise of wealth or fame, is worth the surrender of a people's manhood or the loss of a man's self-respect. We refuse to surrender the leadership of this race to cowards and trucklers. We are men; we will be treated as men. On this rock we have planted our banners. We will never give up, though the trump of doom find us still fighting.

And we shall win. The past promised it, the present foretells it. Thank God for John Brown! Thank God for ... all the hallowed dead who died for freedom! Thank God for all those today, few though their voices be, who have not forgotten the divine brotherhood of all men, white and black, rich and poor, fortunate and unfortunate.

We appeal to the young men and women of this nation, to those whose nostrils are not yet befouled by greed and snobbery and racial narrowness: Stand up for the right, prove yourselves worthy of your heritage and whether born north or south dare to treat men as men. Cannot the nation that has absorbed ten million foreigners into its political life without catastrophe absorb ten million Negro Americans into that same political life at less cost than their unjust and illegal exclusion will involve?

Courage, brothers! The battle for humanity is not lost or losing. All across the skies sit signs of promise. The Slav is rising in his might, the yellow millions are tasting liberty, the black Africans are writhing toward the light, and everywhere the laborer, with ballot in his hand, is voting open the gates of Opportunity and Peace. The morning breaks over blood-stained hills. We must not falter, we may not shrink. Above are the everlasting stars.

Anna Garlin Spencer, *Women Citizens* (1898)

Government is not now merely the coarse and clumsy instrument by which military and police forces are directed; it is the flexible, changing and delicately adjusted instrument of many and varied educative, charitable and supervisory functions, and the tendency to increase the functions of government is a growing one. Prof. Lester F. Ward says: "Government is becoming more and more the organ of the social consciousness and more and more the servant of the social will." The truth of this is shown in the modern public school system; in the humane and educative care of dependent, defective and wayward children; in the increasingly discriminating and wise treatment of the insane, the pauper, the tramp and the poverty-bound; in the provisions for public parks, baths and amusement places; in the bureaus of investigation and control, and the appointment of officers of inspection to secure better sanitary and moral conditions; in the board of arbitration for the settlement of political and labor difficulties; and in the almost innumerable committees and bills, national, State and local, to secure higher social welfare for all classes, especially for the weaker and more ignorant. Government can never again shrink and harden into a mere mechanism of military and penal control.

It is, moreover, increasingly apparent that for these wider and more delicate functions a higher order of electorate, ethically as well as intellectually advanced, is necessary. Democracy can succeed only by securing for its public service, through the rule of the majority, the best leadership and administration the State affords. Only a wise electorate will know how to select such leadership, and only a highly moral one will authoritatively choose such....

When the State took the place of family bonds and tribal relationships, and the social consciousness was born and began its long travel toward the doctrine of "equality of human rights" in government, and the principle of human brotherhood in social organization; man, as the family and tribal organizer and ruler, of course took command of the march. It was inevitable, natural and beneficent so long as the State concerned itself with only the most external and mechanical of social interests. The instant, however, the State took upon itself any form of educative, charitable or personally helpful work, it entered the area of distinctive feminine training and power, and therefore became in need of the service of woman. Wherever the State touches the personal life of the infant, the child, the youth, or the aged, helpless, defective in mind, body or moral nature, there the State enters the "woman's peculiar sphere," her sphere of motherly succor and training, her sphere of sympathetic and self-sacrificing ministration to individual lives. If the service of women is not won to such governmental action (not only through "influence or the shaping of public opinion," but through definite and authoritative exercise), the mother-office of the State, now so widely adopted, will be too often planned and administered as though it were an external, mechanical and abstract function, instead of the personal, organic and practical service which all right helping of individuals must be.

Insofar as motherhood has given to women a distinctive ethical development, it is that of sympathetic personal insight respecting the needs of the weak and helpless, and of quick-witted, flexible adjustment of means to ends in the physical, mental and moral training of the undeveloped. And thus far has mother-hood fitted women to give a service to the modern State which men cannot altogether duplicate....

Whatever problems might have been involved in the question of woman's place in the State when government was purely military, legal and punitive, have long since been antedated. Whatever problems might have been involved in that question when women were personally subject to their families or their husbands, are well-nigh outgrown in all civilized countries, and entirely so in the most advanced. Woman's nonentity in the political department of the State is now an anachronism and inconsistent with the prevailing tendencies of social growth....

The earth is ready, the time is ripe, for the authoritative expression of the feminine as well as the masculine interpretation of that common social consciousness which is slowly writing justice in the State and fraternity in the social order

1. Describe the progressive view of human nature and the course of human history.

2. Given that view, why did they avoid issues of African Americans and women?

3. Compare Washington's views on civil rights with those of Du Bois.

4. Which of the two views worked best during the Progressive Era? Would the same views have worked well in the 1950s and 1960s?

5. Evaluate the views of the anti-suffragists and those of Anna Garland Spencer. Which do you think best promoted the interests of women?

CHAPTER 24

The Nation at War, 1901–1920

SUMMARY

In 1915, the British steamship *Lusitania* was sunk by a German submarine off the coast of Ireland with 1,200 fatalities, horrifying Americans. The tragedy embroiled the United States more deeply in the European crisis, and despite Wilson's commitment to peace and neutrality, America went to war in 1917.

A New World Power

After 1901, the United States became much more involved in international issues through its economic expansion. Policymaking was left almost entirely to the president because most Americans paid little attention to foreign affairs. From 1901 to 1920, American foreign policy was aggressive and nationalistic, intervening in Europe, the Far East, Latin America, and dominating the Caribbean.

Building the Panama Canal

The strong desire for an isthmian canal to connect the Atlantic and Pacific Oceans led to a major departure in U.S.-Latin American relations. President Roosevelt, convinced that America should achieve a more active international status, moved to consolidate American power in the Caribbean and Central America. He intervened in affairs in Colombia-Panama in order to secure the canal zone, and the Hay-Bunau-Varilla Treaty gave the United States control of the canal zone and guaranteed the independence of Panama. Roosevelt's actions angered many in Latin America.

With American interests entrenched in the Caribbean, the president issued the Roosevelt Corollary to the Monroe Doctrine. It threatened Latin American nations with American intervention should they fail to keep their finances in order. In particular, Roosevelt was reacting to the tendency of Latin American nations to default on their debts to European nations, thereby inviting European intervention in the area—something Roosevelt wanted to prevent.

Ventures in the Far East

American action in the Far East was shaped by the Open Door Policy and its possession of the Philippine Islands. After war broke out between Russia and Japan, Roosevelt sought to balance Russian and Japanese power in the Far East by mediating the conflict. The Taft-Katsura Agreement recognized Japanese control of Korea in exchange for a promise from the Japanese not to invade the Philippines. In 1908, after assuaging Japanese resentment over anti-Japanese action in the American West, Roosevelt sent the enlarged naval fleet around the world, with a stop in Tokyo, as a show of strength.

Taft and Dollar Diplomacy
Under President Taft, American business and financial interests were extended abroad through "dollar diplomacy," replacing European loans with American loans. Taft's initiatives in the Far East led to intense rivalry and increased tension with Japan.

Foreign Policy Under Wilson
Confident of his own abilities and very idealistic, President Wilson foresaw a world freed from the threats of militarism, colonialism, and war. He stressed morality rather than money, advocating a course of diplomacy that would bring about peace and the spread of democracy.

Troubles Across the Border
Revolution and lingering political instability caused Wilson to become embroiled in Mexican political turbulence. When the conservative General Huerta assassinated the reformer Madero, Wilson refused to recognize him, asserting a new policy toward revolutionary regimes that required not only the exercise of power but also the demonstration of a "just government based on law." Tensions mounted between the United States and Mexico. When revolutionary leader Pancho Villa began attacking Americans, Wilson responded with military intervention further arousing the ire of Mexico. Distracted by affairs in Europe, Wilson withdrew the military from Mexico.

Toward War
The assassination of Austro-Hungarian Archduke Franz Ferdinand set into motion a chain of events that by August 1914 had brought the major European nations to war. Stunned as he was, Wilson called on the American people to remain impartial.

The Neutrality Policy
At the outset of war, Wilson envisioned the nation's role as that of a peacemaker and pillar of democracy. Americans were sharply divided in sentiment, but most sympathized with the British and French and considered German aggression largely responsible for the war. Except in Latin America, the United States had a well-established tradition of isolationism, and Americans accepted neutrality as the desirable course. Progressivism also mitigated against involvement as most reformers preferred to focus on domestic problems.

Freedom of the Seas
Maintaining the nation's neutrality, American firms tried to trade with both the Allies and Germany. For the most part, Britain was careful to disrupt German trade without disrupting Anglo-American relations. Other than U-boats, Germany did little to disrupt American trade with the Allies, and American goods flooded European ports, especially in Britain and France, resulting in great profits at home and increasing commercial ties with the Allies.

The U-Boat Threat
Germany's use of the dreaded submarines posed a direct threat to American shipping. Until 1917, Germany agreed not to fire on American ships. The issue then became one of American passengers on foreign ships. The sinking of the *Lusitania* and the *Arabic* outraged Americans and forced President Wilson to pressure the German government. After the French steamer *Sussex* was sunk, Wilson threatened to sever relations with Germany, and German Kaiser Wilhelm issued a pledge promising that German submarines would only target enemy naval vessels.

The Election of 1916
The "preparedness" advocates led by Theodore Roosevelt called for readiness in case of war and spoke out against pacifist sentiment in the country. Facing pressure from both sides, Wilson advocated preparedness while championing his record of peace. Wilson defeated the Republican candidate Charles Evans Hughes in 1916. Winning by a very narrow margin, Wilson continued to pledge his commitment to peace even while he advocated preparedness.

The Final Months of Peace
In January 1917, Wilson called upon the European nations to submit to a "peace without victory" and a peace between equals, but renewed German submarine attacks severely threatened relations with the United States. Public indignation against Germany soared after the exposure of the Zimmermann telegram, which encouraged a Mexican-German alliance and German support in a Mexican war against the United States. Prompted by continued sinking of American ships, Wilson at last demanded military intervention.

Over There
A wave of patriotism swept the country as hundreds of thousands of troops departed for Europe, and antiwar protest at home was crushed.

Mobilization
Wilson selected "Black Jack" Pershing to lead the American Expeditionary Force (AEF). Preferring a draft as more efficient and democratic, Congress passed the Selective Service Act, eventually drafting over two million men, including black men, into the army.

War in the Trenches
A massive German offensive was launched in March 1918 against western Europe, but the American-supported Allied lines held. By autumn, German forces were in headlong retreat, and in November, Germany agreed to armistice terms. Within the month, Austria-Hungary, Turkey, and Bulgaria also were finished.

Over Here
All aspects of the economy and of society were needed to fight the war, and Wilson was able to mobilize the whole country both economically and emotionally.

The Conquest of Convictions
At home, the Committee on Public Information launched a propaganda campaign to evoke hatred for Germany and support for the war. Wilson encouraged the emerging vigilante repression of antiwar sympathizers and enacted and enforced the Espionage Act and the Sedition Act against those who opposed the war effort.

A Bureaucratic War
The War Industries Board was established to oversee all aspects of industrial production. Herbert Hoover headed the Food Administration, which fixed prices and encouraged Americans to plant "victory gardens," while the Fuel Administration rationed coal and oil and introduced daylight savings time. Government involvement in American life had never been greater. Liberty bonds were sold, and taxes on individuals and corporations were boosted.

Labor in the War
The war secured the partnership between labor and government, and union membership swelled to more than four million by 1919. The War Labor Board standardized wages and hours and protected the rights of workers to organize and collectively bargain. Women and African Americans found economic opportunities that had never before existed. Companies sent agents into the South to recruit black labor, setting off a great migration of blacks to northern industrial areas, and growing competition for jobs and housing led to an increase in racial tensions. The United States emerged from the war as the greatest economic power in the world.

The Treaty of Versailles
Wilson's plan for peace contained in his Fourteen Points outlined a far-reaching, nonpunitive settlement. Although England and France reluctantly submitted to much of Wilson's idealistic plans, they were skeptical of its promises for world peace.

A Peace at Paris
In a dramatic break from tradition, Wilson himself attended the peace conference where he unveiled his lofty goals for a lasting peace, including national self-determination in Europe and the creation of a League of Nations. Several of Wilson's important principles were sacrificed, however, as enormous reparations were heaped upon Germany, its Asian and African colonies were divided up among other European nations, and the doctrine of self-determination was violated in the establishment of Poland and Czechoslovakia. Additionally, there was no mention of disarmament, free trade, or freedom of the seas.

Rejection in the Senate
Because the treaty limited the power of Congress in some respects, senators with strong reservations were committed to opposing it. Wilson's refusal to budge on a few crucial points and his inability to campaign for it with his usual zest (he suffered a debilitating stroke) led to the treaty's final rejection. Republican Warren G. Harding's election in 1920 assured the final demise of the treaty.

Conclusion: Postwar Disillusionment

World War I, feared before it started, popular while it lasted, and hated when it ended, confirmed the nation's disillusionment with war and international commitment. The war and its aftermath also killed the progressive spirit of reform that had dominated the first two decades of the century.

LEARNING OBJECTIVES

After mastering this chapter, you should be able to:

1. Discuss the new role of the United States in Latin America and the various diplomatic approaches of Roosevelt, Taft, and Wilson.

2. Describe the problems Wilson faced in Mexico and whether he handled them responsibly.

3. List and explain the causes of the war in Europe and American reactions to the war.

4. Compare and contrast the arguments of the preparedness advocates and the pacifists.

5. Understand the factors that brought the United States into the war and the extent to which German belligerence in the North Atlantic was responsible.

6. Compare American military involvement and wartime losses with those of the major European nations.

7. Determine the reasons for the final military collapse of Germany.

8. Show the ways in which the wartime partnership between citizens and government worked and how the war affected women and African Americans.

9. Specify the steps by which America mobilized for war.

10. Explain the effects of patriotic fervor and anti-German sentiment on the American public.

11. Summarize the activities of the War Industries Board, the Committee on Public Information, and the War Labor Board.

12. Explain the concessions or sacrifices that Wilson had to make to the other European leaders regarding the peace structuring.

13. Define the different goals of the victorious nations at the Paris Peace Conference, and explain how Wilson's goals were incorporated into the treaty.

14. Discuss the reasons for the failure of Wilsonian global idealism and the Versailles treaty.

15. Reflect on American disillusionment and the decline of the progressive spirit as the 1920s set in.

GLOSSARY

To build your social science vocabulary, familiarize yourself with the following terms:

1. **ultimatum** a proposition or demand with strong consequences for rejection. "… almost an ultimatum—warning Germany that the United States would view similar sinking as 'deliberately unfriendly.'"

2. **protectorates** governments established by a major power over a dependent country. "Roosevelt also established protectorates in Cuba and Panama."

3. **status quo** the way things presently exist. " ... in which they promised to maintain the status quo in the Pacific ..."

4. **militarism** a condition of aggressive military preparedness or strong military buildup. "... Wilson believed in a principled, ethical world in which militarism, colonialism, and war were brought under control."

5. **neutrality** a policy of remaining unaligned with any one side in an international conflict. "Wilson immediately proclaimed neutrality ..."

7. **pacifist** one who categorically opposes war. " ... while pacifists denounced any attempt at military readiness."

8. **conscription** a forced contribution or draft of persons for military duty. "Wilson turned to conscription, which he believed was both efficient and democratic."

9. **self-determination** the right of a people or nation to choose their own form of government and leaders. " ... and they were skeptical of the principle of self-determination."

10. **reparations** payments made for damages caused. "... it made Germany accept responsibility for the war and demanded enormous reparations ..."

11. **belligerent** warring or warlike. "... neutral countries were permitted to trade in nonmilitary goods with all belligerent countries."

12. **bellicose** inclined toward quarreling or aggressive arguments. "Bellicose as always, Teddy Roosevelt led the preparedness campaign."

13. **assimilated** made similar or integrated. "Society assimilated some of the shifts, but social and economic tensions grew ..."

14. **arbitration** intervention by an impartial third party in disputes with the decision usually binding. "League members pledged to submit to arbitration every dispute ..."

IDENTIFICATION

Briefly identify the meaning and significance of the following terms:

1. *Lusitania*_____

_____

2. Roosevelt Corollary_____

_____

3. dollar diplomacy_____

_____

4. moral diplomacy_____

_____

5. Selective Service Act_____

_____

6. Zimmermann Telegram_____

_____

7. John J. "Black Jack" Pershing_____

_____

8. Sedition Act_____

_____

9. War Industries Board_____

_____

10. League of Nations_____

_____

MATCHING

A. Match the following diplomatic measures with the appropriate description:

_____1. Hay-Herran Convention

a. recognized Japan's control of Korea in return for her non-interference in the Philippines

_____2. Hay-Bunau-Varilla Treaty

b. was convened by Roosevelt to end the war between Japan and Russia

_____3. Taft-Katsura Agreement

c. contained a promise by the Germans not to fire on nonmilitary ships in the North Atlantic

_____4. Portsmouth Conference

d. in agreement with Colombia, gave the U.S. the right to dig a canal and a ninety-nine year lease

_____5. *Sussex* Pledge

e. gave U.S. control over the Panama Canal zone in return for U.S. guarantee of Panamanian independence

f. increased American suspicion of German intervention in Mexico

B. Match the following public figures with the appropriate description:

_____1. George Creel

a. head of the wartime Fuel Administration who introduced daylight savings time

_____2. Bernard Baruch

b. Socialist party leader who was imprisoned for denouncing capitalism and the war

_____3. Herbert Hoover

c. head of the Food Administration who supplied food to American armies overseas

_____4. Eugene V. Debs

d. leader of the Committee on Public Information to publicize the war effort

_____5. Harry A. Garfield

e. person who ran the War Industries Board, which determined manufacturing priorities

f. head of the War Labor Board, which standardized hours and wages

137

COMPLETION

Answer the question or complete the statement by filling in the blanks with the correct word or words.

1. The secretary of state who chose to resign rather than sign a note demanding certain pledges from Germany after the sinking of the *Lusitania* was _____.

2. To consolidate the country's new position in the Caribbean and to strengthen America's two-ocean navy, Roosevelt desired _____.

3. With the _____, the United States and Japan promised to maintain the status quo in the Pacific and support Chinese independence.

4. Rejecting "dollar diplomacy," Wilson initially intended to follow a course of _____ to settle international disputes by right rather than might.

5. The longtime president of Mexico who invited foreign investments into the Mexican economy was_____.

6. At the outbreak of war in Europe, Wilson proclaimed _____ and asked the American people to remain impartial in thought and action.

7. The new weapon that violated traditional rules of warfare and strained United States-German relations was the _____.

8. The issue that dominated the presidential election of 1916 was _____ or _____.

9. The Mexican leader whom Wilson refused to recognize, calling him instead "the butcher," was _____.

10. When Du Bois spoke of blacks as being more proud and militant after the war, he used the term _____ to describe them.

TRUE/FALSE

Mark the following statements either T (True) or F (False):

_____1. The Hay-Pauncefote Treaty gave the United States and Britain joint ownership of the proposed isthmian canal.

_____2. The new approach to Latin American affairs promised by Wilson was to elevate human rights and national integrity.

_____3. Because the Philippines were strategically crucial to American interests in the Pacific, Congress decided to fortify the islands promptly after acquisition.

_____4. William Jennings Bryan was appointed secretary of state by Wilson primarily because of his previous experience in foreign affairs through the State Department.

_____5. Many progressives called for U.S. neutrality in World War I because the war went against the spirit of progressivism.

_____6. Because he had fought so doggedly for neutrality, Wilson was able to sympathize with those Americans who opposed the U.S. entry into the war in 1917.

_____7. Because of the Zimmermann telegram and the possibility of war with Mexico as well as because of the universal hatred for Mexicans by southwestern Americans, Congress tightened immigration restrictions from south of the border after 1917.

_____8. The fact that most African Americans actively supported the war effort had a calming effect on racial tensions at home after the war.

_____9. In selecting a peace delegation for the Treaty of Versailles, President Wilson bypassed Henry Cabot Lodge and Elihu Root because he felt he could not control them.

_____10. After much political wrangling, Wilson finally managed to convince Congress to accept the Treaty of Versailles before he left office.

MULTIPLE CHOICE

Circle the one alternative that *best* completes the statement or answers the question.

1. The Roosevelt Corollary
    a. promised an American empire in the Caribbean.
    b. warned European nations to eliminate all economic interests in Latin America.
    c. warned of American intervention in Latin American affairs when necessary.
    d. acquired Cuba for the United States as a territory.

2. The approach of President Taft toward foreign affairs was to
    a. increase military buildup and involvement.
    b. promote American financial and business interests.
    c. oppose all non-democratic regimes.
    d. attract European capital and loans to Latin America.

3. According to Woodrow Wilson, the objectives and pursuits of the American people should be
    a. moral principle, preservation of peace, and extension of democracy.
    b. military power and increased armaments.
    c. material interests and "dollar diplomacy."
    d. overwhelming concern for domestic progressive issues to the sacrifice or preclusion of foreign problems.

4. One of the major reasons for the war in Europe in 1914 was
    a. the fear of Britain and France toward the rising power of Russia.
    b. the fear of creeping communist revolutions throughout Europe.
    c. the breakup of the Austro-Hungarian empire and the desire for additional territories by her southeastern European neighbors.
    d. a web of entangling alliances that could cause a local problem to escalate into a major war.

5. At the outset of the European war, most Americans
    a. accepted neutrality as advisable and moral.
    b. favored entering the war on the side of Britain and France.
    c. blamed Britain for the war because of its extensive imperial system.
    d. were unconcerned with events in Europe.

6. The preparedness advocates called for
    a. American entry into the war at any cost.
    b. naval destroyers to accompany merchant vessels across the North Atlantic.
    c. Roosevelt to run for the presidency in 1916.
    d. military readiness in case of war.

7. The Committee on Public Information was responsible for
   a. giving the American people clear and objective reasons why the United States was compelled to intervene in the war.
   b. distributing news items to the major daily papers and other media.
   c. using the arts, advertising, and film industries to publicize the war and launching a propaganda campaign to popularize the war effort against the barbaric Germans.
   d. keeping a watchful eye on antiwar sympathizers and publicly discrediting them.

8. The effect of the war on organized labor was to
   a. bring labor into partnership with the federal government and greatly increase union membership.
   b. allow the government to forbid strikes or work slowdowns.
   c. weaken labor because most workers were called into the armed forces.
   d. allow women to unionize on the same basis as men.

9. African American participation in the war could best be described in which of the following ways?
   a. African Americans were not allowed in the armed forces in any capacity.
   b. African Americans were enlisted in support and supply units but were not allowed in combat.
   c. More than forty thousand African Americans served in combat but were commonly discriminated against when they returned home.
   d. African Americans were fully integrated into the armed forces and treated the same as white troops for the most part.

10. Which of the following was not a major goal of Wilson's at the Paris Peace Conference?
    a. enforcement of enormous financial reparations upon the Germans
    b. national self-determination for European ethnic and nationalist groups
    c. a League of Nations to settle international disputes
    d. reduction of tensions through disarmament and establishment of free trade

11. The Hay-Bunau-Varilla Treaty granted
    a. the United States control of a canal zone through Panama.
    b. the United States and Britain joint ownership of the canal.
    c. the United States a ninety-nine year lease on a canal zone in return for payments to Columbia.
    d. Columbia preferential treatment in using the canal.

12. Progressives in the United States believed all of the following about World War I EXCEPT
    a. it would bring an end to reform.
    b. Germany was a barbarous nation that needed to be defeated.
    c. they did not necessarily see England as on the right side given its large international finance industry.
    d. it would kill millions of the workers their reforms were designed to help.

13. The German policy that was most directly responsible for bringing the United States into the war was the
    a. support for Mexico with arms and money during the punitive expedition.
    b. decision to renew unrestricted submarine warfare in the North Atlantic against American vessels.
    c. sinking of the *Lusitania.*
    d. revelation of wartime objectives including territorial gains in Europe and Africa.

14. The key issue in the 1916 presidential campaign was
    a. that Wilson had kept us out of war and that Hughes was perceived to be more aggressive toward Germany.
    b. the proposed extension of suffrage to women.
    c. whether civil rights for African Americans continued in the progressive agenda.
    d. whether we would eventually come into the European war on the side of Germany or on the side of Britain and France.

15. Wilson's attitude toward antiwar dissent after American entry was to
    a. tolerate it because of his own moral revulsion to war.
    b. crack down on super patriotic vigilantism directed against antiwar sympathizers.
    c. encourage repression and humiliation of antiwar sympathizers.
    d. refuse to concern himself because of the greater importance of directing the war in Europe.

THOUGHT QUESTIONS

To check your understanding of the key issues of this period, solve the following problems:

1. Neutrality, although the United States policy for the first three years of the war in Europe, was not actually neutral. What were the problems in remaining neutral?

2. Several factors prompted U.S. entry into the war against Germany in 1917. What do you consider to be the most important reasons for intervention?

3. How did mobilization change the habits and patterns of American society at home? To what extent did the federal government become "big brother" to the economy during the war?

4. W.E.B. Du Bois spoke of a "New Negro" during the war years. How did the war change the expectations and directions of blacks in a still predominantly white-dominated society?

5. How did the war damage the progressive, humanitarian spirit in America? How did disillusionment affect the U.S. at home, as well as in its relations with other countries?

6. How would you compare the Latin American policies of Presidents Roosevelt and Wilson? What problems with Mexico did Wilson's attitude of condescension and morality create?

7. Wilson attempted to apply his lofty ideals of morality and self-determination to the world arena after the war. Why were his goals difficult to achieve, and why specifically did the Senate reject his treaty?

CRITICAL THINKING QUESTIONS

After reading Boy Scouts of America from "Boy Scouts Support the War Effort" (1917), and Newton D. Baker, "The Treatment of German Americans" (1918), and F. J. Grimke, "Address of Welcome to the Men Who Have Returned from the Battlefront," (1919) answer the following questions:

Boy Scouts of America from, "Boy Scouts Support the War Effort" (1917)

To the Members of the Boy Scouts of America!

Attention, Scouts! We are again called upon to do active service for our country! Every one of the 285,661 Scouts and 76,957 Scout Officials has been summoned by President Woodrow Wilson, Commander-in-Chief of the Army and Navy, to serve as a dispatch bearer from the Government at Washington to the American people all over the country. The prompt, enthusiastic, and hearty response of every one of us has been pledged by our [Scout] President, Mr. Livingstone. Our splendid record of accomplishments in war activities promises full success in this new job.

This patriotic service will be rendered under the slogan: "EVERY SCOUT TO BOOST AMERICA" AS A GOVERNMENT DISPATCH BEARER. The World War is for liberty and democracy.

America has long been recognized as the leader among nations standing for liberty and democracy. American entered the war as a sacred duty to uphold the principles of liberty and democracy.

As a democracy, our country faces great danger-not so much from submarines, battleships and armies, because, thanks to our allies, our enemies have apparently little chance of reaching our shores.

Our danger is from within. Our enemies have representatives everywhere; they tell lies; they mispresent the truth; they deceive our own people; they are a real menace to our country.

Already we have seen how poor Russia has been made to suffer because her people do not know the truth. Representatives of the enemy have been very effective in their deceitful efforts to make trouble for the Government.

Fortunately here in America our people are better educated-they want the truth. Our President recognized the justice and wisdom of this demand when in the early stages of the war he created the Committee on Public Information. He knew that the Government would need the confidence, enthusiasm and willing service of every man and woman, every boy and girl in the nation. He knew that the only possible way to create a genuine feeling of partnership between the people and its representatives in Washington was to take the people into his confidence by full, frank statements concerning the reasons for our entering the war, the various steps taken during the war and the ultimate aims of the war.

Neither the President as Commander-in-Chief, nor our army and navy by land and sea, can alone win the war. At this moment the best defense that America has is an enlightened and loyal citizenship. Therefore, we as scouts are going to have the opportunity of rendering real patriotic service under our slogan.

"EVERY SCOUT TO BOOST AMERICA" AS A GOVERNMENT DISPATCH BEARER.

Here is where our service begins. We are to help spread the facts about America and America's part in the World War. We are to fight lies with truth.

We are to help create public opinion "just as effective in helping to bring victory as ships and guns," to stir patriotism, the great force behind the ships and guns. Isn't that a challenge for every loyal Scout?

"EVERY SCOUT TO BOOST AMERICA" AS A GOVERNMENT DISPATCH BEARER: HOW?

As Mr. George Creel, the Chairman of the Committee on Public Information, says in his letter, scouts are to serve as direct special representatives of the Committee on Public Information to keep the people informed about the War and its causes and progress. The Committee has already prepared a number of special pamphlets and other will be prepared. It places upon the members of the Boy Scouts of America the responsibility of putting the information in these pamphlets in homes of the American people. Every Scout will be furnished a credential card by his Scoutmaster. Under the direction of our leaders, the Boy Scouts of America are to serve as an intelligence division of the citizens' army, always prepared and alert to respond to any call which may come from the President of the United States and the Committee on Public Information at Washington.

… Each Scoutmaster is to be furnished with a complete set of all of the government publications, in order that all of the members of his troop may be completely informed. Each scout and scout official is expected to seize every opportunity to serve the Committee on Public Information by making available authoritative information. It is up to the Boy Scouts to see that as many people as possible have an intelligent understanding of any and all facts incident to our present national crisis and the World War....

        PAMPHLETS NOW READY FOR CIRCULATION

        Note: A set will be sent to every Scoutmaster. You will need to know what is in these pamphlets so as to act as a serviceable bureau of information and be able to give each person the particular intelligence he seeks.

Newton D. Baker, "The Treatment of German-Americans" (1918)

The spirit of the country seems unusually good, but there is a growing frenzy of suspicion and hostility toward disloyalty. I am afraid we are going to have a good many instances of people roughly treated on very slight evidence of disloyalty. Already a number of men and some women have been "tarred and feathered," and a portion of the press is urging with great vehemence more strenuous efforts at detection and punishment. This usually takes the form of advocating "drum-head courts-martial" and "being stood up against a wall and shot," which are perhaps none too bad for real traitors, but are very suggestive of summary discipline to arouse mob spirit, which unhappily does not take time to weigh evidence.

        In Cleveland a few days ago a foreign-looking man got into a street car and, taking a seat, noticed pasted in the window next to him a Liberty Loan poster, which he immediately tore down, tore into small bits, and stamped under his feet. The people in the car surged around him with the demand that he be lynched, when a Secret Service man showed his badge and placed him under arrest, taking him in a car to the police station, where he was searched and found to have two Liberty Bonds in his pocket and to be a non-English Pole. When an interpreter was procured, it was discovered that the circular which he had destroyed had had on it a picture of the German Emperor, which had so infuriated the fellow that he destroyed the circular to show his vehement hatred of the common enemy. As he was unable to speak a single word of English, he would undoubtedly have been hanged but for the intervention and entirely accidental presence of the Secret Service agent.

        I am afraid the grave danger in this sort of thing, apart from its injustice, is that the German Government will adopt retaliatory measures. While the Government of the United States is not only responsible for these things, but very zealously trying to prevent them, the German Government draws no fine distinctions.

F. J. Grimke, "Address of Welcome to the Men Who Have Returned from the Battlefront" (1919)

Young gentlemen, I am glad to welcome you home again after months of absence in a foreign land in obedience to the call of your country-glad that you have returned to us without any serious casualties.

        I am sure you have acquitted yourself well; that in the record that you have made for yourselves, during your absence from home, there is nothing to be ashamed of, nothing that will reflect any discredit upon the race with which you are identified....

        While you were away you had the opportunity of coming in contact with another than the American type of white man; and through that contact you have learned what it is to be treated as a man, regardless of the color of your skin or race identity. Unfortunately you had to go away from home to receive a man's treatment, to breathe the pure, bracing air of liberty, equality, fraternity. And, while it was with no intention of bringing to you that knowledge, of putting you where you could get that kind of experience, but simply because they couldn't very well get along without you, I am glad nevertheless, that you were sent. You know now that the mean, contemptible spirit of race prejudice that curses this land is not the spirit of other lands; you know now what it is to be treated as a man. And, one of the things that I am particularly hoping for, now that you have had this experience, is that you have come back determined, as never before, to keep up the struggle for our rights until, here in these United States, in this boasted land of the free and home of the brave, every man, regardless of the color of his skin, shall be accorded a man's treatment.

        Your trip will be of very little value to the race in this country unless you have come back with the love of liberty, equality, fraternity burning in your souls.... In the struggle that is before us, you can do a great deal in helping to better conditions. You, who gave up everything-home, friends, relatives-you who took your lives in your hands and went forth to lay them, a willing sacrifice upon the altar of your country and in the interest of democracy throughout the world, have a right to speak-to speak with authority; and that right you must exercise.

        We, who remained at home, followed you while you were away, with the deepest interest; and, our hearts burned with indignation when tiding came to us, as it did from time to time, of the manner in which you were treated by those over you, from whom you had every reason, in view of the circumstances that took you abroad and what it was costing you, to expect decent, humane treatment, instead of the treatment that was accorded you. The physical hardships, incident to a soldier's life in times of war, are trying enough, are hard enough to bear-and, during this world war, on the other side of the water, I understand they were unusually hard. To add to these the insults, the studied insults that were heaped upon you, and for no reason except that you were colored, is so shocking that were it not for positive evidence, it would be almost unbelievable....

I know of nothing that sets forth this cursed American race prejudice in a more odious, execrable light than the treatment of our colored soldiers in this great world struggle that has been going on, by the very government that ought to have shielded them from the brutes that were over them....

If it was worth going abroad to make the world safe for democracy, it is equally worth laboring no less earnestly to make it safe at home. We shall be greatly disappointed if you do not do this-if you fail to do your part.

1. What is the inherent contradiction or paradox in the article taken from "Boy Scouts Support the War Effort"?

2. Does the call for support from Boy Scouts have any element of vigilantism or what Newton D. Baker calls "drum-head courts-martial"? Would a member of the Boy Scouts be free to oppose the war?

3. In what ways was Newton Baker both promoting anti-German sentiment and denouncing it?

4. What race of soldier is Grimke addressing? How does he believe the war experience at home and abroad affected American race relations?

CHAPTER 25

Transition to Modern America, 1919–1928

SUMMARY
The 1920s were marked by rapid economic and urban growth and rapid social change, inspiring tensions as rural America resisted many of these far-reaching changes.

The Second Industrial Revolution
Based on mass production, the moving assembly line, and the marketing of consumer goods, the economy of the 1920s experienced phenomenal growth.

The Automobile Industry
The automobile industry, one of the most important of the 1920s, significantly affected American culture, stimulating other industries like steel, rubber, paint, glass, and oil and changing the nation's physical landscape. The subtle changes in industry also illustrated an inherent instability within a consumer goods-driven economy—once consumers purchase a longer-life item, they no longer need to buy it, which removes them from the market.

Patterns of Economic Growth
Other industries not connected to automobiles also boomed, including the electrical industry, radio broadcasting, motion picture production, the development of light metals like aluminum, and the production of synthetic materials like rayon and cellophane. The large corporation run by a professional manager dominated business in the 1920s, and the most distinctive feature of business during the era was an emphasis on marketing and advertising. Despite the economic progress of new industries, some elements of the economy fared poorly, including traditional industries like railroads, coal, cotton textiles, and agriculture. While the middle and upper classes experienced prosperity, workers and minorities did not.

City Life in the Roaring Twenties
Still another important feature of the 1920s was the rapid rise of the city and the consequent changes in society. Skyscrapers were the most visible feature of the new cities and became a symbol of progress and a new metropolitan way of life.

Women and the Family
Women continued to work outside of the home in increasing numbers, though they were confined to low-paying jobs and excluded, for the most part, from the professions. Families changed as a result of falling birthrates (through easier access to birth control) and rising divorce rates, as married women continued to work after marriage. Young men and women, who previously would have joined the workforce as teenagers, discovered adolescence as they attended high school and rebelled against parental authority. Though women had achieved the vote, the feminist movement continued

to be active, lobbying for full equality under the law. For many young women, the assertiveness of the feminist movement translated into rebellion against Victorian social mores rather than crusading for social progress.

Popular Culture in the Jazz Age

The cultural revolution also prompted the rise of organized crime, spectator sports, and a sexual revolution. Much of the rise in crime can be attributed to prohibition as more and more Americans were willing to break the law to acquire alcohol, and rival bootleggers competed with each other for control of the market. The arts flourished as well, highlighted by the Harlem Renaissance and by the works of authors Ernest Hemingway and F. Scott Fitzgerald.

The Conservative Counterattack

Insecurity in the face of all this social upheaval caused rural and small-town America to reject the dominance of the city. Anti-immigrant activity increased as did movements aimed at cultural and political conformity and a return to traditional values.

The Fear of Radicalism

Tradition-minded Americans feared the specter of bolshevism and anarchism and tried to eliminate radicalism from American life, abusing civil liberties in the process. Their fear was fed by the recent Russian Revolution and several violent strikes in the spring and summer of 1919. Public outcry led to government action in the deportation of hundreds of immigrants suspected of communist ties. By 1920 the scare abated as the extremism of the government's reaction sunk in. Even so, the 1920s continued to be colored by nativism, bigotry, and intolerance.

Prohibition

Many associated alcohol with alien cultures and the new urban ways. The Eighteenth Amendment prohibiting the manufacture, sale, and transportation of alcoholic beverages was ratified in 1918. The Volstead Act, passed in January 1920, implemented prohibition. Enforcement was lax, however, and there was widespread noncompliance with the law, especially among the middle and upper classes.

The Ku Klux Klan

The phenomenal growth of such groups as the Ku Klux Klan was also a reaction to the new urban culture. Such groups tried to preserve what they thought was sacred and pure and to limit the rights of blacks, aliens, non-Protestants, and anyone who refused to conform to their standards. A different Klan from that of the Reconstruction Era, the 1920s Klan found members throughout the nation and were open and active in politics. The Klan fell when some of its more violent activities, misuse of funds, and a sex scandal came to light. Despite the virtual disappearance of the Klan, the hatred and nativism it represented continued.

Immigration Restriction

Nativists successfully restricted foreign immigration, and Congress passed a series of laws aimed at limiting immigration, especially from southern and eastern Europe and Asia. The restrictive legislation on immigration was the most lasting achievement of the rural counterattack, lasting until the 1960s.

The Fundamentalist Controversy
Some Americans found solace and security in supporting fundamentalist Christianity or in opposing theories of evolution being taught in the public schools. The Scopes Trial was the most notable of the challenges to evolution.

Republican Politics
Though the Republicans appeared to control the decade by winning the presidency from 1921 to 1933, rural-urban tensions dominated and shaped the course of politics during the 1920s, and Democrats gained significant numbers of urban and immigrant voters.

Harding, Coolidge, and Hoover
The Republicans dominated the White House with three popular presidents: Warren G. Harding, Calvin Coolidge, and Herbert Hoover. Harding died in office before news of corruption within his administration reached the public. Coolidge oversaw a prospering economy so, consistent with his conservative ideology, did little as president to change things. Hoover, a former Secretary of Commerce, was more active as president. He did not view government and business as antagonists and tried to foster a cooperative spirit between the two.

A New Kind of Conservatism
After capturing the White House in the election of 1920, the Republican party returned to traditional conservative policies, passing a program of higher tariffs, lower taxes, and spending cuts. Growing problems as the decade progressed, such as farm overproduction, challenged these policies. By the end of the 1920s, government and private businesses became close partners. The number of government employees nearly doubled and the federal government became more involved in the economy.

The Election of 1928
The election of 1928 symbolized the decade, pitting Democrat Al Smith, a Catholic, urban, "wet" son of immigrants, against Republican Herbert Hoover, an old-stock, "dry" Protestant from Iowa. Hoover won easily, but the Democrats won majorities in the nation's twelve largest cities, indicating the emergence of a new Democratic electorate.

Conclusion: The Old and The New
The 1920s represented the transition of the United States to the modern era. Despite the prosperity and progress of the era, the foundation was unstable.

LEARNING OBJECTIVES

After mastering this chapter, you should be able to:

1. Explain the importance of the automobile industry during the 1920s.

2. Understand what factors contributed to economic growth during the 1920s.

3. List the weaknesses of the American economy in the 1920s.

4. Discuss the impact of the rise of the city.

6. Describe the main features of the conservative reaction of the 1920s.

8. Outline the personalities and contributions of the key political figures of the 1920s.

7. Analyze the election of 1928.

8. Discuss the policies of the Republican party during the 1920s.

9. Describe the changes wrought in the American family in the 1920s.

GLOSSARY

To build your social science vocabulary, familiarize yourself with the following terms:

1. **gross national product** the total market value of all goods and services produced in a country during one year. "The gross national product rose by 40 percent."

2. **per capita** relating to any statistical measurement in which an aggregate is divided by the total population. "... per-capita income increased by 30 percent ..."

3. **dialect** a regional version of a language. "... the advent of radio and films which promoted a standard national dialect ..."

4. **tabloids** newspapers that exploit sex and violence for mass appeal. "... the new urban tabloids—led by the *New York Daily News*—delighted in telling their readers about love nests and kept women."

5. **bigotry** the practice of stubborn attachment to racial hatred. "... symbolized the bigotry and intolerance that lasted through the twenties."

6. **bolshevism** principles of the Russian Communist party. "The heightened nationalism of World War I ... found a new target in bolshevism."

7. **nativism** policies and principles of groups in the United States that oppose open immigration, especially of non-Anglo-Saxon Protestants. "... the recurring demons of nativism and hatred ..."

8. **fundamentalist sect** a Christian denomination that believes in a literal interpretation of the Bible. "… aggressive fundamentalist sects … grew rapidly."

9. **ethnic** relating to a group with common culture or customs. "... it was deeply resented by ethnic groups such as the Germans ..."

10. **bloc** a collection of groups united to further a common cause. "The farm bloc supported the higher tariffs...."

IDENTIFICATION

Briefly identify the meaning and significance of the following terms:

1. Model T _____

_____

2. flappers _____

_____

3. Harlem Renaissance _____

_____

4. Al Capone _____

_____

5. Babe Ruth _____

_____

6. National Origins Quota Act _____

_____

7. Sacco and Vanzetti _____

_____

8. Scopes Trial _____

_____

9. Teapot Dome Scandal _____

_____

10. Herbert Hoover _____

_____

MATCHING

A. Match the following cultural icon with the appropriate description:

_____1.   Jack Dempsey

_____2.   Charles Lindbergh

_____3.   Clara Bow

_____4.   F. Scott Fitzgerald

_____5.   Gertrud Ederle

a.   movie star heartthrob for millions of American women

b.   swam across the English Channel

c.   boxer

d.   flew solo across the Atlantic Ocean

e.   writer who chronicled the experience of the post-World War I generation

f.   "vamp" and "It" girl who set the model for feminine seductiveness

B. Match the following acts with the appropriate description:

_____1.   Eighteenth Amendment

_____2.   Nineteenth Amendment

_____3.   Sheppard-Towner Act

_____4.   Volstead Act

_____5.   Fordney-McCumber Act

a.   gave women the right to vote

b.   provided money for maternal and infant health care

c.   proposed to raise tariffs to a highly protectionist level

d.   prohibited the manufacture and sale of alcoholic beverages

e.   implemented prohibition and defined an illegal beverage as any above one percent alcohol by volume

f.   limited immigration mainly to people from northwestern Europe

COMPLETION

Answer the question or complete the statement by filling in the blanks with the correct word or words.

1. Henry Ford first used the technique of mass production with a moving assembly line to produce the _____.

2. An early comic serial radio production featuring two black Vaudevillians was called
_____.

3. The most distinctive feature of the new consumer-oriented economy was the emphasis on
_____.

4. The man who completed the first solo flight of the Atlantic was
_____.

5. Some urban women expressed independence through the _____image, which included rouged cheeks, short hair, short skirts, and dancing the Charleston.

6. "The business of America is business" was proclaimed by _____ as a vision for conservative America during the 1920s.

7. The attorney general who led an attack on suspected anarchists and Communists in 1919 was _____.

8. The _____concerned the teaching of evolution in Tennessee public schools.

9. The corrupt official in the Teapot Dome scandal was Interior Secretary
_____.

10. The Democratic candidate in the election of 1928 was _____
_____.

TRUE/FALSE

Mark the following statements either T (True) or F (False):

_____1.   Mass production was not an important factor in the consumer-goods revolution.

_____2.   Agriculture fared best during the economic boom of the 1920s.

_____3.   The number of women doctors increased dramatically during the 1920s.

_____4.   The automobile industry stimulated other American industries during the 1920s.

_____5.   Automobiles became a part of the increasingly sexualized culture by providing a place for young couples to escape parental supervision.

_____6.   There was a drop in the birthrate in the 1920s.

_____7.   The Palmer raids were successful because officials were careful to arrest only bona fide Bolsheviks.

_____8.   The tariff policies of the Republicans of the 1920s favored lowering rates on imported goods.

_____9.   Republican policy of the 1920s advocated cutting taxes and government spending.

_____10. Republican presidents effectively cut the number of government bureaucrats in half during the 1920s.

MULTIPLE CHOICE

Circle the one alternative that *best* completes the statement or answers the question.

1. Which of the following was *not* an element of the economic changes of the 1920s?
    a. mass production
    b. moving assembly line
    c. high profits in agriculture
    d. consumer goods revolution

2. As Secretary of the Treasury, Andrew Mellon
    a. sought to increase corporate income taxes.
    b. raised the highest income tax bracket.
    c. reduced government spending.
    d. All of the above.

3. The government passed immigration acts in the 1920s that resulted in
    a. increased Mexican immigration.
    b. reduced northern and western European immigration.
    c. increased southern and eastern European immigration.
    d. increased Asian immigration.

4. Prohibition resulted in all of the following EXCEPT
    a. a decline in drinking.
    b. breeding a profound disrespect for the law.
    c. a flourishing bootlegging industry.
    d. an attitude among the wealthy and middle-class that drinking was not fashionable.

5. The Ku Klux Klan of the 1920s targeted
    a. blacks.
    b. Catholics.
    c. immigrants.
    d. All of the above.

6. The American family in the 1920s experienced
    a. declining divorce rates.
    b. increasing birthrates.
    c. declining birthrates.
    d. a declining rate of working wives.

7. The election of Warren G. Harding in 1920 meant that
    a. business would have no power in Washington.
    b. morality would be paramount in the actions of the new president.
    c. reform was not as popular as it had been.
    d. there would be an increase in social and political reform.

8. The end of the Red Scare came about as a result of
   a. the acquittal of Sacco and Vanzetti.
   b. its own extremism, as well as courageous public officials.
   c. the passage of the Nineteenth Amendment.
   d. the work of evangelist Billy Sunday.

9. The National Origins Quota Act of 1924 was
   a. a reaction to the increase of Nordic immigration.
   b. a response by some to a general rise in rates of immigration.
   c. an attempt by some to establish racial purity as an immigration policy.
   d. an effort to increase immigration from southeastern Europe.

10. The Scopes Trial indicated that
    a. traditional religious beliefs were stronger than ever.
    b. fundamentalism died after the trial.
    c. Darwin's theory was proved wrong.
    d. None of the above.

11. The Red Scare was caused by all of the following EXCEPT
    a. heightened nationalism after World War I.
    b. the number of actual communists in the United States rose to over one million.
    c. a wave of strikes in the spring and summer of 1919.
    d. the success of the Russian Revolution.

12. During his presidency, Warren G. Harding
    a. allowed some friends to abuse their power.
    b. exposed and tried to clean up the Teapot Dome scandal.
    c. was deeply involved in corruption and bribes.
    d. was not well liked, but was an effective president.

13. As president, Calvin Coolidge
    a. was friendly to American business interests.
    b. was as corrupt as Harding.
    c. worked hard and long at being a good president.
    d. ran for another term as president and barely won.

14. Republican policies of the 1920s favored
    a. low tariffs, low taxes, and cuts in government spending.
    b. high tariffs, high taxes, and cuts in government spending.
    c. high tariffs, low taxes, and cuts in government spending.
    d. low tariffs, high taxes, and increases in government spending.

15. All of the following apply to 1928 Democratic presidential nominee Al Smith EXCEPT
    a. he was Catholic.
    b. he was associated with big-city machine politics.
    c. he was for prohibition.
    d. he was a descendant of immigrants.

THOUGHT QUESTIONS

To check your understanding of the key issues of this period, solve the following problems:

1. How was the economic revolution of the 1920s different from the changes of the latter nineteenth century?

2. List the elements of American life that were changed by the automobile.

3. What groups did not share in the prosperity of the 1920s?

4. Compare the women's movement of the 1920s with other similar movements in American history.

5. Hoover called prohibition a "noble experiment." What were the results of that experiment? Were they noble or ignoble?

6. Summarize the policies of the Republican presidents of the 1920s. What were the results of these policies?

CRITICAL THINKING EXERCISE

After reading Comprehensive Immigration Law (1924), Bartolomeo Vanzetti, Court Statement (1927), and Advertisements (1925, 1927), answer the following questions:

Comprehensive Immigration Law (1924)

By the President of the United States of America

A Proclamation

Whereas it is provided in the act of Congress approved May 26, 1924, entitled "An act to limit the immigration of aliens into the United States, and for other purposes" that "The annual quota of any nationality shall be two per centum of the number of foreign-born individuals of such nationality resident in continental Untied States as determined by the United States Census of 1890, but the minimum quota of any nationality shall be 100 (Sec. 11 a)....

"The Secretary of State, the Secretary of Commerce, and the Secretary of Labor, jointly, shall, as soon as feasible after the enactment of this act, prepare a statement showing the number of individuals of the various nationalities resident in continental United States as determined by the United States Census of 1890, which statement shall be the population basis for the purposes of subdivision (a) of section 11 (Sec. 12 b).

"Such officials shall, jointly, report annually to the President the quota of each nationality under subdivision (a) of section 11, together with the statements, estimates, and revisions provided for in this section. The President shall proclaim and make known the quotas so reported." (Sec.12 e).

Now, therefore I, Calvin Coolidge, President of the United States of America acting under and by virtue of the power in me vested by the aforesaid act of Congress, do hereby proclaim and make known that on and after July 1, 1924, and throughout the fiscal year 1924-1925, the quota of each nationality provided in said act shall be as follows:

COUNTRY OR AREA OF BIRTH QUOTA 1924–1925

Afghanistan – 100
Albania – 100
Andorra – 100
Arabian peninsula (1, 2) – 100
Armenia – 124
Australia, including Papua, Tasmania, and all islands appertaining to Australia (3, 4) – 121
Austria – 785
Belgium (5) – 512
Bhutan – 100
Bulgaria – 100
Cameroon (proposed British mandate) – 100
Cameroon (French mandate) – 100
China – 100
Czechoslovakia – 3,073
Danzig, Free City of – 228
Denmark (5, 6) – 2,789
Egypt – 100
Estonia – 124
Ethiopia (Abyssinia) – 100
Finland – 170
France (1, 5, 6) – 3,954
Germany – 51,227
Great Britain and Northern Ireland (1, 3, 5, 6)0s34,007
Greece – 100
Hungary – 473
Iceland – 100
India (3) – 100
Iraq (Mesopotamia) – 100
Irish Free State (3) – 28,567
Italy, including Rhodes, Dodecanesia, and Castellorizzo (5) – 3,845
Japan – 100
Latvia – 142
Liberia – 100
Liechtenstein – 100
Lithuania – 344
Luxemburg – 100
Monaco – 100
Morocco (French and Spanish Zones and Tangier) – 100
Muscat (Oman) – 100
Nauru (proposed British mandate) (4) – 100
Nepal – 100
Netherlands (1, 5, 6) – 1648
New Zealand (including appertaining islands (3, 4) – 100
Norway (5) – 6,453
New Guinea, and other Pacific Islands under proposed Australian mandate (4) – 100
Palestine (with Trans-Jordan, proposed British mandate) – 100
Persia (1) – 100
Poland – 5,982
Portugal (1, 5) – 503
Ruanda and Urundi (Belgium mandate) – 100

159

Rumania – 603
Russia, European and Asiatic (1) – 2,248
Samoa, Western (4) (proposed mandate of New Zealand) – 100
San Marino – 100
Siam – 100
South Africa, Union of (3) – 100
South West Africa (proposed mandate of Union of South Africa) – 100
Spain (5) – 131
Sweden – 9,561
Switzerland – 2,081
Syria and The Lebanon (French mandate) – 100
Tanganyika (proposed British mandate) – 100
Togoland (proposed British mandate) – 100
Togoland (French mandate) – 100
Turkey – 100
Yap and other Pacific islands (under Japanese mandate) (4) – 100
Yugoslavia – 671

GENERAL NOTE. The immigration quotas assigned to the various countries and quota-areas should not be regarded as having any political significance whatever, or as involving recognition of new governments, or of new boundaries, or of transfers of territory except as the United States Government has already made such recognition in a formal and official manner.... Calvin Coolidge.

Bartolomeo Vanzetti, Court Statement (1927)

Now, I should say that I am not only innocent of all these things, not only have I never committed a real crime in my life-though some sins but not crimes-not only have I struggled all my life to eliminate crimes, the crimes that the officials and the official moral condemns, but also the crime that the official moral and the official law sanctions and sanctifies-the exploitation and the oppression of the man by the man, and if there is a reason why I am here as a guilty man, if there is a reason why you in a few minutes can doom me, it is this reason and none else....

We were tried during a time that has now passed into history. I mean by that, a time when there was a hysteria of resentment and hate against the people of our principles, against the foreigner, against slackers....

Well, I have already said that I not only am not guilty ... but I never commit a crime in my life-I have never stole and I have never killed and I have never spilt blood, and I have fought against crime and I have fought and have sacrificed myself even to eliminate the crimes the law and the church legitimate and sanctify.

This is what I say: I would not wish to a dog or to a snake, to the most low and misfortunate creature of the earth-I would not wish to any of them what I have had to suffer for things that I am not guilty of. But my conviction is that I have suffered for things I am guilty of. I am suffering because I am a radical and indeed I am a radical; I have suffered because I was an Italian, and indeed I am an Italian; I have suffered more for my family and for my beloved than for myself; but I am so convinced to be right that if you could execute me two times, and if I could be reborn two other times, I would live again to do what I have done already.

I have finished. Thank you.

Advertisements (1925, 1927)

Advertisement for Berkey & Gay Furniture Company (1925)

Do they know Your son at MALUCIO's?

There's a hole in the door at Malucio's. Ring the bell and a pair of eyes will look coldly out at you. If you are known you will get in. Malucio has to be careful.

There have been riotous nights at Malucio's. Tragic nights, too. But somehow the fat little man has managed to avoid the law.

Almost every town has its Malucio's. Some, brightly disguised as cabarets-others, mere back street filling stations for pocket flasks.

160

But every Malucio will tell you the same thing. His best customers are not the ne'er-do-wells of other years. They are the young people-frequently, the best young people of the town.

Malucio has put one over on the American home. Ultimately he will be driven out. Until then THE HOME MUST BID MORE INTELLIGENTLY FOR MALUCIO's BUSINESS.

There are many reasons why it is profitable and wise to furnish the home attractively, but one of these, and not the least, is-Malucio's.

The younger generation is sensitive to beauty, princely proud, and will not entertain in homes of which it is secretly ashamed.

But make your rooms attractive, appeal to the vaulting pride of youth, and you may worry that much less about Malucio's-and the other modern frivolities that his name symbolizes.

A guest room smartly and tastefully furnished-a refined and attractive dining room-will more than hold their own against the tinsel cheapness of Malucio's.

Nor is good furniture any longer a luxury for the favored few. THE PRESCOTT suite shown above, for instance, is a moderately priced pattern, conforming in every detail to the finest Berkey & Gay standards.

In style, in the selection of rare and beautiful woods, and in the rich texture of the finish and hand decorating, it reveals the skill of craftsmen long expert in the art of quality furniture making.

The PRESCOTT is typical of values now on display at the store of your local Berkey & Gay dealer. Depend on his showing you furniture in which you may take deep pride-beautiful, well built, luxuriously finished, and moderately priced.

There is a Berkey & Gay pattern suited to every home-an infinite variety of styles at prices ranging all the way from $350 to $6,000.

Advertisement for Eveready Flashlight and Battery (1927)

The Song that STOPPED!

A child of five skipped down the garden path and laughed because the sky was blue. "Jane," called her mother from the kitchen window, "come here and help me bake your birthday cake." Little feet sped. "Don't fall," her mother warned.

Jane stood in the kitchen door and wrinkled her nose in joy. Her gingham dress was luminous against the sun. What a child! Dr. and Mrs. Wentworth cherished Jane.

"Go down to the cellar and get mother some preserves ... the kind you like."

"The preserves are in the cellar," she chanted, making a progress twice around the kitchen. "Heigh-ho a-derry-o, the preserves are ..." her voice grew fainter as she danced off. "... in the ..."

The thread of song snapped. A soft *thud-thud*. Fear fluttered Mrs. Wentworth's heart. She rushed to the cellar door.

"Mother!" ... a child screaming in pain. Mrs. Wentworth saw a little morsel of girlhood lying in a heap of gingham and yellow hair at the bottom of the dark stairs.

The sky is still blue. But there will be no birthday party tomorrow. An ambulance clanged up to Dr. Wentworth's house today. Jane's leg is broken.

If a flashlight had been hanging on a hook at the head of the cellar stairs, this little tragedy would have been averted. If Jane had been taught to use a flashlight as carefully as her father, Dr. Wentworth, had taught her to use a tooth-brush, a life need not have been endangered.

An Eveready Flashlight is always a convenience and often a life-saver. Keep one about the house, in the car; and take one with you wherever you go. Keep it supplied with fresh Eveready Batteries-the longest-lasting flashlight batteries made. Eveready Flashlights, $1.00 up.

161

1. Why was 1890 chosen as a base year for the immigration quotas? What parts of the world received the most immigrant allowances? Why?

2. Compare the Comprehensive Immigration Law of 1924 and the comments of Vanzetti at his trial. Could there have been prejudice against him?

3. Were Sacco and Vanzetti presumed innocent until proven guilty?

4. Compare the appeal of the furniture advertisement and the Comprehensive Immigration Law of 1924. What are the key similarities?

5. To what human emotion does the flashlight and battery advertisement appeal?

6. What other contradiction is explored in Baker's article "The Treatment of German Americans"? What did the treatment of the non-English-speaking Pole reveal about the status of nativism in America?

7. What is your reaction to the fact that sometimes German prisoners of war were treated better than black American soldiers who fought for their country? What is Grimke's suggestion to these veterans?

8. Using examples from all three readings, write an essay on the subject of "World War I was fought to make the world safe for democracy."

CHAPTER 26

Franklin D. Roosevelt and the New Deal, 1929–1939

SUMMARY
After a great rise in the stock market, the 1929 crash brought about an economic depression, which had to be dealt with first by Hoover, and then, more successfully, by Franklin Delano Roosevelt.

The Great Depression
The economy of the United States collapsed after 1929, creating the single worst panic and era of unemployment in the nation's history.

The Great Crash
The consumer revolution of the 1920s relied on increased productivity and prosperity, but after 1924, productivity began to outpace consumption, causing a slight recession in 1927. Corporate and government leaders failed to heed this warning sign, however, and from 1927 to 1929, the stock market experienced a sharp increase known as the *great bull market*. Based on easy credit, inflated currency, and margin loans, the strength of the stock market obscured the economic problems looming on the horizon. The bubble burst in the fall of 1929 in the great stock market crash. The crash soon spilled over into the larger economy—banks and businesses failed, workers lost their jobs, and consumers came up short.

The Effect of the Depression
This was the start of a decade of terrible economic conditions, and few escaped its material or psychological impact. Ironically, the poor survived because they had experience with existing in poverty while the middle class took what was perhaps the hardest hit. Eventually, the Great Depression became the worst economic downturn in the nation's history.

Fighting the Depression
Ending the depression became the most important political issue of the 1930s, as first a Republican president and then a Democrat tried to achieve economic recovery. Though they failed solve the nation's economic problems, the Democrats did succeed in renewing Americans' hope for the future and alleviating some individual suffering.

The Emergence of Roosevelt
Hoover at first hoped the economy would work itself out, then emphasized voluntary solutions to the economic ills of the nation, using government only minimally. As the depression deepened, he began getting the government more and more involved in the economy, but his efforts failed to stop the deterioration.

163

In 1932, the voters elected Democrat Franklin D. Roosevelt, the former governor of New York who promised a "new deal" for the country, to the presidency in a landslide.

The Hundred Days

With a clear understanding of the responsibilities of political leadership, Roosevelt called Congress into special session in order to solve the banking crisis. After this success, he proceeded to pass several significant reforms in the first three months of his initial term. Though some of his programs were somewhat radical, the tone of Roosevelt's New Deal was reform and restore, not drastic change.

Steps toward Recovery

Roosevelt pushed several acts through Congress, attempting to instigate industrial and agricultural recovery. The National Recovery Administration was meant to foster cooperation between government, business, and labor as a means of achieving economic progress while the Agricultural Adjustment Administration was an effort to subsidize farmers back into prosperity.

Reforming American Life

After pressure developed for more fundamental reform, Roosevelt responded by suggesting permanent changes in the economic arrangements and institutions of the United States.

Challenges to FDR

Several liberal critics, including most notably Father Charles Coughlin, Francis Townsend, and Huey Long, complained that the New Deal was not solving the problems of the still-ailing economy. They suggested that more radical reforms were in order.

Social Security

In response to this criticism from the left, Roosevelt secured passage of the Social Security Act, which provided modest pensions, unemployment insurance, and financial assistance to the handicapped, needy elderly, and dependent children. The Social Security Act was a landmark piece of legislation for FDR, creating a system to provide for the welfare of individuals in the new industrial society.

The Impact of the New Deal

Roosevelt's New Deal program, succeeded in improving some, if not all, elements of American society, but did not initiate radical change. In short, the New Deal was a modest success but not an overwhelming victory. The most important advances came for organized labor while women and minorities in nonunionized industries were largely neglected.

The Rise of Organized Labor

The New Deal resulted in a dramatic increase in union membership, especially among the unskilled laborers who worked in the nation's steel and automobile industries. Miners and workers in other mass production factories also became more unionized as a result of the New Deal. Workers in the service industries still remained largely unorganized.

The New Deal Record on Help to Minorities
With only a few exceptions, the New Deal did not address the problems of the nation's minorities. While some New Deal programs helped African Americans and other minorities survive the depression, they did little to address racial injustice and discrimination. Indeed, some New Deal programs actively discriminated against non-white Americans. Native Americans, long neglected by the federal government, fared better than they had in many years with the passage of the Indian Reorganization Act that emphasized tribal unity and authority.

The New Deal's End
After five years of significant success, Roosevelt could no longer secure the passage of new reforms and his New Deal came to an end. Despite the end of the New Deal, Roosevelt was extremely popular and had revived American optimism despite the continuation of the Depression.

The Supreme Court Fight
Roosevelt's effort to reorganize the Supreme Court so that it would act more favorably on his New Deal programs failed in Congress and weakened the president's position with Congress. Senators and Representatives that had reluctantly supported FDR's programs before now felt free to oppose them.

The New Deal in Decline
A recession in 1937 that dissolved the slow but steady improvement in the economy under Roosevelt's New Deal revived the Republican party and strengthened opposition to Roosevelt's programs in Congress.

Conclusion: The New Deal and American Life
The New Deal did not cure the problems of the Depression, nor did it radicalize the nation's economy. And while its benefits were not distributed evenly among the American populace, the New Deal did ease many Americans' suffering while at the same time relieving the psychological impact of the depression on the public. The New Deal also made some permanent reforms in the American system and left the Democratic party as the majority party for decades to come.

LEARNING OBJECTIVES

After mastering this chapter, you should be able to:

1. Explain the causes of the "great bull market" and the stock market crash.

2. Describe the material and psychological effects of the Great Depression.

3. Discuss President Hoover's attempts to end the Depression.

4. Analyze the New Deal legislation passed in the "Hundred Days."

5. Differentiate between Roosevelt's programs for reform and recovery.

6. List and evaluate New Deal reforms.

7. Compare and contrast the programs of the various critics of the New Deal.

8. Show how the New Deal affected labor, women, and minorities.

9. Narrate the events and explain the significance of Roosevelt's attempt to "pack the court."

10. Discuss the factors that ended the New Deal.

GLOSSARY

To build your social science vocabulary, familiarize yourself with the following terms:

1. **speculative** pertaining to buying stocks or goods at risk, hoping for great gains in the future. "People bet their savings on speculative stocks."

3. **durable goods** long-lasting goods, typically automobiles and appliances. "... a natural consequence as more and more people already owned these durable goods."

4. **margin** in the stock market, the amount of the broker's loan to an investor to encourage the purchase of stock. "Corporations used their large cash reserves to supply money to brokers who in turn loaned it to investors on margin ..."

5. **stoop labor** a type of hard farm labor in which the worker must bend over at the waist for long hours. "... angry citizens, now willing to do stoop labor in the fields ..."

6. **vagrants** those who have no home. "... the number of vagrants increased ..."

7. **nuances** small gradations in meaning or significance. "he had little patience with philosophical nuances."

8. **solvent** able to pay all debts. "Other banks, once they became solvent, would open later."

9. **allocate** to assign or distribute for a particular purpose. "allocate acreage among individual farmers."

10. **collective bargaining** the process of negotiating the terms of work between management and a union representing all the workers. "... the guarantee of collective bargaining by unions..."

11. **morass** something sticky or impeding. "The NRA quickly bogged down in a huge bureaucratic morass."

12. **anti-Semitism** prejudice, discrimination, or hostility against Jews. "... Coughlin appealed to the discontented with a strange mixture of crank monetary schemes and anti-Semitism."

IDENTIFICATION

Briefly identify the meaning and significance of the following terms:

1. Bonus Army_____

_____

2. National Recovery Administration (NRA)_____

_____

3. Agricultural Adjustment Act (AAA)_____

_____

4. Black Thursday_____

_____

5. The Hundred Days _____

_____

6. Indian Reorganization Act_____

_____

7. Social Security Act_____

_____

8. "court packing" scheme_____

_____

9. John L. Lewis_____

_____

10. "the Roosevelt Recession"_____

_____

MATCHING

A.   Match the following legislation or agencies to the appropriate description:

_____1. Tennessee Valley Authority   **a.**   created the National Labor Relations Board to oversee union elections

_____2. Works Progress Administration   **b.**   led by African American woman Mary McLeod Bethune

_____3. Civilian Conservation Corps   **c.**   built dams and flood controls in seven southeastern states

_____4. National Youth Administration   **d.**   loaned money to financial institutions to save them from bankruptcy

_____5. Wagner Act   **e.**   a massive 1935 emergency relief measure

f.   employed city youths to work in the country on public parks and recreational sites

B.   Match the following individuals with the appropriate description:

_____1. Charles Coughlin   **a.**   African American who served in Roosevelt's Interior Department

_____2. Francis Townsend   **b.**   energetic leader of the NRA

_____3. Huey Long   **c.**   Roosevelt's Secretary of Agriculture who addressed the issue of farmers' overproduction

_____4. William H. Hastie   **d.**   Detroit Roman Catholic radio commentator who became a critic of the New Deal

_____5. Hugh Johnson   **e.**   colorful senator from Louisiana who started the "share the wealth" movement

f.   doctor who proposed a pension for the elderly

COMPLETION

Answer the question or complete the statement by filling in the blanks with the correct word or words.

1. President Roosevelt's ambitious plan of relief and reform during the Great Depression was called the _____.

2. World War I veterans were forced out of the shacks in Washington D.C. by General _____.

3. Section 7a of the New Deal's industrial recovery legislation protected the rights of _____.

4. The blue eagle was a symbol of cooperation with the _____.

5. Roosevelt's secretary of agriculture was _____.

6. The National Union for Social Justice was the idea of _____.

7. The legislation that guaranteed unions the rights of collective bargaining was the _____.

8. Flamboyant Louisiana Senator _____ started a "Share the Wealth" movement in 1934

9. John L. Lewis's group, which was expelled from the American Federation of Labor, became known as the _____.

10. The leader in the Senate opposition to the court-packing plan was Montana's _____.

TRUE/FALSE

Mark the following statements either T (True) or F (False):

_____ 1. Most Americans were active traders in the stock market when it collapsed in 1929.

_____ 2. President Hoover did nothing to try to solve the problems of the Depression.

_____ 3. The basic cause of the Great Depression was the inability of Americans to consume what was produced in American factories.

_____ 4. The Agricultural Adjustment Act allowed the government to set production quotas for certain crops.

_____ 5. Mexican immigration was encouraged during the Great Depression in order that businesses could benefit from inexpensive labor.

_____ 6. The New Deal reform legislation tried to correct all of the nation's social and economic injustices.

_____ 7. The greatest successes of the New Deal were the attempts to aid minorities.

_____ 8. The Indian Reorganization Act of 1934 stressed tribal unity.

_____ 9. President Roosevelt wanted to reform and restore the American economic system, not drastically change it.

_____ 10. The economic successes of 1937 indicated that the New Deal had cured the Depression.

MULTIPLE CHOICE

Circle the one alternative that *best* completes the statement or answers the question.

1. One of the reasons for the "great bull market" was that
   a. a majority of Americans bought and sold stock.
   b. the productivity of the American economy was well distributed among the population.
   c. investors could get easy credit for broker's loans.
   d. the Federal Reserve Board raised the discount rate.

2. Herbert Hoover's solution to the Depression was to
   a. at first do nothing, but then move to voluntary cooperation among businesses to maintain wages and employment.
   b. provide no help at all.
   c. help all levels of the economy, but in an amount consistent with a balanced budget.
   d. lower tariffs and thus increase foreign trade.

3. The purpose of the Agricultural Adjustment Act was to
   a. ensure that no one starved.
   b. raise farm income by restricting production.
   c. socialize America's farms.
   d. protect the rights of farm tenants and sharecroppers.

4. The significance of the Works Progress Administration was that it
   a. was a relief program that immediately helped some suffering families.
   b. was the idea of Huey Long's.
   c. established the rights of unions to organize and bargain collectively.
   d. became a permanent federal agency.

5. Father Charles Coughlin attacked the New Deal, suggesting that
   a. everyone over sixty should receive $200 per month.
   b. money should be inflated and the banks nationalized.
   c. there should be a "share the wealth" program.
   d. the nation should encourage Jewish immigration from Germany.

6. The Social Security Act provided for all of the following *except*
   a. old-age pensions.
   b. unemployment compensation.
   c. welfare grants.
   d. aid to the nation's migrants.

7. During the New Deal, organized labor
   a. received support from the government, but declined in members.
   b. received support from government and gained membership.
   c. won most of its major goals with no violent strikes.
   d. took a united and aggressive approach to organizing the unskilled.

8. The New Deal handled past inequities to minorities by
   a. passing civil rights legislation.
   b. making sure that all programs were "color-blind."
   c. confronting squarely the racial injustice in federal relief programs.
   d. none of the above

9. President Roosevelt
   a. was a relative political novice.
   b. was not flexible in his political outlook.
   c. had the ability to persuade and motivate others.
   d. All of the above.

10. Which of the following is an accurate evaluation of the New Deal?
    a. It was clearly socialist in intent and impact.
    b. It was moderate and relatively ineffective economically, but did produce sweeping political changes, putting the Democratic party in the majority.
    c. It was a successful revolution that achieved the goal of equal opportunity and social justice.
    d. It achieved little except for equality for women and minorities.

11. Which of the following was *not* a cause of the Great Depression?
    a. More goods were produced than consumers could use.
    b. There were unstable economic conditions in Europe.
    c. Many U.S. corporations were mismanaged.
    d. High taxes for the social security system took too high a percentage of the federal budget.

12. The National Recovery Administration tried to guarantee
    a. minority rights
    b. freedom from unions.
    c. codes of fair practice.
    d. no government interferences.

13. As the first lady, Eleanor Roosevelt
    a. held a cabinet position.
    b. led the National Recovery Adminstration.
    c. was seldom seen or heard.
    d. worked for civil rights of minorities.

14. Long-term effects of New Deal programs included all of the following EXCEPT
   a. a recognition that government had a responsibility to provide welfare for those who could not help themselves.
   b. growth in labor unions to balance corporate power.
   c. providing an outlet to economic aid for unorganized "forgotten men."
   d. a minimum wage law that provided a much needed floor for many workers.

15. The effect of the "court-packing" scheme was to
   a. end the power of the Supreme Court.
   b. increase the number of judges on the court to fifteen.
   c. weaken the president's relations with Congress.
   d. jeopardize Roosevelt's popularity with older Americans.

THOUGHT QUESTIONS

To check your understanding of the key issues of this period, solve the following problems:

1. Compare and contrast the first and second New Deals. Comment on possible explanations for the different approaches.

2. "The differences between Hoover and Roosevelt were more appearance than reality." Comment. To what extent is this true, and in what ways is it false?

3. What were the permanent changes of the New Deal? Were these changes for the better or not?

4. Compare the New Deal with other reform movements, such as populism and progressivism.

5. Comment on the extent to which Roosevelt's personality affected the course of the New Deal.

6. What set of factors ended Roosevelt's legislative successes? What could he have done to preserve and extend his influence?

CRITICAL THINKING EXERCISE

Using material in Chapter 26 of the text and the primary sources provided below, please answer the questions that follow the documents, Ruth Shallcross, "Shall Married Women Work?" (1936), Louise Mitchell, "Slave Markets in New York City" (1940), and Joseph D. Bibb, "Flirting with Radicalism

Ruth Shallcross, "Shall Married Women Work?" (1936)

Legislative Action

Within the last few years, bills have been introduced in the legislatures of twenty-six states against married woman workers. Only one of these passed. This was in Louisiana, and it was later repealed. Six other states have either joint resolutions or governors' orders restricting married women's right to work. Three other states have made a general practice of prohibiting married women from working in public employment …

Extent of Discrimination

The National Federation of Business and Professional Women's Clubs made a survey early in 1940 of local employment policies. This was part of a general study which assembled all materials relating to the employment of married women. The survey shows that married women are most likely to find bars against them if they seek jobs as school teachers, or as office workers in public utilities or large manufacturing concerns. Only a very small number of department stores refuse jobs to married women. However, in 1939, the *Department Store Economist* reported that the sentiment against married women "is growing stronger." Opposition, it was found, came from customers, labor organizations, women's clubs, and miscellaneous groups of the unemployed. Despite this opposition, "nearly all stores are either doubtful whether it would be a wise plan to announce publicly a policy against hiring or retaining married women, or believe it would not be helpful to public relations." This attitude may reflect the fact that married women's employment has been advantageous to department stores because the necessary part-time arrangements suited both parties well. Single women usually want full-time employment, but many married women prefer to work only a few hours each day …

Kinds of Bars

The bars against married women are of different kinds—all of which exist for some school teachers. They may take the form of refusal to hire married women (the most frequent), of dismissal upon marriage, delay in granting promotion, or actual demotion, and either permanent or temporary dismissal when pregnant. Discrimination is often difficult to detect; a married woman may assume that her marriage is the cause of her inability to hold a job, or to get a new one, when the real reason may lie in her lack of ability, personality, or training.

The National Education Association has from time to time made surveys of employment policies in local communities with respect to married women teachers. Its material is more complete than any other. Its survey, made in 1931, revealed that 77 percent of the cities reporting made a practice of not employing married women as new teachers, and 63 percent dismissed women teachers upon marriage. Tenure acts protect married teachers from being dismissed in some states. But although tenure acts may protect teachers who marry after being employed, they do not assure a new teacher that marriage will not be a bar to getting a job. The National Education Association reported in 1939 that teachers in at least thirteen states are legally protected by court decisions from being dismissed for being married. Kentucky seems to be the only state where the contract of marriage is deemed "the very basis of the whole fabric of society" and hence is not an obstacle to employment …

Studies show that men have been affected by unemployment to a much greater extent than have women, because unemployment has been more acute in the heavy industries (steel, oil, mining, etc.) where men are mostly employed.… The administrative and clerical jobs connected with these industries, which are partially filled by women, have not been eliminated to anything like the same degree as production jobs.

Consumer and service industries (textile, food, beauty parlors, telephone service, to name only a few), where women are mostly to be found, were not affected seriously as heavy industries by the Depression. The government's recovery measures, based on artificially increasing purchasing power, chiefly stimulated the consumer and service industries, thus opening up relatively more opportunities for women than men. As a result, women have fared better than men in getting new jobs …

State and federal employment offices also give evidence of the relative ease with which women have obtained jobs compared with men, and indicate that men have been unemployed for longer periods of time than have women. One study of a community of 14,000 people in the West makes this point specific. Women's work in the town increased during the early years of the Depression in the needle trades and textiles, as well as in the service occupations, while men's work in glass declined

175

sharply. Another study in a steel town showed much the same thing. Few of the people who oppose married women's employment seem to realize that a coal miner or steel worker cannot very well fill the jobs of nursemaids, cleaning women, or the factory and clerical occupations now filled by women. Unhappily, men accustomed to work in the heavy industries have not been able to fill the jobs in consumer and service industries. Retraining of these men has been practically negligible, and could not have been done in time to benefit them immediately. Expenditures for defense are now once more increasing opportunities in heavy industries, so we may expect to see a fundamental change in the situation in the coming months.

Louise Mitchell, "Slave Markets in New York City" (1940)

Every morning, rain or shine, groups of women with brown paper bags or cheap suitcases stand on street corners in the … bargain for their labor.

They come as early as 7 in the morning, wait as late as four in the afternoon with the hope that they will make enough to buy supper when they go home. Some have spent their last nickel to get to the corner and are in desperate need. When the hour grows later, they sit on boxes if any are around. In the afternoon their labor is worth only half as much as in the morning. If they are lucky, they get about 30 cents an hour scrubbing, cleaning, laundering, washing windows, waxing floors and woodwork all day long; in the afternoon, when most have already been employed, they are only worth the degrading sum of 20 cents an hour. Once hired on the "slave market," the women often find after a day's backbreaking toil, that they worked longer than was arranged, got less than was promised, were forced to accept clothing instead of cash and were exploited beyond human endurance. Only the urgent need for money makes them submit to this routine daily.

Throughout the county, more than two million women are engaged in domestic work, the largest occupational group for women. About half are Negro women …

Though many Negro women work for as little as two dollars a week and as long as 80 hours a week … they have no social security, no workmens' compensation, no old age security.…

The Women's Bureau in Washington points out that women take domestic work only as a last resort. Largely unprotected by law, they find themselves at the mercy of an individual employer. Only two states, Wisconsin and Washington, have wage or hour legislation. But enforcement is very slack.…

The tradition of street corner markets is no new institution in this city. As far back as 1834, the statute books show a place was set aside on city streets, where those seeking work could meet with those who wanted workers. This exchange also functions for male workers.… At present, markets flourish in the Bronx and Brooklyn, where middle-class families live. However, this method of employment is also instituted in Greenwich Village, Richmond and Queens.…

The prosperity of the nation can only be judged by the living standards of its most oppressed group. State legislatures must pass laws to protect the health and work of the domestic. A world of education is still needed, both for employees and employers.

Many civic and social organizations are now working toward improving conditions of domestics. Outstanding among these is the Bronx Citizens Committee for Improvement of Domestic Employees. The YWCA and many women's clubs are interested in the problem. Mayor LaGuardia ... must be forced to end these horrible conditions of auction block hiring with the most equitable solution for the most oppressed section of the working class—Negro women.

Joseph D. Bibb, "Flirting with Radicalism"

Contrary to the conciliatory policies of ... our conservative leaders and erstwhile voicers of black public opinion, the overtures of the Communists and other radical political and economic groups to Negroes are not falling on deaf ears. In most of these cases, the prophecies are begotten of the wish, but the evidence to the contrary is too apparent everywhere about us to be contradicted on such slim rebuttal and words. When thousands of colored men and women gather every night of the week at the open air forums held by these radical groups in the parks and on the street corners of nearly all of our large cities to listen with rapt attention and enthusiasm to doctrines of a radical reorganization of our political and economic organization, the evidence to the contrary of the declaration that "Negroes will never take to Communis[m]" is too strong to be ignored. When Negro miners in the coal and iron districts join in strikes and face starvation to cast their lot with the brother workers, no mere mouthing of platitudes will suffice to hoodwink the thinking masses of our people. When the enslaved and peon-ized sharecroppers of the South dare bravely a certain threat of rope and faggot to follow radical leadership with organized demands for a newer and squarer deal, it fairly shouts from the house tops that the working Negro is part and parcel of the seething discontent which has swept across the entire world.

The rottenness, the injustice, the grim brutality and cold unconcern of our present system has become too irksome to the man farthest down to be longer endured in silence and pacifism. It is high time that those who would stem a revolution busied themselves in sweeping and lasting cures to the cancerous sores which fester upon our body politic and fiercely competitive society. The Communists have framed a program of social remedies which cannot fail to appeal to the hungry and jobless millions, who live in barren want, while everywhere about them is evidence of restricted plenty in the greedy hands of the few. Safety and security, peace and plenty are the things most dear to the hearts of the inarticulate lowly, and these are the things which the radicals hold out as bait to the masses, white as well as black. To argue that they cannot give them but begs the question, for the obvious answer is that our present systems HAVE not given them, and offer no promise of them.

If our two major parties would stem this rising tide of Communism, let them take steps to provide for such immediate needs as are virtually hurling the masses into the ranks of radicalism. Food, shelter and clothing, adequate employment are the only answer to the challenge of Communism, not mere word of mouth denials. The demand among both black and white alike is insisting for improvement—or change.

1. After reading the text, compare the effects of the Great Depression on white males, African Americans, and women.

2. After reading the text, describe the major relief and reform efforts of the New Deal. Did they address the needs of whites, minorities and women equally?

3. According to Ruth Shallcross, how did the public and private sectors respond to the employment needs of women during the Great Depression? Explain that response.

4. What did Louise Mitchell mean by "Slave Market"? Why did it exist?

5. Compare Joseph Bibb's radicalism with the New Deal's reformism as you described it in question 2 above.

CHAPTER 27

America and the World, 1921–1945

SUMMARY

Refusing to assume an important role in world affairs after the end of World War I, the United States became more and more isolationist throughout the 1920s. In the 1930s, as conflict brewed in Europe and Asia, the United States' commitment to isolationism grew deeper until 1941 when Nazism and Japanese imperialism forced a foreign policy reversal and entrance into the second World War. At the conclusion of World War II, the United States remained highly involved in world affairs and took a leading role in maintaining world order.

Isolationism

Because of the Great Depression and the fear of involvement in another European war, the United States followed an isolationist policy in the 1930s despite the increasing militarism of Japan and the rise to power of Adolf Hitler in Germany and Benito Mussolini in Italy. In 1937, when these three powers allied themselves as the Axis Powers, thereby posing a threat not only to Europe but to the entire world, the United States continued its isolationist policies until it was almost too late.

The Lure of Pacifism and Neutrality

Looking back at World War I as a meaningless effort, many Americans sought security in pacifism and legal neutrality. They wanted a way to ensure that the United States would not be drawn into another European conflict. Young people especially wanted to avoid war as peace movements swept across college campuses. After a Senate investigation into unsavory business practices in the munitions industry, a series of neutrality laws were passed that tried to limit the ways that Americans could be drawn into a conflict. Though publicly committed to neutrality, Roosevelt tried to limit the nation's retreat into isolationism.

War in Europe

Events in Europe made American neutrality increasingly unrealistic and difficult to maintain, making the neutrality acts harder to support.

The Road to War

From 1939 to 1941, the United States moved ever closer to war as the nation's sympathy and support went to England and France.

From Neutrality to Undeclared War

As the war worsened in Europe, President Roosevelt pushed the country closer to participation. He clearly favored the Allied cause and convinced Congress to relax the strict neutrality acts in order to aid the British. After the success of the German *blitzkrieg* put England at risk, Roosevelt asked for a peace-time draft and began the Lend-Lease program to get war supplies to the British. Although there was some opposition to Roosevelt's actions, the American populace became more and more convinced of the need for some kind of intervention. This stance only intensified as Germany and the United States engaged in an undeclared naval war.

Showdown in the Pacific

While war raged in Europe, Japan continued to expand in Asia, especially into British and French colonies. When the United States responded with economic sanctions, Japan sent diplomats to Washington to discuss peace proposals. At the same time they readied for a surprise attack on Pearl Harbor, plunging the United States into war.

Turning the Tide Against the Axis

In both Europe and Asia, the early days of the war were discouraging for Americans. It took two years for the Allies to halt the advance of the Axis powers. They then faced the daunting task of driving them back and liberating the conquered territories.

Wartime Partnerships

Most importantly, the alliance of the United States and Britain was a genuine coalition with unified command and strategy. Relations with other members of the United Nations coalition were more strained. China objected to the decision to defeat Germany first, having been at war with Japan since 1937. And relations with the Soviet Union were also uneasy as they took the worst fury of the German *blitzkrieg* alone while Britain and the United States could do little more than promise future help.

Halting the German Blitz

The United States and Britain invaded first North Africa and then Italy, while the Soviet Union stopped the Germans at Stalingrad.

Checking Japan in the Pacific

In Asia, the United States Navy gained control of the central Pacific by July of 1942.

The Home Front

The war wrought vast changes in American society and ended the decade of depression. The need for war materials was met by American industries working at full capacity. Women and minorities moved into jobs previously closed to them as men went to war. The nation's economic recovery led to FDR's reelection to a fourth term in 1940.

The Arsenal of Democracy

Though American soldiers were certainly important to the Allied victory, American industry was the single most important contribution of the nation to the war effort. The rapid increase in production led to many problems including shortages of critical materials like aluminum, steel, and copper. In 1942, the War Production Board was formed to answer such complex logistical concerns. One result of the wartime economic expansion was increased incomes for both workers and farmers.

A Nation on the Move

The war motivated millions to migrate, young men to training camps and then overseas and defense workers to booming industrial cities. Such movement created problems in housing and family life, but also offered opportunities, especially to African Americans, Hispanic Americans, and women. Though African Americans experienced some social and economic gains, their progress was limited by continued and even inflamed racial prejudices. The internment of Japanese Americans into concentration camps was another sad counterpoint to the economic progress of the war years.

Victory

After the offensives of the Axis powers had been stopped, the war ended quickly. The Germans were thoroughly defeated and forced to surrender unconditionally.

War Aims and Wartime Diplomacy

With the end of the war came the end of the alliance between the United States and the Soviet Union. Tensions between the two nations emerged from a mutual distrust, the Soviet Union's perception of an Allied delay in opening a second front, and vastly different goals concerning the rebuilding of postwar Europe.

Triumph and Tragedy in the Pacific

Though the war in Europe was over, the war in the Pacific continued until President Harry S Truman ordered the dropping of two atomic bombs on Japan.

Conclusion: The Transforming Power of War

World War II had a significant impact on American life. It was the first time the United States reached its full military potential. The United States emerged from the war the strongest nation in the world and fully committed to a global role. The war also brought about economic recovery and unprecedented prosperity while establishing political and demographic trends.

LEARNING OBJECTIVES

After mastering this chapter, you should be able to:

1. Explain the causes and effects of the isolationism of the 1930s.

2. Trace the background of war in Europe in the 1930s.

3. Discuss the factors that led to conflict in Asia.

4. Analyze the goals of the Allies in forming the wartime coalition.

5. Discuss the military strategy that stopped the advance of the Germans.

6. Describe how the United States took control of the central Pacific in 1942.

7. Discuss the changes the war brought about in domestic economic development.

8. Describe the impact of the war on minorities, women, and labor unions.

9. Evaluate the performance of the United States in wartime diplomacy.

10. Discuss the Allied strategy of the last days of World War II.

11. Discuss the seeds of Soviet-American tension fostered by the war.

GLOSSARY

To build your social science vocabulary, familiarize yourself with the following terms:

1. **pacifists** those who oppose war or the unrestricted use of the military. "... especially among pacifists who had advocated the outlawing of war ..."

2. **bilateral** in diplomacy, pertaining to an action or treaty involving two nations. "An unhappy Briand, who had wanted a bilateral treaty with the United States ..."

3. **charismatic** having a magnetic personality or attraction. "A shrewd and charismatic leader, Hitler capitalized on both domestic discontent and bitterness ..."

4. **Reich** German word for rule, kingdom, or reign. "... uniting all Germans into a Greater Third Reich that would last a thousand years ..."

5. **belligerents** nations engaged in war. "... ban arms sales and loans to belligerents ..."

6. **coup** a sudden and decisive forcible change in the government of a nation. "... he seized Austria in a bloodless coup."

7. **Anglophiles** those who favor or have an affinity for the people and institutions of Britain. "Eastern Anglophiles, moderate New Dealers, and liberal Republicans made up the bulk of the membership ..."

8. **depreciation** (in taxation) a tax break based on the fact that machinery wears out or loses value. "The WPB allowed business rapid depreciation, and thus huge tax credits ..."

9. **detention** restraint or confinement. "Herded into hastily built detention centers ..."

10. **Balkan** an area of south central Europe, a peninsula bounded by the Aegean and Adriatic seas. "As his armies overran Poland and the Balkan countries ..."

11. **capitulation** a surrender with stated conditions. "... Japan signed a formal capitulation agreement ..."

IDENTIFICATION

Briefly identify the meaning and significance of the following terms:

1. Kellogg-Briand Pact _____

_____

2. isolationism _____

_____

3. Nye Committee _____

_____

4. America First Committee _____

_____

5. Lend-Lease Program _____

_____

6. War Production Board _____

_____

7. Fair Employment Practices Committee _____

_____

8. "Zoot Suit" Riots _____

_____

9. Yalta Conference _____

_____

10. Manhattan Project _____

_____

MATCHING

A. Match the following world leaders with the appropriate description:

_____1. Haile Selassie

_____2. Chiang Kai-shek

_____3. Hideki Tojo

_____4. Charles de Gaulle

_____5. Joseph Stalin

a. dictator of Italy before and during World War II

b. emperor of Ethiopia during the Italian invasion

c. leader of the Soviet Union during World War II

d. leader of the Nationalist Chinese during World War II

e. Japanese army militant who became premier in 1941

f. leader of exile government known as the Free French

B. Match the following leaders with the appropriate description:

_____1. Cordell Hull

_____2. Gerald Nye

_____3. William Allen White

_____4. Donald Nelson

_____5. A. Philip Randolph

a. head of the Committee to Defend America by aiding the Allies

b. aviator-hero and member of the America First Committee

c. Secretary of State under President Franklin D. Roosevelt

d. African-American labor leader who demanded equal employment opportunities during World War II

e. Sears, Roebuck executive and head of the War Production Board

f. senator who sponsored the neutrality acts of 1935, 1936, and 1937

COMPLETION

Answer the question or complete the statement by filling in the blanks with the correct word or words.

1. The 1928 treaty intended to outlaw war was the _____.

2. In 1937 the totalitarians nations of Germany, Italy, and Japan signed an anti-Comintern pact establishing them as the _____.

3. The German strategy of lightning war was called _____.

4. To avoid a two-front war, Hitler signed the _____ with Russia.

5. The _____ was the result of Nazi racial policies of genocide.

6. The German Afrika Korps was led by _____.

7. The American leader of the naval attack on key Japanese islands in the Pacific was _____.

8. An example of America being the arsenal for democracy was Henry Ford's _____ plant that built B-24 bombers.

9. In December 1944, the _____in the Ardennes Forest delayed Eisenhower's advance into Germany.

10. A committee headed by _____ suggested dropping an atomic bomb on a Japanese city.

TRUE/FALSE

Mark the following statements either T (True) or F (False):

_____1.   The emergency of the Great Depression convinced most Americans of the need to be more active in international affairs.

_____2.   Hitler came to power in Germany in 1933 by capitalizing on domestic discontent and bitterness over World War I.

_____3.   The Nye Committee's report buttressed American isolationism by blaming the nation's involvement in World War I on bankers and munitions makers.

_____4.   Economic depression and the threat of war made the United States more isolationist in the 1930s.

_____5.   Americans were eager to oppose the rise of fascism in Europe in the 1930s.

_____6.   The battle of El Alamein was a major Allied victory in southeast Asia.

_____7.   President Roosevelt believed that a German victory threatened American security.

_____8.   Because of Pearl Harbor, the United States decided to defeat the Japanese first before attacking Germany.

_____9.   The Soviet Union suffered more losses of life and property than did the other Allies fighting the Nazi threat.

_____10.   President Truman considered for several months the decision to drop the atomic bomb.

MULTIPLE CHOICE

Circle the one alternative that *best* completes the statement or answers the question.

1. After Japan invaded southern Indochina, the United States
   a. declared war only on Japan.
   b. froze Japanese assets.
   c. sent massive military aid to China.
   d. declared war on Japan and Germany.

2. All of the following are true about Pearl Harbor EXCEPT
   a. the battle dragged on all day.
   b. eight battleships were sunk.
   c. warning messages about an attack failed to reach Pacific bases on time.
   d. it led to the United States declaring war on Japan the next day.

3. In the summer of 1943, Allied forces invaded Europe through
   a. France.
   b. Spain.
   c. Greece.
   d. Sicily and Italy.

4. The turning point in the Pacific war came at
   a. the Philippines.
   b. Guadalcanal.
   c. Midway.
   d. Iwo Jima.

5. In the 1930s, Japan, Germany, and Italy were
   a. strongly anticommunist, but threatened the rest of the world too.
   b. no threat to their neighbors.
   c. supporters of the League of Nations.
   d. satisfied with the world status quo.

6. Which of the following was not an element of the pacifist movement of the 1930s?
   a. the novel *All Quiet on the Western Front*
   b. the efforts of rich families such as the Krupps and the DuPonts
   c. American youth on college campuses
   d. the "merchants-of-death" thesis

7. The neutrality acts
   a. tried to insulate the United States from European problems.
   b. had no impact on European affairs.
   c. received the strong support of President Roosevelt.
   d. limited the war to Europe and Asia.

8. Increasing defense expenditures, the peacetime draft, and lend-lease indicated that Americans
   a. wanted to declare war on Germany.
   b. feared the results of German victory.
   c. wanted to respond to Pearl Harbor.
   d. desired to dominate Latin America.

9. The effect of the attack on Pearl Harbor was to
   a. divide the country politically on foreign policy.
   b. bring about war with Japan but not Germany.
   c. shock Americans into an awareness of the Axis threat.
   d. all of the above.

10. The wartime Allied coalition was
    a. especially close and effective between the United States and Britain.
    b. based on American and Free French cooperation.
    c. no more effective than the Berlin-Rome-Tokyo Axis.
    d. difficult because the United States had not recognized the Soviet Union.

11. At the meeting of the Western Allies at Casablanca it was decided that
    a. the war in Europe was successful enough to avoid a beachhead assault.
    b. use of the atomic bomb would be restricted to Asia.
    c. Russia would create a "second front" with Germany.
    d. they would fight the Axis powers until they achieved an unconditional surrender.

12. Americans who stayed at home during World War II
    a. had to make major adjustments in their lives.
    b. found that society changed little.
    c. seldom moved.
    d. could at least enjoy the abundance of consumer goods.

13. Which of the following was not a U.S. problem of the war years?
    a. a housing shortage
    b. racial problems in integrated combat units
    c. racial discrimination in industry
    d. an increased divorce rate

14. Japanese Americans were
    a. treated as badly as Germany treated Jews.
    b. often denied their liberty and their property.
    c. allowed to fight but only in the Pacific.
    d. treated differently depending on whether they were first- or second-generation immigrants.

15. The United States used atomic bombs to defeat
    a. Germany.
    b. Italy.
    c. the Soviet Union.
    d. Japan.

THOUGHT QUESTIONS

To check your understanding of the key issues of this period, solve the following problems:

1. To what extent did the American retreat from responsibility in foreign affairs aid the rise of dictators in the 1930s?

2. Considering the reasons for conflict in Asia, how surprising was the attack on Pearl Harbor?

3. What were the long-range effects of World War II on American society?

4. What was the role of historical interpretation in the foreign policy of the 1930s, specifically the neutrality acts?

5. What were the various goals of the Allied powers? How did these different goals affect the coalition, the strategy, and the outcome of the war?

6. Do you think that President Roosevelt "sold us out" at the Yalta Conference? What was the Soviet perspective on Eastern Europe?

7. What is the significance of the Holocaust to American and world history?

8. In retrospect, was the decision to use the atomic bombs a wise one?

CRITICAL THINKING EXERCISE

After reading Albert Einstein, Letter to President Roosevelt (1939), Franklin Delano Roosevelt, "The Four Freedoms" (1941), and "A Woman Remembers the War" (1984), answer the following:

Albert Einstein, Letter to President Roosevelt (1939)

Albert Einstein
Old Grove Rd. Nassau Point
Peconic, Long Island

August 2nd, 1939

F. D. Roosevelt,
President of the United States,
White House
Washington, D. C.

Sir:

Some recent work by E. Fermi and L. Szilard, which has been communicated to me in manuscript, leads me to expect that the element uranium may be turned into a new and important source of energy in the immediate future. Certain aspects of the situation which has arisen seem to call for watchfulness and, if necessary, quick action on the part of the Administration. I believe therefore that it is my duty to bring to your attention the following facts and recommendations:

In the course of the last four months it has been made probable-through the work of Joliot in France as well as Fermi and Szilard in America-that it may become possible to set up a nuclear chain reaction in a large mass of uranium, by which vast amount of power and large quantities of new radium-like elements would be generated. Now it appears almost certain that this could be achieved in the immediate future.

This new phenomenon would also lead to the construction of bombs, and it is conceivable-though much less certain-that extremely powerful bombs of a new type may thus be constructed. A single bomb of this type, carried by boat and exploded in a port, might very well destroy the whole port together with some of the surrounding territory. However, such bombs might very well prove to be too heavy for transportation by air.

The United States has only very poor ores of uranium in moderate quantities. There is some good ore in Canada and the former Czechoslovakia, while the most important source of uranium is the Belgian Congo.

In view of this situation you may think it desirable to have some permanent contact maintained between the Administration and the group of physicists working on chain reactions in America. One possible way of achieving this might be for you to entrust with this task a person who has your confidence and who could perhaps serve in an inofficial capacity. His task might comprise the following:

a) to approach Government Departments, keep them informed of the further development, and put forward recommendations for Government action, giving particular attention to the problem of securing a supply of uranium ore for the United States:

b) to speed up the experimental work, which is at present being carried on within the limits of the budgets of University laboratories, by providing funds, if such funds be required, through his contacts with private persons who are willing to make contributions for this cause, and perhaps also by obtaining the co-operation of industrial laboratories which have the necessary equipment.

I understand that Germany has actually stopped the sale of uranium from the Czechoslovakian mines which she has taken over. That she should have taken such early action might perhaps be understood on the ground that the son of the German Under-Secretary of State, von Weizsacker, is attached to the Kaiser-Wilhelm-Institut in Berlin where some of the American work on uranium is now being repeated.

Yours very truly,

[signed] Albert Einstein

Franklin D. Roosevelt, "The Four Freedoms" (1941)

Armed defense of democratic existence is now being gallantly waged in four continents. If that defense fails, all the population and all the resources of Europe, Asia, Africa and Australasia will be dominated by the conquerors. The total of those populations and their resources ... greatly exceeds the sum total of the population and the resources of the whole of the Western Hemisphere-many times over.

In times like these it is immature-and incidentally untrue-for anybody to brag that an unprepared America, single-handed, and with one hand tied behind its back, can hold off the whole world.

No realistic American can expect from a dictator's peace international generosity, or return of true independence, or world disarmament, or freedom of expression, or freedom of religion-or even good business....

The need of the moment is that our actions and our policy should be devoted primarily-almost exclusively-to meeting this foreign peril. For all our domestic problems are now a part of the great emergency.

Just as our national policy in internal affairs has been based upon a decent respect for the rights and the dignity of all our fellow men within our gates, so our national policy in foreign affairs has been based on a decent respect for the rights and dignity of all nations, large and small. And the justice of morality must and will win in the end.

Our national policy is this:

First, by an impressive expression of the public will and without regard to partisanship, we are committed to all-inclusive national defense.

Second, by an impressive expression of the public will and without regard to partisanship, we are committed to full support of all those resolute peoples, everywhere, who are resisting aggression and are thereby keeping war away from our hemisphere. By this support, we express our determination that the democratic cause shall prevail, and we strengthen the defense and security of our own nation.

Third, by an impressive expression of the public will and without regard to partisanship, we are committed to the proposition that principles of morality and considerations for our own security will never permit us to acquiesce in a peace dictated by aggressors and sponsored by appeasers. We know that enduring peace cannot be bought at the cost of other people's freedom....

I also ask this Congress for authority and for funds sufficient to manufacture additional munitions and war supplies of many kinds, to be turned over to those nations which are now in actual war with aggressor nations.

Our most useful and immediate role is to act as an arsenal for them as well as for ourselves. They do not need man power. They do need billions of dollars' worth of the weapons of defense....

Let us say to the democracies, "We Americans are vitally concerned in your defense of freedom. We are putting forth our energies, our resources, and our organizing powers to give you the strength to regain and maintain a free world. We shall send you, in ever-increasing numbers, ships, planes, tanks, guns. This is our purpose and our pledge." ...

There is nothing mysterious about the foundations of a healthy and strong democracy. The basic things expected by our people of their political and economic systems are simple.

They are:

> Equality of opportunity for youth and for others.
> Jobs for those who can work.
> Security for those who need it.
> The ending of special privilege for the few.
> The preservation of civil liberties for all.
> The enjoyment of the fruits of scientific progress in a wider and constantly
> rising standard of living.

These are the simple and basic things that must never be lost sight of in the turmoil and unbelievable complexity of our modern world. The inner and abiding strength of our economic and political systems is dependent upon the degree to which they fulfill these expectations....

In the future days, which we seek to make secure, we look forward to a world founded upon four essential human freedoms.

The first is freedom of speech and expression everywhere in the world.

The second is freedom of every person to worship God in his own way everywhere in the world.

The third is freedom from want, which, translated into world terms, means economic understandings which will secure to every nation a healthy peacetime life for its inhabitants everywhere in the world.

The fourth is freedom from fear-which, translated into world terms, means a world-wide reduction of armaments to such a point and in such a thorough fashion that no nation will be in a position to commit an act of physical aggression against any neighbor-anywhere in the world.

That is no vision of a distant millennium. It is a definite basis for a kind of world attainable in our own time and generation. That kind of world is the very antithesis of the so-called new order of tyranny which the dictators seek to create with the crash of a bomb.

To that new order we oppose the greater conception-the moral order. A good society is able to face schemes of world domination and foreign revolutions alike without fear.

Since the beginning of our American history we have been engaged in change-in a perpetual peaceful revolution-a revolution which goes on steadily, quietly adjusting itself to changing conditions-without the concentration camp or the quicklime in the ditch. The world order which we seek is the cooperation of free countries, working together in a friendly, civilized society.

"A Woman Remembers the War" (1984)

When the war started I was twenty-six, unmarried, and working as a cosmetics clerk in a drugstore in Los Angeles. I was running the whole department, handling the inventory and all that. It seemed asinine, though, to be selling lipstick when the country was at war. I felt that I was capable of doing something more than that toward the war effort.

There was also a big difference between my salary and those in defense work. I was making something like twenty-two, twenty-four dollars a week in the drugstore. You could earn a much greater amount of money for your labor in defense plants. Also it interested me. There was a certain curiosity about meeting that kind of challenge, and here was an opportunity to do that, for there were more and more openings for women.

So I went to two or three plants and took their tests. And they all told me I had absolutely no mechanical ability. I said, "I don't believe that." So I went to another plant, A.D.E.I. I was interviewed and got the job. This particular plant made the hydraulic-valve system for the B-17. And where did they put women? In the burr room. You sat at a workbench, which was essentially like a picnic table, with a bunch of other women, and you worked grinding and sanding machine parts to make them smooth. That's what you did all day long. It was very mechanical and it was very boring. There were about thirty women in the burr room, and it was like being in a beauty shop every day. I couldn't stand the inane talk. So when they asked me if I would like to work someplace else in the shop, I said I very much would.

They started training me. I went to a blueprint class and learned how to use a micrometer and how to draw tools out of the tool crib and everything else. Then one day they said, "Okay, how would you like to go into the machine shop?"

I said, "Terrific."

And they said, "Now, Adele, it's going to be a real challenge, because you'll be the only women in the machine shop." I thought to myself, well, that's going to be fun, all those guys and Adele in the machine shop. So the foreman took me over there. It was a big room, with a high ceiling and fluorescent lights, and it was very noisy. I walked in there, in my overalls, and suddenly all the machines stopped and every guy in the shop just turned around and looked at me. It took, I think, two weeks before anyone even talked to me. The discrimination was indescribable. They wanted to kill me.

My attitude was, "Okay, you bastards, I'm going to prove to you I can do anything you can do, and may be better than some of you." And that's exactly the way it turned out. I used to do the rework on the pieces that the guy on the shift before me had screwed up. I finally go assigned to nothing but rework.

Later they taught me to run an automatic screwing machine. It's a big mother, and it took a lot of strength just to throw that thing into gear. They probably thought I wasn't going to be able to do it. But I was determined to succeed. As a matter of fact, I developed the most fantastic biceps from throwing that machine into gear. Even today I still have a little of that muscle left.

Anyway, eventually some of the men became very friendly, particularly the older ones, the ones in their late forties or fifties. They were journeymen tool and die makers and were so skilled that they could work anywhere at very high salaries. They were sort of fatherly, protective. They weren't threatened by me. The younger men, I think, were.

Our plant was an open shop, and the International Association of Machinists was trying to unionize the workers. I joined them and worked to try to get the union in the plant. I proselytized for the union during lunch hour, and I had a big altercation with the management over that. The employers and my lead man and foreman called m in the office and said, "We have a right to fire you."

I said, "On what basis? I work as well or better than anybody else in the shop except the journeymen."

They said, "No, not because of that. Because you're talking for the union on company property. You're not allowed to do that."

I said, "Well, that's just too bad, because I can't get off the grounds here. You won't allow us to leave the grounds during lunch hour. And you don't pay me for my lunch hour, so that time doesn't belong to you, so you can't tell me what to do." And they backed down.

I had one experience at the plant that really made me work for the union. One day while I was burring I had an accident and ripped some cartilage out of my hand. It wasn't serious, but it looked kind of messy. They had to take me over to the industrial hospital to get my hand sutured. I cam back and couldn't work for a day or two because my hand was all bandaged. It wasn't serious, but it was awkward. When I got my paycheck, I saw that they had docked me for the times I was in the industrial hospital. When I saw that I was really mad.

It's ironic that when the union finally got into the plant, they had me transferred out. They were anxious to get rid of me because after we got them in I went to a few meetings and complained about it being a Jim Crow union. So they arranged for me to have a higher rating instead of a worker's rating. This allowed me to make twenty-five cents an hour more, and I got transferred to another plant. By this time I was married. When I became pregnant I worked for about three months more, then I quit.

For me defense work was the beginning of my emancipation as a woman. For the first time in my life I found out that I could do something with my hands besides bake a pie. I found out that I had manual dexterity and the mentality to read blueprints and gauges, and to be inquisitive enough about things to develop skills other than the conventional roles that women had at that time. I had the consciousness-raising experience of being the only woman in this machine shop and having the mantle of challenge laid down by the men, which stimulated my competitiveness and forced me to prove myself. This, plus working in the union, gave me a lot of self-confidence.

1. What element of Albert Einstein's argument for a better-funded atomic research effort was most effective? Why?

2. Later Albert Einstein wished that he had not sent this letter. Why?

3. Is Roosevelt's speech "The Four Freedoms" effective? Compare this argument for involvement with President Wilson's case for preparedness and war in 1915–1917.

4. What was the impact of the woman working in a defense plant on her self-esteem?

5. Looking back from the 1980s to the early 1940s, the woman views that older time through the filter of the women's rights movement. Can you cite examples from the memoir that indicate possible subsequent influence on her memory of the war years?

CHAPTER 28

The Onset of the Cold War, 1945–1960

SUMMARY
Postwar antagonism gradually led the United States and the Soviet Union into the Cold War. The contrasts between the countries were dramatically represented in their leaders—Truman, who believed in the innate goodness of America, and Stalin, the hard-headed realist who was determined to protect Russia's wartime conquests.

The Cold War Begins
The two countries split over three issues: control of Europe, postwar economic aid, and the control of atomic weapons.

The Division of Europe
The Allies first disagreed over the division of Europe, with each side intent on imposing its values in the areas liberated by its military. The division of Germany between the West (where the U.S., Britain, and France exercised authority) and the East (under the Soviets) was most crucial. Had the West regarded Stalin simply as a cautious leader who was trying to protect Russia rather than an aggressive dictator leading a communist drive for world domination, the tension between the two sides might not have escalated into the Cold War.

The Atomic Dilemma
The United States proposed only a gradual abolition of nuclear arms in the Baruch Plan, thus preserving America's atomic monopoly, while the Soviets proposed immediate nuclear disarmament. Because both proposals were based on each nation's self-interest, attempts to agree on mutual reduction of atomic weapons failed.

Containment
U.S. foreign policy leaders initiated a major departure in American foreign affairs from the traditional policy of isolationism to one of containment, arguing that only strong and sustained resistance could halt Soviet expansionism.

The Truman Doctrine
In 1947, President Truman asked Congress for economic and military aid to Greece and Turkey to prevent possible communist revolutions. In providing this aid, the United States assumed what had been Great Britain's role—that of a leading Western power in the eastern Mediterranean—and established that the United States would support any nation that was resisting communist takeover. This, the issuance of the Truman Doctrine, marked the beginning of the Cold War.

The Marshall Plan

The American government also decided to contain Soviet influence by financing postwar European recovery as a check on communist power. Through the Marshall Plan, the United States paid for the industrial revival in Western Europe and ended the threat that all Europe might drift into the communist orbit because of economic desperation.

The Western Military Alliance

In 1949, the United States entered into the North Atlantic Treaty Organization (NATO), a pact for collective self-defense, with ten European nations and Canada. The move represented an overreaction to Soviet aggression, and tensions between the former allies escalated as NATO intensified Russian fears of the West.

The Berlin Blockade

When the Russians blockaded the western access to Berlin, the Truman government responded with an airlift, which maintained the American position in that German city and contributed to Truman's surprising reelection victory in 1948. The Berlin crisis signaled the end of the initial phase of the Cold War—Europe was divided and the rivalry between the Soviets and Americans was about to spread to the rest of the world.

The Cold War Expands

In the late 1940s and the early 1950s, the Cold War expanded. Both sides built up their military might, and diplomatic competition spread from Europe to Asia.

The Military Dimension

Committed to winning the growing conflict with Russia, the American government unified its armed services and initiated a massive military buildup, especially in its air force. The National Security Act created the Department of Defense, the Central Intelligence Agency, and the National Security Council. A new national defense policy—NSC-68—took form that was based on the premise that the Soviet Union sought "to impose its absolute authority over the rest of the world" thereby "mortally challenging the United States."

The Cold War in Asia

In Asia, the United States consolidated its Pacific sphere, but failed to avert the Chinese civil war in which Mao Tse-tung and the Communists drove Chiang Kai-shek and the Nationalists from the mainland to Formosa (renamed Taiwan). The United States refused to recognize the legitimacy of the communist government of China and turned its focus to Japan as its main ally in Asia.

The Korean War

The showdown of the Cold War in Asia came in June 1950 when the North Koreans invaded South Korea, perhaps without Soviet approval, leading to war. The United States secured UN support for a police action to defend South Korea. An attempt to drive the Communists out of North Korea failed, however, and the war settled into a stalemate near the 38th parallel. The most significant result of the war might have been the massive rearming of America and the implementation of NSC-68.

The Cold War at Home

President Truman tried, for the most part unsuccessfully, to revive the New Deal reform tradition after World War II. The Cold War controlled American attention, and the Republicans used dissatisfaction with the postwar economy and fear of communism in the United States to revive its political fortunes.

Truman's Troubles

Truman's apparent lack of political vision and his fondness for appointing cronies to high office were major weaknesses. Also, the postwar mood of the country was not conducive to further reform. As the economy settled into postwar normality, Truman found himself caught in the middle between union demands for higher wages and the public demand that consumer prices be kept down.

Truman Vindicated

Facing pressure from within his own party (Southern Democrats bolted over a proposed civil rights measure to form the Dixiecrat Party) as well as Republican attacks on his domestic policies, Truman's reelection hopes in 1948 seemed dubious. The president benefited, however, from Thomas Dewey's passive campaign and the indecisiveness of the Republican Congress. Reminding the voters of the past successes of the New Deal and of his aggressiveness in the Cold War, Truman confounded the pollsters by winning a decisive victory.

The Loyalty Issue

Fear of Communists led to a government loyalty program and unrelenting investigations by the House Un-American Activities Committee. Former State Department official Alger Hiss was convicted of perjury after allegations of espionage. Thousands of government workers were dismissed by the Loyalty Review Board for dubious loyalty, and following Soviet detonation of an atomic bomb, Julius and Ethel Rosenberg were executed for conspiring with the Soviets.

McCarthyism in Action

Playing on heightened American fears, Senator Joseph McCarthy engaged in tireless pursuits of communist conspirators. He received great support among the American populace because he offered a simple solution to the complicated problems of the Cold War. McCarthy directed his accusations everywhere, from the State Department to the U.S. Army, and would-be critics, fearful of arousing suspicion, remained quiet.

The Republicans in Power

Promising to clean up corruption and to bring the Korean War to an honorable end, Republican Dwight Eisenhower won election as president in 1952. In 1953 Eisenhower succeeded in reaching an agreement with the North Koreans for an armistice. McCarthy eventually overreached himself when he accused the upper echelons of the Army of communist ties, leading to his public humiliation and censure following Senate hearings in 1954.

Conclusion: The Continuing Cold War

During his eight years as president, Eisenhower managed to keep the United States out of war, but the momentum of the Cold War continued. The Eisenhower administration contributed to the escalation of the Cold War by lending aid to forces resisting a communist takeover in South Vietnam and covert actions in Latin America and the Middle East, all of which contributed to global tension in the coming decades.

LEARNING OBJECTIVES

After mastering this chapter, you should be able to

1. Explain the origins of the Cold War between the United States and the Soviet Union following World War II.

2. Evaluate the responses of the Truman administration to the onset of the Cold War.

3. Discuss the origins, developments, and results of the Korean War.

4. Assess Truman's action in the Berlin Crisis. What were his alternatives? Did he make the right choice?

5. Discuss the Marshall Plan and the Truman Doctrine. How effective were they as foreign policies?

6. Explain the reasons for Truman's surprise reelection as president in 1948.

7. Evaluate Truman's success in extending the New Deal policies of FDR.

8. Explain the rise and fall of McCarthyism in the United States from 1950 to 1954.

9. Account for the election of Dwight D. Eisenhower as president in 1952.

10. Discuss Eisenhower's leadership as president during the Korean War and the years of McCarthyism.

GLOSSARY

To build your social science vocabulary, familiarize yourself with the following terms:

1. **reparations** payments by a defeated nation to victors for war damages and losses. "Truman and Stalin clashed ... over such difficult issues as reparations ..."

2. **coalition** union or alliance, often temporary, among factions, parties, or nations. "Communist regimes replaced coalition governments ..."

3. **coup** a successful decisive action, especially the overthrow of a government. "a coup in Czechoslovakia ... gave the Soviets a strategic foothold in Central Europe."

4. **demobilization** disbandment, especially of military forces. "Eisenhower ... cited the rapid demobilization of American armed forces ..."

5. **appeasement** bringing peace, especially when done with conciliatory concessions. "Recalling the lesson of Munich, he opposed appeasement ..."

6. **trusteeship** control of the administration of a territory, usually by appointment of an international organization. "A trusteeship arrangement ... merely disguised the fact that the United States held full control over the ... islands."

7. **mediation** the attempt to resolve differences through an intermediary. "Political mediation had failed, military intervention was out of the question."

8. **collective security** pertaining to the organization of a group of nations to guarantee the security of each member nation. "the President ... secured a resolution ... calling on the member nations to engage in a collective security action."

9. **tactical** pertaining to maneuvers for gaining an advantage over an adversary. "he waited ready to dazzle an opponent with tactical mastery."

10. **intelligence** secret information, usually about an adversary. "the act created the Central Intelligence Agency (CIA) to coordinate the intelligence-gathering activities ..."

11. **legitimacy** a state of lawfulness according to accepted standards. "the state department refused to recognize the legitimacy of the new regime in Peking."

12. **bipartisan** involving cooperation or agreement between two parties (usually, in American history, Republicans and Democrats). "The Republicans, committed to support the bipartisan policy of containment."

13. **red herring** something used to divert attention from the basic issue. "Although Truman tried to dismiss the loyalty issue as a 'red herring'."

IDENTIFICATION

Briefly identify the meaning and significance of the following terms:

1. Potsdam Conference _____

_____

2. Iron Curtain_____

_____

3. NATO_____

_____

4. Truman Doctrine_____

_____

5. NSC-68_____

_____

6. Taft-Hartley Act of 1947_____

_____

7. McCarthyism_____

_____

8. Adlai Stevenson_____

_____

9. Berlin Crisis_____

_____

10. Marshall Plan_____

_____

MATCHING

A. Match the following American leaders with the appropriate description:

_____ 1. Bernard Baruch

    a. head of Policy Planning Staff who drafted NSC-68

_____ 2. George C. Marshall

    b. senator who suggested that Truman "scare hell" out of Americans to get their backing for aid to countries resisting communism

_____ 3. Dean Acheson

    c. secretary of state who offered American economic aid to rebuild western Europe

_____ 4. George Kennan

    d. undersecretary of state who hoped to see the U.S. take Britain's role as a leading world power

_____ 5. Arthur M. Vandenberg

    e. financier who drafted a plan that preserved America's monopoly of the atomic bomb

    f. head of Policy Planning Staff who first advocated U.S. containment of Soviet power

B. Match the following Cold War figures with the appropriate description:

_____ 1. Andrei Gromyko

    a. Chinese communist leader who won control of the Chinese mainland

_____ 2. Mao Zedong

    b. North Korean who launched attack on South Korea in 1950

_____ 3. Kim Il-Sung

    c. Vietnamese nationalist whose Saigon government received backing by the U.S.

_____ 4. Syngman Rhee

    d. conservative nationalist leader of South Korea

_____ 5. Chiang Kai-shek

    e. Russian diplomat who proposed a total ban on atomic bombs

    f. nationalist leader in southern China who fought unsuccessfully against a communist takeover

COMPLETION

Answer the question or complete the statement by filling in the blanks with the correct word or words.

1. The government of _____placed an "iron curtain" around Eastern Europe by placing communist regimes in countries like Poland and Bulgaria between 1946 and 1947.

2. When the British informed the United States it could no longer provide aid to the eastern Mediterranean nations of _____ and _____ in 1947, President Truman announced a policy pledging American support to any countries resisting communism.

3. The Berlin airlift helped President Truman win reelection in 1948 over Republican candidate _____.

4. Following the Soviet explosion of the atomic bomb in 1949, the United States planned for building of the more destructive _____ bomb.

5. Truman convened the United Nations Security Council in June 1950 to protest the military aggression of _____.

6. Members of the Democratic splinter group who bolted from the party in 1948 and nominated Strom Thurmond for the presidency were known as _____.

7. The most famous case of possible American espionage involved prominent U.S. State Department official _____.

8. The Wisconsin Senator who led the search for communists in the U.S. government and elsewhere in society was _____.

9. The televised _____ hearings of 1954 proved to be the climax of the anti-communist crusade.

10. Soon after being elected president, Eisenhower traveled to _____in an effort to bring the war there to an end.

TRUE/FALSE

Mark the following statements either T (True) or F (False).

_____1. When compared to the blunt and belligerent Stalin, Harry Truman seemed cautious and cunning.

_____2. The Russians refused to participate in the Marshall Plan because they saw it as an attempt to weaken their control of eastern Europe.

_____3. NSC-68 argued that the United States could afford to spend no more than thirty percent of its gross national product for military security.

_____4. As the spheres of influence were defined at Yalta, China fell between the American and Russian spheres.

_____5. Secretary of State Dean Acheson argued that the civil war in China was beyond the control of the government of the United States.

_____6. Secretary Acheson and General MacArthur warned President Truman of the dangers of Chinese entrance into the Korean War.

_____7. The most important issue in the 1948 presidential election was the waging of the Cold War.

_____8. When it became apparent that the communist Chinese forces were winning the struggle for China, the response of the United States was full-scale military intervention in support of Chiang Kai-shek.

_____9. When General MacArthur called for a renewed offensive in Korea, President Truman decided to relieve the popular commander and bring him home.

_____10. The defection of the Dixiecrats from the Democratic party and the unpopularity of Truman's reform policies led to a Republican victory in the 1948 presidential election.

MULTIPLE CHOICE

Circle the one alternative that *best* completes the statement or answers the question.

1. Which of the following was *not* a major postwar issue between the United States and the Soviet Union?
   a. the division of Europe
   b. the punishment of German war criminals
   c. postwar economic aid
   d. control of atomic weapons

2. With his Truman Doctrine speech President Truman hoped to
   a. "scare hell" out of Americans so they would support the policy of containment.
   b. "scare hell" out of the Russians to take advantage of the American atomic monopoly.
   c. provide economic assistance for the rebuilding of Europe.
   d. establish a Western military alliance to "contain" communism.

3. Which of the following did *not* coincide with the U.S. policy of containment?
   a. extension of lend-lease aid to the Soviet Union
   b. extension of economic aid to western Europe
   c. offering of protection to Greece and Turkey
   d. establishment of the North Atlantic Treaty Organization (NATO)

4. Truman responded to the Russian blockade of Berlin in 1948 by
   a. yielding to the blockade with a vigorous protest in the United Nations.
   b. airlifting supplies into the city.
   c. sending American tanks through the blockade.
   d. escalating the conflict with a counter blockade of Soviet positions.

5. The National Security Act of 1947 created the
   a. Department of Defense.
   b. Central Intelligence Agency (CIA).
   c. National Security Council.
   d. all of the above

6. The most significant result of the Korean War was the
   a. massive rearmament by the United States.
   b. American determination to avoid land wars in Asia.
   c. firing of General Douglas MacArthur.
   d. unification of the military services.

7. The Marshall Plan was
   a. General Marshall's plan to defeat the communists in the Korean War.
   b. General Marshall's plan to defeat the communists in China.
   c. a massive economic aid program to rebuild western Europe after World War II.
   d. a bold attempt to turn the Soviet Union into a capitalist nation.

8. The postwar mood of the American people could best be described as one that
   a. desired the extension of New Deal reforms.
   b. wished to back away from global efforts to halt the spread of communism.
   c. favored the retention of wartime price and wage controls.
   d. favored swift conversion to a peacetime economy.

9. McCarthy drew a disproportionate backing from which of the following groups?
   a. upper-middle-class businesspeople and professionals
   b. writers, teachers, artists, and other intellectuals
   c. working-class Irish, Polish, and Italian Catholics
   d. farmers, Hispanics, and African Americans

10. Bernard Baruch and General Eisenhower insisted on preserving American postwar monopoly on atomic weapons to
   a. offset the Soviets' conventional military strength.
   b. intimidate the Russians in important diplomatic negotiations.
   c. turn back a Soviet plan for world conquest.
   d. balance the American government's budget by reducing defense costs.

11. The principal goal of Eisenhower's foreign policy was to
   a. liberate eastern Europe from communist control.
   b. relax tensions and initiate disarmament.
   c. prevent the fall of China to the Communists.
   d. win the arms race with a technological breakthrough.

12. As a result of the Army-McCarthy hearings,
   a. McCarthy was publicly ridiculed and censured by the Senate.
   b. most of McCarthy's allegations were found to be accurate.
   c. McCarthy was subsequently tried and convicted of perjury.
   d. the army responded by purging its ranks of revealed Communists.

13. The U.S. Cold War policy of containment is best defined as
   a. an attempt to provoke a Soviet attack, thus winning sympathy for the United States around the world.
   b. provoking a war between China and the Soviet Union.
   c. taking an aggressive military stance toward the Soviet Union.
   d. a patient, long-term attempt to halt Soviet expansion while forcing them to adopt more peaceful policies.

14. As a result of the communist takeover of China, the United States
    a. refused to recognize the new communist government and instead maintained relations with the exiled nationalist government in Formosa.
    b. focused on Japan as becoming their main Asian ally.
    c. Neither a nor b.
    d. Both a and b.

15. The Taft-Hartley Act of 1947 did all of the following EXCEPT
    a. shift labor-management power relations more toward labor.
    b. outlawed closed shops.
    c. outlawed secondary boycotts.
    d. allowed the president to intervene if strikes threatened national security.

THOUGHT QUESTIONS

To check your understanding of the key issues of this period, solve the following problems:

1. What were the causes of the Cold War? Which side was more to blame for it—the United States or the Soviet Union?

2. How did the Truman administration respond to the onset of the Cold War? Was he successful? Explain.

3. Why was Truman's reelection as president in 1948 such a surprise? Was Truman a successful president in domestic affairs?

4. Why did the Cold War escalate during the late 1940s and early 1950s? What were the major consequences?

5. What factors contributed to the rise and fall of Joseph McCarthy as a political power in the U.S. from 1950 to 1954? What lessons might be learned from the experience of McCarthyism?

6. Explain the objectives of President Eisenhower's foreign policy and evaluate its long-term as well as short-term success.

CRITICAL THINKING EXERCISE

Read the following selections: "Testimony Before the House Un-American Activities Committee" (1947) by Ronald Reagan and the Wheeling Speech in 1950 by Joseph McCarthy. Answer the questions following the reading selections.

Ronald Reagan, "Testimony Before the House Un-American Activities Committee" (1947)

The Committee met at 10:30 A.M. [October 23, 1947], the Honorable J. Parnell Thomas (Chairman) presiding.

THE CHAIRMAN: The record will show that Mr. McDowell, Mr. Vail, Mr. Nixon, and Mr. Thomas are present. A Subcommittee is sitting.

Staff members present: Mr. Robert E. Stripling, Chief Investigator; Messrs. Louis J. Russell, H. A. Smith, and Robert B. Gatson, Investigators; and Mr. Benjamin Mandel, Director of Research.

MR. STRIPLING: When and where were you born, Mr. Reagan?

MR. REAGAN: Tampico, Illinois, February 6, 1911.

MR. STRIPLING: What is your present occupation?

MR. REAGAN: Motion-picture actor.

MR. STRIPLING: How long have you been engaged in that profession?

MR. REAGAN: Since June 1937, with a brief interlude of three and a half years-that at the time didn't seem very brief.

MR. STRIPLING: What period was that?

MR. REAGAN: That was during the late war.

MR. STRIPLING: What branch of the service were you in?

MR. REAGAN: Well, sir, I had been for several years in the Reserve as an officer in the United States Calvary, but I was assigned to the Air Corp.

MR. STRIPLING: Are you the president of the guild at the present time?

MR. REAGAN: Yes, sir....

MR. STRIPLING: As a member of the board of directors, as president of the Screen Actors Guild, and as an active member, have you at any time observed or noted within the organization a clique of either Communists or Fascists who were attempting to exert influence or pressure on the guild?

MR. REAGAN: Well, sir, my testimony must be very similar to that of Mr. [George] Murphy and Mr. [Robert] Montgomery. There has been a small group within the Screen Actors Guild which has consistently opposed the policy of the guild board and officers of the guild, as evidenced by the vote on various issues. That small clique referred to has been suspected of more or less following the tactics that we associated with the Communist Party.

MR. STRIPLING: Would you refer to them as a disruptive influence within the guild?

MR. REAGAN: I would say that at times they have attempted to be a disruptive influence.

MR. STRIPLING: You have no knowledge yourself as to whether or not any of them are members of the Communist Party?

MR. REAGAN: No, sir, I have no investigative force, or anything, and I do not know.

MR. STRIPLING: Has it ever been reported to you that certain members of the guild were Communists?

MR. REAGAN: Yes, sir, I have heard different discussions and some of them tagged as Communists.

MR. STRIPLING: Would you say that this clique has attempted to dominate the guild?

MR. REAGAN: Well, sir, by attempting to put over their own particular views on various issues....

MR. STRIPLING: Mr. Reagan, there has been testimony to the effect here that numerous Communist-front organizations have been set up in Hollywood. Have you ever been solicited to join any of those organizations or any organization which you consider to be a Communist-front organization?

MR. REAGAN: Well, sir, I have received literature from an organization called the Committee for a Far-Eastern Democratic Policy. I don't know whether it is Communist or not. I only know that I didn't like their views and as a result I didn't want to have anything to do with them....

MR. STRIPLING: Would you say from your observation that this is typical of the tactics or strategy of the Communists, to solicit and use the names of prominent people to either raise money or gain support.

MR. REAGAN: I think it is in keeping with their tactics, yes, sir.

MR. STRIPLING: Do you think there is anything democratic about those tactics?

MR. REAGAN: I do not, sir.

MR. STRIPLING: Mr. Reagan, what is your feeling about what steps should be taken to rid the motion-picture industry of any Communist influences?

MR. REAGAN: Well, sir, ninety-nine percent of us are pretty well aware of what is going on, and I think, within the bounds of our democratic rights and never once stepping over the rights given us by democracy, we have done a pretty good job in our business of keeping those people's activities curtailed. After all, we must recognize them at present as a political party. On that basis we have exposed their lies when we came across them, we
have opposed their propaganda, and I can certainly testify that in the case of the Screen Actors Guild we have been eminently successful in preventing them from, with their usual tactics, trying to run a majority of an organization with a well-organized minority. In opposing those people, the best thing to do is make democracy work....

Sir, I detest, I abhor their philosophy, but I detest more than that their tactics, which are those of the fifth column, and are dishonest, but at the same time I never as a citizen want to see our country become urged, by either fear or resentment of this group that we ever compromise with any of our democratic principles through that fear or resentment. I still think that democracy can do it.

Speech of Joseph McCarthy, Wheeling, West Virginia, February 9, 1950

Ladies and gentlemen, tonight as we celebrate the one hundred forty-first birthday of one of the greatest men in American history, I would like to be able to talk about what a glorious day today is in the history of the world. As we celebrate the birth of this man who with his whole heart and soul hated war, I would like to be able to speak of peace in our time—of war being outlawed—and of world-wide disarmament. These would be truly appropriate things to be able to mention as we celebrate the birthday of Abraham Lincoln.

Five years after a world war has been won, men's hearts should anticipate a long peace—and men's minds should be free from the heavy weight that comes with war. But this is not such a period—for this is not a period of peace. This is a time of "the cold war." This is a time when all the world is split into two vast, increasingly hostile armed camps—a time of a great armament race.

Today we can almost physically hear the mutterings and rumblings of an invigorated god of war. You can see it, feel it, and hear it all the way from the Indochina hills, from the shores of Formosa, right over into the very heart of Europe itself.

The one encouraging thing is that the "mad moment" has not yet arrived for the firing of the gun or the exploding of the bomb which will set civilization about the final task of destroying itself. There is still a hope for peace if we finally decide that no longer can we safely blind our eyes and close our ears to those facts which are shaping up more and more clearly . . . and that is that we are now engaged in a show-down fight . . . not the usual war between nations for land areas or other material gains, but a war between two diametrically opposed ideologies.

The great difference between our western Christian world and the atheistic Communist world is not political, gentlemen, it is moral. For instance, the Marxian idea of confiscating the land and factories and running the entire economy as a single enterprise is momentous. Likewise, Lenin's invention of the one-party police state as a way to make Marx's idea work is hardly less momentous.

Stalin's resolute putting across of these two ideas, of course, did much to divide the world. With only these differences, however, the east and the west could most certainly still live in peace.

The real, basic difference, however, lies in the religion of immoralism . . . invented by Marx, preached feverishly by Lenin, and carried to unimaginable extremes by Stalin. This religion of immoralism, if the Red half of the world triumphs—and well it may, gentlemen—this religion of immoralism will more deeply wound and damage mankind than any conceivable economic or political system.

Karl Marx dismissed God as a hoax, and Lenin and Stalin have added in clear-cut, unmistakable language their resolve that no nation, no people who believe in a god, can exist side by side with their communistic state.

Karl Marx, for example, expelled people from his Communist Party for mentioning such things as love, justice, humanity or morality. He called this "soulful ravings" and "sloppy sentimentality." . . .

Today we are engaged in a final, all-out battle between communistic atheism and Christianity. The modern champions of communism have selected this as the time, and ladies and gentlemen, the chips are down—they are truly down.

Lest there be any doubt that the time has been chosen, let us go directly to the leader of communism today—Joseph Stalin. Here is what he said—not back in 1928, not before the war, not during the war—but 2 years after the last war was ended: "To think that the Communist revolution can be carried out peacefully, within the framework of a Christian democracy, means one has either gone out of one's mind and lost all normal understanding, or has grossly and openly repudiated the Communist revolution." . . .

Ladies and gentlemen, can there be anyone tonight who is so blind as to say that the war is not on? Can there by anyone who fails to realize that the Communist world has said the time is now? . . . that this is the time for the show-down between the democratic Christian world and the communistic atheistic world?

Unless we face this fact, we shall pay the price that must be paid by those who wait too long.

Six years ago, . . . there was within the Soviet orbit, 180,000,000 people. Lined up on the antitotalitarian side there were in the world at that time, roughly 1,625,000,000 people. Today, only six years later, there are 800,000,000 people under the absolute domination of Soviet Russia—an increase of over 400 percent. On our side, the figure has shrunk to around 500,000,000. In other words, in less than six years, the odds have changed from 9 to 1 in our favor to 8 to 5 against us.

This indicates the swiftness of the tempo of Communist victories and American defeats in the cold war. As one of our outstanding historical figures once said, "When a great democracy is destroyed, it will not be from enemies from without, but rather because of enemies from within." . . .

The reason why we find ourselves in a position of impotency is not because our only powerful potential enemy has sent men to invade our shores . . . but rather because of the traitorous actions of those who have been treated so well by this Nation. It has not been the less fortunate, or members of minority groups who have been traitorous to this Nation, but rather those who have had all the benefits that the wealthiest Nation on earth has had to offer . . . the finest homes, the finest college education and the finest jobs in government we can give.

This is glaringly true in the State Department. There the bright young men who are born with silver spoons in their mouths are the ones who have been most traitorous. . . .

I have here in my hand a list of 205 . . . a list of names that were made known to the Secretary of State as being members of the Communist Party and who nevertheless are still working and shaping policy in the State Department. . . .

As you know, very recently the Secretary of State proclaimed his loyalty to a man guilty of what has always been considered as the most abominable of all crimes—being a traitor to the people who gave him a position of great trust—high treason. . . .

He has lighted the spark which is resulting in a moral uprising and will end only when the whole sorry mess of twisted, warped thinkers are swept from the national scene so that we may have a new birth of honesty and decency in government.

1.   Does Reagan believe that the Communist party had exerted an influence in the motion picture industry? Why was he called to testify?

2.   Why do you think Hollywood was a particular target of the House Un-American Activities Committee?

3.   According to Reagan, what steps should be taken by the country to rid the motion picture industry of any communist influences?

4.   How does McCarthy compare communist nations to the United States?

5.   In what ways does McCarthy evoke fear and a hope of peace in his speech? Is the tone of McCarthy's speech comparable to Reagan's testimony?

CHAPTER 29

Affluence and Anxiety, 1945–1960

SUMMARY

In postwar America, new affluence replaced the poverty and hunger of the Great Depression, and people flocked to suburbs like Levittown to escape the city and to raise their growing families. International events and the possibility of nuclear war contributed to increasing feelings of anxiety among the populace. The 1950s also saw the beginning of African Americans' push for equality in the face of the nation's growing affluence.

The Postwar Boom

An intensified demand for consumer goods and heavy government spending stimulated economic growth from the late 1940s through the 1950s. Although the rate of economic growth slowed in the second half of the 1950s, most Americans had far more real income during this era than ever before.

Postwar Prosperity

By 1950, production caught up with demand and the gross national product reached a point 50 percent higher than in 1940. The baby boom and expanding suburbia stimulated consumerism as fear of another depression dissipated. In the American workplace, higher pay and shorter hours remained as permanent standards. Slowdowns in economic growth occurred in the second half of the decade and older manufacturing regions like New England suffered a degree of decline, but the expansion of the Cold War and the growth of the military-industrial complex in the South and West provided sufficient economic stimuli to make the American standard of living the highest in the world.

Life in the Suburbs

The newly affluent postwar generation shed their identities to live in look-alike homes and embrace the new culture of the suburbs. Life in these communities depended on the automobile as people commuted to work and school and shopped in shopping centers and malls that popped up across the country. The home and nuclear family became the focus of American activity and aspiration as homemaking and child rearing became primary vocations for suburban women. Nonetheless, the number of wives working outside of the home doubled between 1940 and 1960 as women strove to contribute necessary funds to the maintenance of the suburban household.

The Good Life?

Despite an abundance of material goods and increased leisure time, many Americans questioned the quality of their lives.

Areas of Greatest Growth

One of the institutions that flourished in the postwar years was organized religion as Americans became divided into three segments—Catholics, Protestants, and Jews. The tremendous increase in the number of school-aged children created enormous growth and an overwhelming strain on local school districts. The number of young adults attending college increased precipitously. The greatest growth came in the medium of television, which became the most popular entertainment source. Though at first it was a source of artistic innovation, it quickly became a safe conveyor of the consumer culture.

Critics of the Consumer Society

With affluence and prosperity came an abundance of introspection and self-criticism. The disenchantment with consumer culture was epitomized by the emergence of beatnik writers like Jack Kerouac and abstract expressionist artists like Jackson Pollock.

The Struggle Over Civil Rights

The Cold War helped to arouse the national conscience in favor of civil rights for African Americans. Although benefiting economically from World War II, blacks continued to live in blighted neighborhoods and to be segregated from white society. The denunciation of Soviet human rights abuses while African Americans were kept in a state of second-class citizenship sparked calls for change.

Civil Rights as a Political Issue

Although President Truman had failed to push his civil rights package through Congress over southern opposition, he did succeed in adding civil rights to the liberal agenda. Additionally, he strengthened the civil rights division of the Justice Department, making legal attempts to challenge Jim Crow laws more likely to succeed. Most importantly, Truman desegregated the armed forces.

Desegregating the Schools

The Supreme Court took the lead in reversing the late nineteenth century's "separate but equal" decisions. In *Brown* v. *Board of Education of Topeka,* the Court ordered the nation's public schools to admit African-American students for the first time. Though President Eisenhower sent troops into Little Rock, Arkansas, to enforce the ruling, on the whole the lack of presidential support weakened the desegregation process. A permanent Commission for Civil Rights was established to protect voting rights, however. Though southern "massive resistance" made these efforts largely ineffective, the actions of the Supreme Court and Congress marked a turning point in national policy toward racial justice.

The Beginnings of Black Activism

More dynamic than the Supreme Court and Congress were the actions of African Americans themselves. In Montgomery, Alabama, Rosa Parks and Dr. Martin Luther King Jr. led a successful boycott against the city's segregated bus system. Drawing from sources such as Gandhi, King developed the concept of passive resistance. In 1960 "sit-ins" and other direct but peaceful demonstrations led by SCLC and SNCC succeeded in desegregating many public facilities.

Conclusion: Restoring National Confidence

Though the 1950s ended with a national mood that was less troubled than when the decade began, the United States was neither as tranquil or confident as it could have been. Though Americans no longer feared a reoccurrence of the Great Depression, new fears emerged about the hollowness of the new abundance and the contradiction that American race relations posed for national promises of equality, democracy, and freedom.

LEARNING OBJECTIVES

After mastering this chapter, you should be able to:

1. Explain how Levittown was symptomatic of American conformity and consumerism of the postwar years.

2. Describe the problems of reconverting to a peacetime economy and the reasons for the surge of the economy after 1946.

5. Discuss the objectives, victories, and failures of the civil rights movement in the 1950s.

6. Summarize the contributions of Martin Luther King Jr. to the civil rights movement during the 1950s.

7. Explain the effects of suburban life on American families and American women in particular.

8. Explain the effects of suburban life on the landscape of the nation.

9. What was the baby boom and how did it impact the nation?

10. Describe the critics that emerged to the consumer culture that dominated the nation.

11. Identify the reasons why the pace of desegregation of the schools was slow.

GLOSSARY

To build your social science vocabulary, familiarize yourself with the following terms:

1. **conformity** the tendency to correspond or behave alike. "They condemned the conformity, charging the newly affluent with forsaking traditional American individualism ..."

2. **affluence** material abundance or comfort. "... the American people had achieved an affluence that finally erased the lingering memories of the Great Depression."

3. **gross national product** the total sum of goods and services produced in a nation during a year. "... and the gross national product (GNP) reached $318 billion ..."

4. **real income** income after accounting for inflation. "... the average American family had twice as much real income to spend ..."

5. **disposable income** remaining income after taxes. "... per-capita disposable income rose by $500 ..."

6. **feminism** organized movement for political, economic, and social equality for women. "The nuclear family, typical of the suburb, did nothing to encourage the development of feminism."

8. **desegregation** the process of removing the characteristics of segregation, that is, of integrating or assimilating. "The process of desegregating the schools proved to be agonizingly slow."

9. **passive resistance** a posture or attitude of peaceful opposition or unwillingness to cooperate with authority. "Drawing on sources as diverse as Gandhi and Henry David Thoreau, King came out of the bus boycott with the concept of passive resistance."

10. **neo-orthodoxy** a movement after World War II that affirmed the absolute sovereignty of God and challenged liberal theology. " ... the emergence of neo-orthodoxy in Protestant seminaries ... "

11. **suburbia** the social customs of suburban life. "A number of widely read books explored the flaws in the new suburbia."

12. **sit-ins** acts of protest involving remaining on the premises of an establishment that practices discrimination; a common practice during the civil rights movement. "Other students, both whites and blacks, joined in similar 'sit-ins' across the South ..."

IDENTIFICATION

Briefly identify the meaning and significance of the following terms:

1. Levittown_____

_____

2. baby boom_____

_____

3. *Sputnik*_____

_____

4. *Baby and Child Care*_____

_____

5. Commission on Civil Rights_____

_____

6. *Brown* v. *Board of Education of Topeka*_____

_____

7. Martin Luther King Jr._____

_____

8. abstract expressionism_____

_____

9. passive resistance_____

_____

10. Fair Employment Practices Committee_____

_____

MATCHING

A. Match the following figures involved in the early civil rights movement with the appropriate description:

_____1. Rosa Parks

a. NAACP lawyer who challenged the 1896 Supreme Court decision (*Plessy* v. *Ferguson*) that upheld separate but equal public facilities

_____2. Martin Luther King Jr.

b. Chief justice of the Supreme Court appointed by President Eisenhower who wrote the landmark decision in *Brown* v. *Board of Education Topeka*

_____3. Orville Faubus

c. Black seamstress who in 1955 challenged a city ordinance by refusing to give up her bus seat to a white person

_____4. Earl Warren

d. Governor of Arkansas who in 1957 called out the National Guard to prevent black children from attending Little Rock's Central High School

_____5. Thurgood Marshall

e. Led a massive protest against the jailing of Rosa Parks in Montgomery, Alabama

f. Appointed a presidential commission on civil rights in 1946

B. Match the following writers with the appropriate description:

_____1. Jack Kerouac

a. ideas contributed to rise of neo-orthodoxy in Protestant seminaries

_____2. Benjamin Spock

b. influential Beat generation writer, a literary group that rejected the materialistic 1950s

_____3. Rod Serling

c. wrote book on baby and child care

_____4. Norman Vincent Peale

d. religious writer whose positive gospel urged people to "start thinking faith, enthusiasm, and joy"

_____5. Reinhold Niebuhr

e. playwright who created notable dramas in early days of television

f. condemned the racial hostility that the all-white suburbs created

COMPLETION

Answer the question or complete the statement by filling in the blanks with the correct word or words.

1. Levittown answered the postwar American desire to move to_____, away from the central city.

2. The_____ region of the United States benefited enormously from the growth of the aircraft and electronic industries.

3. Although most of his civil rights initiatives were thwarted, Truman was successful in ordering the desegregation of the _____.

4. In 1959, the nation was shocked to hear the Columbia University professor Charles Van Doren cheated on the popular television game show _____.

5. Some of the largest advances came in the new cultural medium of the _____ which at first was artistically innovative but became a safe conveyor of consumer culture.

6. In *Brown v. Board of Education of Topeka* the Supreme Court ruled that segregation violated the

    _____.

7. The first action of the civil rights movement is typically noted to be the

    _____.

8. The philosophy Martin Luther King Jr. borrowed from Gandhi and applied to the civil rights movement was _____.

9. In the South, racial _____ was enforced at all places of public entertainment.

10. Painter _____ challenged Americans' ideas about the form and function of art.

TRUE/FALSE

Mark the following statements either T (True) or F (False):

_____1. During the decade of the 1950s, population growth in the inner city kept pace with the growth of suburbia.

_____2. Togetherness became a key concept among suburban families in the 1950s.

_____3. With more men entering the work force after the war, the number of wives working outside the home decreased.

_____4. Beat writers and abstract expressionist artists embraced conformity and consumerism in their work.

_____5. Reflecting the basic conservative attitudes of the 1960s, the Warren Court issued several decisions that assisted prosecutors and police in the war against crime.

_____6. Although President Truman failed to achieve significant civil rights legislation, he succeeded in pushing the issue to the forefront of the political agenda.

_____7 One of the most important new directions undertaken by American youth between 1940 and 1960 was away from college education toward technical-vocational training and early entry into the job market.

_____8. The actions of the Supreme Court in *Brown* v. *Board of Education* and Congress in the creation of the Commission on Civil Rights were the most effective efforts made in the 1950s toward achieving African-American equality.

_____9. Groups like SNCC and the SCLC replaced the NAACP's strategy of court rulings for civil rights with direct, but peaceful, confrontation.

_____10. The Southern Christian Leadership Conference competed with Martin Luther King, Jr. for leadership of the Montgomery Bus Boycott.

MULTIPLE CHOICE

Circle the one alternative that *best* completes the statement or answers the question.

1. An accurate description of the social makeup of the suburbs is that
    a. only middle-class people lived there.
    b. they mainly attracted professional types such as doctors and lawyers.
    c. a surprising variety of practically all economic types—excluding mainly the very rich and very poor—resided there.
    d. only the very rich could afford to live there.

2. All of the following were economic problems during the 1950s EXCEPT
    a. per capita disposable income declined.
    b. older manufacturing regions like New England experienced a downturn.
    c. the steel industry's growth fell behind that of the national average.
    d. rural areas like the Great Plains did not share equally in the affluence.

3. In education, the idea that most people could agree upon was
    a. that "progressive" education should be maintained.
    b. that working-class and suburban families shared common goals for their children.
    c. the desirability of a college education.
    d. the federal government should become more involved in local educational decisions.

4. The Student Nonviolent Coordinating Committee was responsible for
    a. coordinating student protests against the war in Korea.
    b. bolstering the sagging fortunes of the NAACP by joining it in the struggle for civil rights.
    c. direct but peaceful confrontation that would heighten the social tension of the civil rights movement.
    d. opposing the efforts of the Southern Christian Leadership Conference.

5. In the years after World War II the United States experienced
    a. an economic boom caused by high rates of consumption and military spending.
    b. a continuation of the unemployment rates of the mid-1930s.
    c. a farm economic boom but widespread urban poverty.
    d. prosperity for businesses located in the Northeast but continued depression in the South and West.

6. Eisenhower's decision to send troops into Little Rock, Arkansas, was in response to
    a. a violent strike of railroad workers.
    b. a direct challenge to the Supreme Court decision in *Brown* v. *Board of Education of Topeka* when the governor of Arkansas used armed troops to turn back African American students in their attempt to attend school.
    c. student protests against the war in Korea.
    d. the beatings of "freedom ride" protesters by local Klansmen and other toughs.

220

7. Women discovered that suburban life in postwar America
   a. encouraged them to develop career skills.
   b. discouraged child bearing.
   c. encouraged them to devote their efforts toward homemaking.
   d. encouraged them to adopt feminist ideas.

8. *Brown* v. *Board of Education of Topeka* determined that
   a. separate educational facilities for the races had to be eliminated.
   b. property owners had to pay school taxes even if they did not have children attending school.
   c. busing could be used to achieve racial balance in the schools.
   d. private schools could continue to bar minority applicants.

9. The main purpose of the Southern Christian Leadership Conference was to
   a. unite conservative religious denominations in the South against federal intrusion into local racial affairs.
   b. settle some of the outstanding theological differences still existing among American churches.
   c. direct the movement against segregation and promote peaceful confrontation against the enemies of racial equality.
   d. educate aspiring religious leaders to the need for moral leadership in the coming years.

10. The 1956 Southern Manifesto denounced the *Brown* decision as
    a. an abuse of judicial power.
    b. reverse racism.
    c. a Republican ploy for political power.
    d. not doing enough to help black students.

11. Martin Luther King, Jr. did all of the following EXCEPT
    a. helped to lead the Montgomery Bus Boycott.
    b. founded the SCLC.
    c. used passive resistance as a weapon.
    d. kept religious principles out of his ideology.

12. Critics of the consumer society of the 1950s in literature were known as the
    a. fair dealers.
    b. abstracts expressionists.
    c. beats.
    d. Kerouacs.

13. All of the following were consequences of suburban living after World War II except
    a. encouragement for feminism.
    b. greater loss of intimate contact with uncles, aunts, and grandparents.
    c. a new affluence replacing the deprivation of the Great Depression.
    d. fulfillment of the desire for more space, comfort, and freedom of action.

14. The sit-in at North Carolina A&T College in 1960 epitomized the activist method of
    a. violent confrontation.
    b. armed intervention.
    c. appealing to the courts.
    d. passive resistance.

15. In the years following World War II the United States experienced
    a. declining church attendance.
    b. increasing church attendance.
    c. increases in church attendance, but only among Catholics.
    d. the popularity of neo-orthodoxy in the suburbs but not in the seminaries.

THOUGHT QUESTIONS

To check your understanding of the key issues of this period, solve the following problems:

1. What were some of the sociological effects of suburban living after the war?

2. What was Martin Luther King Jr. pressing for with passive resistance and civil disobedience? Why were his tactics successful?

3. What, if any, seeds of change do you see being planted in the 1950s?

4. Should the 1950s be considered a decade that brought Americans together or drove them apart?

Critical Thinking Questions

After reading Rosa Parks, "The Montgomery Bus Boycott," (1977), Jo Ann Gibson Robinson, "The Montgomery Bus Boycott," (1955), and Martin Luther King Jr. "The Strategy of Nonviolent Direct Action" (1963), answer the following:

Rosa Parks, "The Montgomery Bus Boycott" (1977)

As I got up on the bus and walked to the seat, I saw that there was only one vacancy that was just back of where it was considered the white section. So this was the seat that I took, next to the aisle, and a man was sitting next to me. Across the aisle there were two women, and there were a few seats at this point in the very front of the bus that was called the white section. I went on to one stop, and I didn't particularly notice the other people getting on. And on the third stop there were some people getting on, and at this point all the front seats were taken. Now in the beginning, at the very first stop I had got on the bus, the back of the bus was filled up with people standing in the aisle, and I don't know why this one vacancy that I took was left, because there were quite a few people already standing toward the back of the bus. The third stop is when all the seats were taken, and this one man was standing, and when the driver looked around and saw he was standing, he asked the four of us, the man in the seat with me and the two women across the aisle, to let him have those front seats.

At his first request, didn't any of us move. Then he spoke again and said, "You'd better make it light on yourselves and let me have those seats." At this point, of course, the passenger who would have taken the seat hadn't said anything. In fact, he never did speak to my knowledge. When the three people, the man who was in the seat with me and the two women, stood up and moved into the aisle, I remained where I was. When the driver saw that I was still there, he asked if I was going to stand up. I told him, no, I wasn't. He said, "Well, if you don't stand up, I'm going to have you arrested." I told him to go on and have me arrested.

He got off the bus and came back shortly. A few minutes later, two policemen got on the bus, and they approached me and asked if the driver had asked me to stand up, and I said yes, and they wanted to know why I didn't. I told them I didn't think I should have to stand up. After I had paid my fare and occupied my seat, I didn't think I should have to give it up. They placed me under arrest then.

Jo Ann Gibson Robinson, "The Montgomery Bus Boycott" (1955)

In the afternoon of Thursday, December 1, [1955] a prominent black woman named Mrs. Rosa Parks was arrested for refusing to vacate her seat for a white man. Mrs. Parks was a medium-sized, cultured mulatto woman; a civic and religious worker; quiet unassuming, and pleasant in manner and appearance; dignified and reserved; of high morals and a strong character. She was—and still is, for she lives to tell the story—respected in all black circles. By trade she was a seamstress, adept and competent in her work.

Tired from work, Mrs. Parks boarded a bus. The "reserved seats" were partially filled, but the seats just behind the reserved section were vacant, and Mrs. Parks sat down in one. It was during the busy evening rush hour. More black and white passengers boarded the bus, and soon all the reserved seats were occupied. The driver demanded that Mrs. Parks get up and surrender her seat to a white man, but she was tired from her work. She remained seated. In a few minutes, police summoned by the driver appeared, placed Mrs. Parks under arrest and took her to jail.

It was the first time the soft-spoken, middle-aged woman had been arrested. She maintained her decorum and poise, and the word of her arrest spread. Mr. E. D. Nixson, a longtime stalwart of our NAACP branch, along with liberal white attorney Clifford Durr and his wife Virginia, went to the jail and obtained Mrs. Parks's release on bond. Her trial was scheduled for Monday, December 5, 1955.

The news traveled like wildfire into every black home. Telephones jangled; people congregated on street corners and in homes and talked. But nothing was done. A numbing helplessness seemed to paralyze everyone. Very few stayed off the buses the rest of that day or the next. There was fear, discontent, and uncertainty. Everyone seemed to wait for someone to *do* something, but nobody made a move. For that day and a half, black Americans rode the buses as before, as if nothing had happened. They were sullen and uncommunicative, but they rode the buses. There was a silent, tension-filled waiting. For blacks were not talking loudly in public places—they were quiet, sullen, waiting. Just waiting!

Thursday evening came and went. Thursday night was far spent, when, at about 11:30 P.M., I sat in my peaceful, single-family dwelling on a side street. I was thinking about the situation. Lost in thought, I was startled by the telephone's ring. Black attorney Fred Gray, who had been out of town all day, had just gotten back and was returning the phone message I had left him about Mrs. Parks's arrest. Attorney Gray, though a very young man, had been one of my most active colleagues in our previous meetings with bus company officials and Commissioner Birmingham. A Montgomery native who had attended Alabama State and been one of my students, Fred Gray had gone on to law school in Ohio before returning to his hometown to open a practice with the only other black lawyer in Montgomery, Charles Langford.

Fred Gray and his wife Bernice were good friends of mine, and we talked often. In addition to being a lawyer, Gray was a trained, ordained minister of the gospel, actively serving as assistant pastor of Holt Street Church of Christ. Tonight his voice on the phone was very short and to the point. Fred was shocked by the news of Mrs. Parks's arrest. I informed him that I already was thinking that the WPC [Women's Political Council] should distribute thousands of notices calling for all bus riders to stay off the buses on Monday, the day of Mrs. Parks's trial. "Are you ready?" he asked. Without hesitation, I assured him that we were. With that he hung up, and I went to work.

I made some notes on the back of an envelope: "The Women's Political Council will not wait for Mrs. Parks's consent to call for a boycott of city buses. On Friday, December 2, 1955, the women of Montgomery will call for a boycott to take place on Monday, December 5."

Martin Luther King Jr., "The Strategy of Nonviolent Direct Action" (1963)

My dear Fellow Clergymen,

While confined here in the Birmingham city jail, I came across your recent statement calling our present activities "unwise and untimely." Seldom, if ever, do I pause to answer criticism of my work and ideas. If I sought to answer all of the criticisms that cross my desk, my secretaries would be engaged in little else in the course of the day, and I would have no time for constructive work. But since I feel that you are men of genuine good will and your criticisms are sincerely set forth, I would like to answer your statement in what I hope will be patient and reasonable terms.

I think I should give the reason for my being in Birmingham, since you have been influenced by the argument of "outsiders coming in." I have the honor of serving as president of the Southern Christian Leadership Conference, an organization operating in every southern state, with headquarters in Atlanta, Georgia. We have some eighty-five affiliate organizations all across the South, one being the Alabama Christian Movement for Human Rights. Whenever necessary and possible, we share staff, educational and financial resources with our affiliates. Several months ago our local affiliate here in Birmingham invited us to be on call to engage in a nonviolent direct-action program if such were deemed necessary. We readily consented, and when the hour came we lived up to our promises. So I am here, along with several members of my staff, because we were invited here. I am here because I have basic organizational ties here.

Beyond this, I am in Birmingham because injustice is here. Just as the eighth century prophets left their little villages and carried their "thus saith the Lord" far beyond the boundaries of their hometowns; and just as the Apostle Paul left his little village of Tarsus and carried the gospel of Jesus Christ to practically every hamlet and city of the Graeco-Roman world, I too am compelled to carry the gospel of freedom beyond my particular hometown. Like Paul, I must constantly respond to the Macedonian call for aid.

Moreover, I am cognizant of the interrelatedness of all communities and states. I cannot sit idly by in Atlanta and not be concerned about what happens in Birmingham. Injustice anywhere is a threat to justice everywhere. We are caught in an inescapable network of mutuality, tied in a single garment of destiny. Whatever affects one directly affects all indirectly. Never again can we afford to live with the narrow, provincial "outside agitator" idea. Anyone who lives in the United States can never be considered an outsider anywhere in this country.

You deplore the demonstrations that are presently taking place in Birmingham. But I am sorry that your statement did not express a similar concern for the conditions that brought the demonstrations into being. I am sure that each of you would want to go beyond the superficial social analyst who looks merely at effects, and does not grapple with underlying causes. I would not hesitate to say that it is unfortunate that so-called demonstrations are taking place in Birmingham at this time, but I would say in more emphatic terms that it is even more unfortunate that the white power structure of this city left the Negro community with no other alternative.

In any nonviolent campaign there are four basic steps: (1) collection of the facts to determine whether injustices are alive, (2) negotiation, (3) self-purification, and (4) direct action. We have gone through all of these steps in Birmingham. There can be no gainsaying of the fact that racial injustice engulfs this community.

Birmingham is probably the most thoroughly segregated city in the United States. Its ugly record of police brutality is known in every section of this country. Its unjust treatment of Negroes in the courts is a notorious reality. There have been more unsolved bombings of Negro homes and churches in Birmingham than any city in this nation. These are the hard, brutal and unbelievable facts. On the basis of these conditions Negro leaders sought to negotiate with the city fathers. But the political leaders consistently refused to engage in good faith negotiation.

Then came the opportunity last September to talk with some of the leaders of the economic community. In these negotiating sessions certain promises were made by the merchants—such as the promise to remove the humiliating racial signs from the stores. On the basis of these promises ... the leaders of the Alabama Christian Movement for Human Rights agreed to call a moratorium on any type of demonstrations. As the weeks and months unfolded we realized that we were the victims of a broken promise. The signs remained. Like so many experiences of the past we were confronted with blasted hopes, and the dark shadow of a deep disappointment settled upon us. So we had no alternative except that of preparing for direct action, whereby we would present our very bodies as a means of laying our case before the conscience of the local and national community. We were not unmindful of the difficulties involved. So we decided to go through a process of self-purification. We started having workshops on nonviolence and repeatedly asked ourselves the questions, "Are you able to accept blows without retaliating?" "Are you able to endure the ordeals of jail?" We decided to set our direct-action program around the Easter season, realizing that with the exception of Christmas, this was the largest shopping period of the year. Knowing that a strong economic withdrawal program would be the by-product of direct action, we felt that this was the best time to bring pressure on the merchants for the needed changes. Then it occurred to us that the March election was ahead and so we speedily decided to postpone action until after election day. When we discovered that [racist police commissioner "Bull"] Connor was in the run-off, we decided again to postpone action so that the demonstrations could not be used to cloud the issues. At this time we agreed to begin our nonviolent witness the day after the run-off.

This reveals that we did not move irresponsibly into direct action. We too wanted to see Mr. Connor defeated; so we went through postponement after postponement to aid in this community need. After this we felt that direct action could be delayed no longer.

You may ask, "Why direct action? Why sit-ins, marches, etc.? Isn't negotiation a better path?" You are exactly right in your call for negotiation. Indeed, this is the purpose of direct action. Nonviolent direct action seeks to create such a crisis and establish such creative tension that a community that has constantly refused to negotiate is forced to confront the issue. It seeks so to dramatize the issue that it can no longer be ignored. I just referred to the creation of tension as a part of the work of the nonviolent resister. This may sound rather shocking. But I must confess that I am not afraid of the word tension. I have earnestly worked and preached against violent tension, but there is a type of constructive nonviolent tension that is necessary for growth. Just as Socrates felt that it was necessary to create a tension in the mind so that individuals could rise from the bondage of myths and half-truths to the unfettered realm of creative analysis and objective appraisal, we must see the need of having nonviolent gadflies to create the kind of tension in society that will help men to rise from the dark depths of prejudice and racism to the majestic heights of understanding and brotherhood. So the purpose of the direct action is to create a situation so crisis-packed that it will inevitably open the door to negotiation. We, therefore, concur with you in your call for negotiation. Too long has our beloved Southland been bogged down in the tragic attempt to live in monologue rather than dialogue.

One of the basic points in your statement is that our acts are untimely. Some have asked, "Why didn't you give the new administration time to act?" The only answer that I can give to this inquiry is that the new administration must be prodded about as much as the outgoing one before it acts. We will be sadly mistaken if we feel that the election of Mr. Boutwell will bring the millennium to Birmingham. While Mr. Boutwell is much more articulate and gentle than Mr. Connor, they are both segregationists, dedicated to the task of maintaining the status quo. The hope I see in Mr. Boutwell is that he will be reasonable enough to see the futility of massive resistance to desegregation. But he will not see this without pressure from the devotees of civil rights. My friends, I must say to you that we have not made a single gain in civil rights without determined legal and nonviolent pressure. History is the long and tragic story of the fact that privileged groups seldom give up their privileges voluntarily. Individuals may see the moral light and voluntarily give up their unjust posture; but as Reinhold Niebuhr has reminded us, groups are more immoral than individuals.

We know through painful experience that freedom is never voluntarily given by the oppressor; it must be demanded by the oppressed. Frankly, I have never yet engaged in a direct-action movement that was "well timed," according to the timetable of those who have not suffered unduly from the disease of segregation. For years now I have heard the word "Wait!" It rings in the ear of every Negro with a piercing familiarity. This "Wait!" has almost always meant "Never." It has been a tranquilizing thalidomide, relieving the emotional stress for a moment, only to give birth to an ill-formed infant of frustration. We must come to see with the distinguished jurist of yesterday that "justice too long delayed is justice denied."

We have waited for more than 340 years for our constitutional and God-given rights. The nations of Asia and Africa are moving with jetlike speed toward the goal of political independence, and we still creep at horse and buggy pace toward the gaining of a cup of coffee at a lunch counter. I guess it is easy for those who have never felt the stinging darts of segregation to say, "Wait." But when you have seen vicious mobs lynch your mothers and fathers at will and drown your sisters and brothers at whim; when you have seen hate-filled policemen curse, kick, brutalize and even kill your black brothers and sisters with impunity; when you see the vast majority of your twenty million Negro brothers smothering in an airtight cage of poverty in the midst of an affluent society; when you suddenly find your tongue twisted and your speech stammering as you seek to explain to your six-year-old daughter why she can't go to the public amusement park that has just been advertised on television, and see tears welling up in her little eyes when she is told that Funtown is closed to colored children, and see the depressing clouds of inferiority begin to form in her little mental sky, and see her begin to distort her little personality by unconsciously developing a bitterness toward white people; when you have to concoct an answer for a five-year-old son asking in agonizing pathos: "Daddy, why do white people treat colored people so mean?"; when you take a cross-country drive and find it necessary to sleep night after night in the uncomfortable corners of your automobile because no motel will accept you; when you are humiliated day in and day out by nagging signs reading "white" and "colored"; when your first name becomes "nigger" and your middle name becomes "boy" (however old you are) and your last name becomes "John," and when your wife and mother are never given the respected title "Mrs."; when you are harried by day and haunted by night by the fact that you are a Negro, living constantly at tiptoe stance never quite knowing what to expect next, and plagued with inner fears and outer resentments; when you are forever fighting a degenerating sense of "nobodiness"; then you will understand why we find it difficult to wait. There comes a time when the cup of endurance runs over, and men are no longer willing to be plunged into an abyss of injustice where they experience the blackness of corroding despair. I hope, sirs, you can understand our legitimate and unavoidable impatience.

You express a great deal of anxiety over our willingness to break laws. This is certainly a legitimate concern. Since we so diligently urge people to obey the Supreme Court's decision of 1954 outlawing segregation in the public schools, it is rather strange and paradoxical to find us consciously breaking laws. One may well ask, "How can your advocate breaking some laws and obeying others?" The answer is found in the fact that there are two types of laws: there are *just* and there are *unjust* laws. I would agree with Saint Augustine that "An unjust law is no law at all."

Now what is the difference between the two? How does one determine when a law is just or unjust? A just law is a man-made code that squares with the moral law or the law of God. An unjust law is a code that is out of harmony with the moral law. To put it in the terms of Saint Thomas Aquinas, an unjust law is a human law that is not rooted in eternal and natural law. Any law that degrades human personality is unjust. All segregation statutes are unjust because segregation distorts the soul and damages the personality. It gives the segregator a false sense of superiority, and the segregaated a false sense of inferiority.... So I can urge men to disobey segregation ordinances because they are morally wrong....

First, I must confess that over the last few years I have been gravely disappointed with the white moderate. I have almost reached the regrettable conclusion that the Negro's great stumbling block in the stride toward freedom is not the White Citizen's Counciler or the Ku Klux Klanner, but the white moderate who is more devoted to "order" than to justice; who prefers a negative peace which is the absence of tension to a positive peace which is the the presence of justice; who constantly says, "I agree with you in the goal you seek, but I can't agree with your methods of direct action"; who paternalistically feels that he can set the timetable for another man's freedom; who lives by the myth of time and who constantly advised the Negro to wait until a "more convenient season." Shallow understanding from people of good will is more frustrating than absolute misunderstanding from people of ill will. Lukewarm acceptance is much more bewildering that outright rejection.

I had hoped that the white moderate would understand that law and order exist for the purpose of establishing justice, and that when they do fail to do this they become dangerously structured dams that block the flow of social progress. I had hoped that the white moderate would understand that the present tenion of the South is merely a necessary phase of the transition from an obnoxious negative peace, where the Negro passively accepted his unjust plight, to a substance-filled positive peace, where all men respect the dignity and worth of human personality. Actually, we who engage in nonviolent direct action are not the creators of tension. We merely bring to the surface the hidden tension that is already alive. We bring it out in the open where it can be seen and dealt with. Like a boil that can never be cured as long as it is covered up but must be opened with all its pus-flowing ugliness to the natural medicines of air and light, injustice must likewise be exposed, with all of the tension its exposing creates, to the light of human conscience and the air of national opinion before it can be cured.

In your statement you asserted that our actions, even though peaceful, must be condemned because they precipitate violence. But can this assertion be logically made? Isn't this like condemning the robbed man because his possession of money precipitated the evil act of robbery? Isn't this like condemning Socrates because his unswerving commitment to truth and his philosophical delvings precipitated the misguided popular mind to make him drink the hemlock? Isn't this like condemning Jesus because His unique God consciousness and never-ceasing devotion to his will precipitated the evil act of crucifixion? We must come to see, as federal courts have consistently affirmed, that it is immoral to urge an individual to withdraw his efforts to gain his basic constitutional rights because the quest precipitates violence. Society must protect the robbed and punish the robber.

I had also hoped that the white moderate would reject the myth of time. I received a letter this morning from a white brother in Texas which said: "All Christians know that the colored people will receive equal rights eventually, but it is possible that you are in too great of a religious hurry. It has taken Christianity almost two thousand years to accomplish what it has. The teachings of Christ take time to come to earth." All that is said here grows out of a tragic misconception of time. It is the strangely irrational notion that there is something in the very flow of time that will inevitably cure all ills. Actually time is neutral. It can be used either destructively or constructively. I am coming to feel that the people of ill will have used time much more effectively than the people of good will. We will have to repent in this generation not merely for the vitriolic words and actions of the bad people, but for the appalling silence of the good people. We must come to see that human progress never rolls in on wheels of inevitability. It comes through the tireless efforts and persistent work of men willing to be co-workers with God, and without this hard word time itself becomes an ally of the forces of social stagnation. We must use time creatively, and forever realize that the time is always ripe to do right. Now is the time to make real the promise of democracy, and transform our pending national elegy into a creative psalm of brotherhood. Now is the time to lift our national policy from the quicksand of racial injustice to the solid rock of human dignity.

You spoke of our activity in Birmingham as extreme. At first I was rather disappointed that fellow clergymen would see my nonviolent efforts as those of the extremist.... But as I continued to think about the matter I gradually gained a bit of satisfaction from being considered an extremist. Was not Jesus an extremist in love—"Love your enemies, bless them that curse you, pray for them that despitefully use you." Was not Amos an extremist for justice—"Let justice roll down like waters and righteousness like a mighty stream." Was not Paul and extremist for the gospel of Jesus Christ—"I bear in my body the marks of the Lord Jesus." Was not Martin Luther an extremist—"Here I stand; I can do none other so help me God." Was not John Bunyan an extremist—"I will stay in jail to the end of my days before I make a Butchery of my conscience." Was not Abraham Lincoln an extremist—"This nation cannot survive half slave and half free." Was not Thomas Jefferson an extremist—"We hold these truths to be self-evident, that all men are created equal." So the question is not whether we will be extremist but what kind of extremist will we be. Will we be extremists for hate or will we be extremists for love? Will we be extremists for the preservation of injustice—or will we be extremists for the cause of justice? In that dramatic scene on Calvary's hill, three men were crucified. We must not forget that all three were crucified for the same crime—the crime of extremism. Two were extremists for immorality, and thusly fell below their environment. The other, Jesus Christ, was an extremist for love, truth, and goodness, and thereby rose above his environment. So, after all, maybe the South, the nation and the world are in dire need of creative extremists.

I had hoped that the white moderate would see this. Maybe I was too optimistic. Maybe I expected too much. I guess I should have realized that few members of a race that has oppressed another race can understand or appreciate the deep groans and passionate yearnings of those that have been oppressed, and still fewer have the vision to see that injustice must be rooted out by strong, persistent and determined action. I am thankful, however, that some of our white brothers have grasped the meaning of this social revolution and committed themselves to it....

Yours for the Cause of Peace and Brotherhood

Martin Luther King Jr.

1. Why was Rosa Parks a fortuitous focus for the beginning of the new civil rights movement?

2. From reading both Rosa Parks' and Jo Ann Gibson Robinson's accounts, can you see elements of why the Montgomery bus boycott was ultimately successful?

3. Based on the teachings of Mahatma Ghandi, Martin Luther King Jr. developed a strategy for black Americans to oppose Jim Crow or segregated public services. What are the key components of this strategy?

4. To whom was Dr. King addressing his rationale? Was it effective?

5. What political and social pressures opposed the early civil rights movement? How would an opponent have responded to each of these three articles?

CHAPTER 30

The Turbulent Sixties, 1960–1968

SUMMARY

The 1960s was an era of angry protests, violent demonstrations, and sweeping social change. Under both Kennedy and Johnson, significant domestic reforms occurred while the continued American involvement in Vietnam led to escalation and eventually stalemate.

Kennedy Intensifies the Cold War

Despite a campaign that focused on domestic issues, foreign affairs took center stage upon John Kennedy's election. The new administration supported containment and authorized a massive buildup of nuclear weapons in an effort to win the Cold War.

Containment in Southeast Asia

Kennedy reacted to Soviet statements promising support for "wars of national liberation" by a combination of financial aid, technical assistance, and counterinsurgency in order to build strong, stable, Western democracies in the less-developed areas of Asia. The most obvious result of this support was the increase of American advisors to South Vietnam from less than 1,000 in 1961 to more than 16,000 in 1963.

Containing Castro: The Bay of Pigs Fiasco

Kennedy gave his approval to a CIA plan developed under Eisenhower to topple Castro by using Cuban exiles as invasion troops. The Bay of Pigs landing proved to be an utter disaster, and Kennedy took full responsibility for the failure.

Containing Castro: The Cuban Missile Crisis

In 1962, the United States faced a much more serious issue regarding the installation of nuclear missiles in Cuba. Kennedy refused to bargain on the missiles and boldly ordered a quarantine of Cuba as the world braced for a possible nuclear showdown. Premier Khrushchev eventually backed down, but the Russians went on a crash nuclear buildup to achieve parity with the United States. Some positive results followed: a limited test ban treaty was signed in 1963; a hot line to speed communication between the nuclear antagonists was installed, and a policy of conciliation replaced that of confrontation. Those gains were offset by a dramatic escalation in the arms race.

The New Frontier at Home

John F. Kennedy took advantage of television debates and a national sense of dissatisfaction to narrowly defeat the Republican candidate Richard Nixon for the presidency in 1960. Kennedy's election marked the arrival of a new generation of leadership. As he had with foreign affairs, Kennedy surrounded himself with the "best and the brightest" advisors on domestic issues. The new administration reflected the president's youth and energy, but Kennedy's greatest asset was his personality and style that endeared him to Americans.

Moving Slowly on Civil Rights

Having promised in his campaign to support desegregation, the president avoided congressional action, focusing instead on executive leadership. His brother and Attorney General, Robert Kennedy, continued the Eisenhower administration's efforts to achieve black voting rights in the South while Vice President Lyndon Johnson headed a presidential Commission on Equal Employment Opportunities. Kennedy also appointed a number of African Americans to high government positions and supported the attempt by James Meredith to gain admission to the University of Mississippi over Governor Ross Barnett's opposition. Not satisfied with the scope of Kennedy's support for black equality, civil rights workers pushed the issue by initiating the first "freedom ride" in 1961 to test the Supreme Court's order to desegregate all bus and train stations used in interstate travel.

"I Have a Dream"

Responding to Dr. King's campaign for racial justice in Birmingham and his eloquent speech from the Lincoln Memorial in 1963, Kennedy finally decided to take the offensive and push for civil rights legislation in Congress. By the time of the president's death, his civil rights bills were on their way to passage. Though Kennedy's record on civil rights was hesitant, he did throw the weight of the presidency behind the civil rights movement, something that had never been done before.

LBJ's Great Society

Vice President Lyndon Johnson moved quickly to fill the void left by Kennedy's death, urging Congress to pass his tax and civil rights bills as a tribute to the fallen president.

Johnson in Action

Although lacking Kennedy's charm and charisma, Johnson possessed far greater ability than his predecessor in dealing with Congress. He sought consensus rather than confrontation. He succeeded in achieving the passage of Kennedy's civil rights measures, and the Civil Rights Act of 1964, which made segregation illegal, was a landmark in the advance of American freedom and equality.

The Election of 1964

Convinced of the detrimental societal effects of poverty, Johnson declared an unconditional "war on poverty" and empowered the new Office of Economic Opportunity to set up a variety of programs to provide assistance to the poor in America. In 1964, Johnson and his "Great Society" program soundly defeated the hawkish Republican Barry Goldwater. The Democrats also achieved huge gains in Congress, breaking the conservative stranglehold.

The Triumph of Reform

Upon inauguration, Johnson began pushing his "Great Society," making health care and educational reforms his top priority. The establishment of Medicare and Medicaid realized Truman's 1949 goal of universal health insurance while the Elementary and Secondary Education Act provided federal monies to school districts throughout the nation. The passage of the Voting Rights Act of 1965 encouraged massive increases in African-American voter registration. Within nine months of being elected in his own right, Johnson achieved the entire

Democratic reform agenda, but difficulties abroad soon stole his attention from domestic concerns.

Johnson Escalates the Vietnam War

Lyndon Johnson shared Kennedy's Cold War view and inherited his military and diplomatic problems. His forcefulness in opposing Castro and the Latin American left brought increasing criticism from many directions, as did his resolve to contain communism in Southeast Asia.

The Vietnam Dilemma

In Vietnam, the United States had supported the South Vietnamese regime of Ngo Dinh Diem against communist insurgents. Kennedy had sent military advisors and substantial military and economic aid. Full-scale American involvement began under Johnson in 1965, after the Gulf of Tonkin Resolution by Congress gave the president the power to take the offensive.

Escalation

Refusing to call for an invasion of the North, Johnson opted for steady military escalation. As his "open-ended commitment" to force a diplomatic solution on Hanoi intensified, American combat missions in the South and air strikes against the North increased. Johnson refused to admit, however, that he had committed the United States to full-scale military involvement, and the situation in Southeast Asia worsened.

Stalemate

Despite massive American escalation, the war remained stalemated in 1968. Westmoreland's wanton use of American firepower to destroy the Vietnamese countryside, wiping out villages and killing civilians, discredited the American cause and increased criticism of the war on the homefront.

Years of Turmoil

With the growth of opposition to the war in Vietnam escalating, the 1960s became the most turbulent decade of the century as those who were dissatisfied with their position in American society—African Americans, women, Native Americans, hippies, Latinos, and students—took to the streets to protest.

Protesting the Vietnam War

Opposition to the war in Vietnam was a central theme for many students. To students the war seemed to symbolize all that was wrong with America. Students held sit-ins and marches demanding an end to the war. Though they failed to end the war, they did change American life.

The Cultural Revolution
Combined with the issues of war and race, the youth of the country seemed to be rejecting all the cultural values of middle-class, middle-aged Americans. Along with opposition to the war and the draft, rock music and drug experimentation were key elements of this counterculture movement that climaxed at the legendary Woodstock concert in Bethel, New York.

"Black Power"
The civil rights movement became more militant and less concerned with racial harmony as the 1960s wore on. Despite the movement's legislative successes, its failure to solve the economic problems of the race along with continued racial discrimination inspired a rejection of King's non-violent tactics. When King was assassinated, urban riots erupted in 125 cities across the nation. The Black Power movement went hand in hand with a movement celebrating pride in black culture and history and the rejection of the term Negro in favor of Afro-American or black.

Ethnic Nationalism
The pride in ethnicity that emerged from the Black Power movement inspired other groups including Mexican Americans and Native Americans to celebrate their own heritage and history. Language classes and programs celebrating ethnic heritage began almost overnight at many colleges and Congress acknowledged the trend with the passage of the Ethnic Heritage Studies Act of 1972.

Women's Liberation
Young women involved in the various civil rights movements of the era found to their dismay that many of their male colleagues saw them only as people to fix the food. Such sexism inspired many to join a growing movement for women's liberation. Recognizing that the condition of women in America created a sense of grievance and discrimination, the work of such authors as Betty Friedan argued that many women were not satisfied with a life that consisted solely of housework and child rearing. The 1964 Civil Rights Act helped women combat employment inequalities while groups like the National Organization for Women emerged to push for full equality for women with the 1972 Equal Rights Amendment. Turned off by some of the more radical views of the feminist movement, the Amendment was not ratified by American voters.

The Return of Richard Nixon
Partially as a reaction to the turmoil of the 1960s, Richard Nixon made a remarkable comeback and won the presidency in 1968.

Vietnam Undermines Lyndon Johnson
As a result of the Viet Cong's surprise offensive during Tet, the lunar New Year, American political and popular support for the war declined rapidly. In March of 1968, President Johnson refused to authorize further military escalation, declared a peace initiative, and announced that he would not run for another term.

The Republican Resurgence

With the wounded Democratic party foundering, and George Wallace, a third-party candidate running on white supremacy, running away with much of the Southern vote, the Republican nominee Richard Nixon easily won the presidency.

Conclusion: The End of an Era

The election of Richard Nixon was a rejection of the politics of protest and the cultural insurgency of the 1960s and a sign that the long-silent majority was fed up with the turmoil of the era. Nixon's election signaled the end the liberal reform impulse that had been born in the midst of the Great Depression. It was also a repudiation of the burgeoning growth of federal power and interventionist foreign policy.

LEARNING OBJECTIVES

After mastering this chapter, you should be able to:

1. Analyze Kennedy's attitude toward the Cold War and nuclear armaments and the possible long-term consequences vis-à-vis the Soviet Union.

2. Summarize the main events and results of the Bay of Pigs landing and the Cuban missile crisis.

3. Compare and contrast the arguments for continued confrontation or conciliation with the Russians in the context of the Cuban missile crisis.

4. Understand the reasons for America's buildup of military strength in Vietnam and how this escalation undermined the Johnson administration.

5. Describe the escalation of America's involvement in the Vietnam War from 1961 to 1968.

6. Explain why and how the year 1968 seemed to mark a turning point in the Vietnam War.

7. Discuss the key elements of Kennedy's New Frontier domestic agenda and his success or failure in enacting it.

8. Explain the domestic successes of Lyndon Johnson.

9. Analyze the key features of the cultural rebellion of the 1960s.

10. Compare the ethnic and women's movements of this era.

11. Summarize the historical factors that led to the return and success of Richard Nixon.

GLOSSARY

To build your social science vocabulary, familiarize yourself with the following terms:

1. **counterinsurgency** organized military and intelligence activity designed to prevent, control, or detect insurrection. "The president took a personal interest in counterinsurgency."

2. **quarantine** a blockade or restraint. "He would proclaim a quarantine of Cuba to prevent the arrival of new missiles ..."

3. **conciliation** agreement or compromise. " ... he shifted from the rhetoric of confrontation to that of conciliation ..."

4. **hawks** those who support war or militancy. "Hawks who had backed Kennedy's military buildup felt that events had justified a policy of nuclear superiority."

5. **junta** a group of people, usually military, in control of a government after a military coup. "When a military junta overthrew a leftist regime in Brazil, ..."

6. **covert** secretive, unannounced or unofficial. "... he expanded American support for covert actions ..."

7. **escalation** buildup or increase. "... critics charged that LBJ wanted a blank check from Congress to carry out the future escalation of the Vietnam War ..."

IDENTIFICATION

Briefly identify the meaning and significance of the following terms:

1. Ngo Dinh Diem _____

_____

2. Bay of Pigs _____

_____

3. Cuban Missile Crisis _____

_____

4. freedom ride _____

_____

5. Gulf of Tonkin Affair _____

_____

6. Students for a Democratic Society (SDS) _____

_____

7. Great Society _____

_____

8. "Black Power" _____

_____

9. Tet Offensive _____

_____

10. Voting Rights Act of 1965 _____

_____

MATCHING

A. Match the following people during the Cuban Missile Crisis with the appropriate identification:

_____1. John McCone

_____2. Nikita Khrushchev

_____3. Anatoly Dobrynin

_____4. Dean Rusk

_____5. Fidel Castro

a. Soviet ambassador to the United States

b. Communist leader of Cuba

c. Premier of the Soviet Union

d. CIA Director who objected to the limiting of U2 flights over Cuba

e. attorney general who heavily influenced President Kennedy's decisions

f. U.S. secretary of state who said: "We're eyeball to eyeball, and I think the other fellow just blinked"

B. Match the following public figures with the appropriate description:

_____1. Dean Rusk

_____2. Robert McNamara

_____3. McGeorge Bundy

_____4. Robert F. Kennedy

_____5. Hubert Humphrey

a. secretary of state under both Kennedy and Johnson

b. MIT economist who became one of Kennedy's most important advisors

c. secretary of defense under President Kennedy

d. U.S. attorney general and Kennedy's most controversial cabinet appointee

e. one of the "best and the brightest" who became Kennedy's national security adviser

f. vice president under Johnson

COMPLETION

Answer the question or complete the statement by filling in the blanks with the correct word or words.

1. The New Frontiersmen appointed by Kennedy were later referred to by journalist David Halberstam as _____.

2. The failed 1961 invasion of Cuba to overthrow Fidel Castro was called the _____.

3. The huge economic aid program called for by Kennedy for Latin America was the _____.

4. South Vietnamese rebels against the regime of Ngo Dinh Diem were known as _____.

5. After the Cuban missile crisis, President Kennedy and Premier Khrushchev agreed to install a _____ for instant communication to prevent any emergency.

6. Senator William Fulbright criticized Johnson's foreign policy and the fallacies of containment with his publication of _____.

7. Johnson complained that the Vietnam conflict, that "bitch of a war," would destroy "the woman I really loved—the _____."

8. The _____ made the segregation of public facilities illegal.

9. The _____ was a central part of LBJ's War on Poverty.

10. Part of the Johnson legislative program was _____, mandated health insurance for Americans over 65 and _____, health care for the indigent.

TRUE/FALSE

Mark the following statements either T (True) or F (False):

_____1.   Because of the problems with Cuba, President Kennedy was unable to increase military and economic aid to South Vietnam.

_____2.   Regarding the Bay of Pigs debacle, Kennedy took personal responsibility for the failure.

_____3.   Compared to President Kennedy, President Johnson lacked the political experience necessary to deal with Congress.

_____4.   After the Cuban missile crisis, the Soviet Union recognized American nuclear superiority and concentrated primarily on conventional weapons.

_____5.   John Kennedy's Alliance for Progress emphasized military rather than economic means in our Latin American policy.

_____6.   "Strategic hamlets" were fire bases in South Vietnam from which American troops launched their operations.

_____7.   Despite the effect of the "I Have a Dream Speech," President Kennedy refused to call for any additional civil rights legislation.

_____8.   Cesar Chavez organized poorly paid agricultural workers – mostly Mexican American – into the National Farm Workers Association.

_____9.   Gradually Johnson escalated the military activity in Vietnam.

_____10. The Tet offensive of February 1968 had virtually no impact on American public opinion.

MULTIPLE CHOICE

Circle the one alternative that *best* completes the statement or answers the question.

1. In *The Feminine Mystique* Betty Friedan argued that
    a. sexual intercourse was a form of male domination.
    b. many American women lacked a sense of identity and rejected the traditional role of homemaker and housewife.
    c. groups like the National Organization for Women hindered women's rights.
    d. women were not capable of doing jobs traditionally done by men.

2. The "Black Power" movement
    a. was led by Martin Luther King, Jr.
    b. was more militant than the movement of the early 1960s.
    c. unified the Civil Rights movement.
    d. All of the above.

3. President Kennedy's solution to the escalating guerrilla fighting in South Vietnam was to
    a. demand the overthrow of the oppressive Diem government.
    b. send thousands of American offensive ground forces to stabilize the region.
    c. continue to support Diem while recognizing that it was ultimately South Vietnam's war to win or lose.
    d. order the first large-scale bombings of North Vietnam.

4. The result of the Cuban missile crisis was that
    a. Khrushchev agreed to remove the missiles in return for the U.S. promise not to invade Cuba.
    b. the United States agreed to allow only defensive nuclear weapons in Cuba.
    c. the Communist government in Cuba collapsed and was replaced by a pro-American republic.
    d. the Soviet Union and the United States broke off all diplomatic and commercial relations.

5. Kennedy responded to Soviet missiles in Cuba by
    a. an invasion of Cuba to seize the missile sites.
    b. an air raid to destroy the missile sites.
    c. a naval occupation of the Cuban port through which Russian missiles and parts passed.
    d. a naval quarantine of Cuba to prevent the shipment of new missiles coupled with nuclear threat to force the removal of missiles already in place.

6. The Gulf of Tonkin resolution resulted in
    a. a declaration of war by Congress on North Vietnam.
    b. Congress's support of Johnson's desire to increase military activity in Vietnam.
    c. the decision to bomb Hanoi and other North Vietnamese locations.
    d. the decision to overthrow the Diem regime.

7. Johnson's failure regarding Vietnam was to
   a. refuse to acknowledge he had committed the U.S. to dangerous military involvement.
   b. begin the process of sending military specialists and equipment into Vietnam.
   c. support the Diem regime.
   d. overstep the president's authority concerning military commitment.

8. Which best describes the Viet Cong?
   a. pro-American elements of the South Vietnamese military
   b. the South Vietnamese regular army
   c. the North Vietnamese regular army
   d. communist guerrillas in South Vietnam

9. Both the Kennedy and Johnson administrations developed a foreign policy based primarily on
   a. their Cold War views.
   b. a strong commitment to the United Nations.
   c. emerging theories of *détente*.
   d. a strong commitment to disarmament.

10. Lyndon Johnson used 20,000 American troops to intervene in
    a. Cuba.
    b. the Dominican Republic.
    c. Mexico.
    d. Argentina.

11. Which of the following events took place during the Johnson administration?
    a. the Tet offensive
    b. the Bay of Pigs invasion
    c. the U-2 incident
    d. All of the above.

12. John F. Kennedy took advantage of which of the following to gain votes in 1960?
    a. sagging national economy and a renewed commitment to the Cold War
    b. his greater name recognition than Nixon
    c. his prior reputation for being a strong civil rights leader
    d. his reputation for being a tougher cold warrior than Nixon

12. Johnson's Great Society represented
    a. conservative support for corporations and wealthy Americans.
    b. an intensifying of the war effort in Vietnam.
    c. extensive tax cuts and defense spending cuts.
    d. long-awaited reforms in health care, federal aid to education, and promotion of civil rights.

13. Most of the actual stimulation of the economy during the Kennedy administration came from
    a. increased social welfare programs.
    b. tax increases to increase federal spending.
    c. the lifting of wage and price controls held over from the Eisenhower years.
    d. greatly increased appropriations for defense and space.

14. All of the following led to Richard Nixon winning the presidency in 1968 EXCEPT
    a. third party candidate George Wallace cut deeply into the normal Democratic majority.
    b. widespread support from African Americans and civil rights protestors.
    c. Johnson's handling of the Vietnam War caused problems for the Democratic nominee, Hubert Humphrey.
    d. Nixon positioned himself as a reconciler who could bring a torn country back together.

THOUGHT QUESTIONS

To check your understanding of the key issues of this period, solve the following problems:

1. Given John Kennedy's military and foreign policy views, would he have followed the Vietnam policies pursued by Lyndon Johnson? Would he have escalated or withdrawn?

2. How do the diplomatic events of the Kennedy administration indicate his commitment to the Cold War?

3. After considering the alternatives, do you think that Kennedy responded correctly to the Cuban missile crisis? What were the long-term consequences of that showdown?

4. Did the Latin American policies of Eisenhower, Kennedy, and Johnson differ significantly? Explain your answer.

5. How do you account for the buildup of American forces in Vietnam? To what degree was Johnson responsible for the tragedy of Vietnam?

6. In what ways were Kennedy's New Frontier and Johnson's Great Society continuations of the New Deal? How were they different?

7. How does the Vietnam conflict connect with the various "movements" of the 1960s?

8. Account for the remarkable comeback of Richard Nixon in 1968.

CRITICAL THINKING QUESTIONS

After reading Betty Friedan, "The Problem That Has No Name," (1963), National Organization For Women, *Statement of Purpose*, (1966), and Frances Sugre, *Diary of a Rent Striker* (1964) answer the following:

Betty Friedan, "The Problem That Has No Name" (1963)

The problem lay buried, unspoken, for many years in the minds of American women. It was a strange stirring, a sense of dissatisfaction, a yearning that women suffered in the middle of the twentieth century in the United States. Each suburban wife struggled with it alone. As she made the beds, shopped for groceries, matched slipcover material, ate peanut butter sandwiches with her children, chauffeured Cub Scouts and Brownies, lay beside her husband at night—she was afraid to ask even of herself the silent question—"Is this all?"

For over fifteen years there was no word of this yearning in the millions of words written about women and for women, in all the columns, books and articles by experts telling women their role was to seek fulfillment as wives and mothers. Over and over women heard in voices of tradition and Freudian sophistication, that they could desire no greater destiny than to glory in their own femininity. Experts told them how to catch a man and how to keep him, how to breastfeed children and handle their toilet training, how to cope with sibling rivalry and adolescent rebellion; how to buy a dishwasher, bake bread, cook gourmet snails, and build a swimming pool with their own hands; how to dress, look, and act more feminine and make marriage more exciting; how to keep their husbands from dying young and their sons from growing into delinquents. They were taught to pity the neurotic, unfeminine, unhappy women who wanted to be poets or physicists or presidents. They learned that truly feminine women do not want careers, higher education, political rights—the independence and the opportunities that the old-fashioned feminists fought for. Some women, in their forties and fifties, still remembered painfully giving up those dreams, but most of the younger women no longer even thought about them. A thousand expert voices applauded their femininity, their adjustment, their new maturity. All they had to do was devote their lives from earliest girlhood to finding a husband and bearing children....

The suburban housewife—she was the dream image of the young American women and the envy, it was said, of women all over the world. The American housewife—freed by science and labor-saving appliances from the drudgery, the dangers of childbirth and the illnesses of her grandmother. She was healthy, beautiful, educated, concerned only about her husband, her children, her home. She had found true feminine fulfillment. As a housewife and mother, she was respected as a full and equal partner to man in his world. She was free to choose automobiles, clothes, appliances, supermarkets; she had everything that women ever dreamed of.

In the fifteen years after World War II, this mystique of feminine fulfillment became the cherished and self-perpetuating core of contemporary American culture. Millions of women lived their lives in the image of those pretty pictures of the American suburban housewife, kissing their husband goodbye in front of the picture window, depositing their station wagonsful of children at school, and smiling as they ran the new electric waxer over the spotless kitchen floor. They baked their own bread, sewed their own and their children's clothes, kept their new washing machines and dryers running all day. They changed the sheets on the beds twice a week instead of once, took the rug-hooking classes in adult education, and pitied their poor frustrated mothers, who had dreamed of having a career. Their only dream was to be perfect wives and mothers; their highest ambition to have five children and a beautiful house, their only fight to get and keep their husbands. They had no thought for the unfeminine problems of the world outside the home; they wanted the men to make the major decisions. They gloried in their role as women, and wrote proudly on the census blank: "Occupation: housewife."

For over fifteen years, the words written for women, and the words women used when they talked to each other, while their husbands sat on the other side of the room and talked shop or politics or septic tanks, were about problems with their children, or how to keep their husband happy, or improve their children's school, or cook chicken or make slipcovers. Nobody argued whether women were inferior or superior to men; they were simply different. Words like "emancipation" and "career" sounded strange and embarrassing; no one had used them for years. When a Frenchwoman named Simone de Beauvoir wrote a book called *The Second Sex*, an American critic commented that she obviously "didn't know what life was all about," and besides, she was talking about French women. The "woman problem" in America no longer existed.

Gradually I came to realize that the problem that has no name was shared by countless women in America. As a magazine writer I often interviewed women about problems with their children, or their marriages, or their houses, or their communities. But after a while I began to recognize the telltale signs of this other problem. I saw the same signs in suburban ranch houses and split-levels on Long Island and in New Jersey and Westchester County; in colonial houses in a small Massachusetts town; on patios in Memphis; in suburban and city apartments; in living rooms in the Midwest. Sometimes I sensed the problem, not as a reporter, but as a suburban housewife, for during this time I was also bringing up my own three children in Rockland County, New York. I heard echoes of the problem in college dormitories and semi-private maternity wards, at PTA meetings and luncheons of the League of Women Voters, at suburban cocktail parties, in station wagons waiting for trains, and in snatches of conversation overheard at Schrafft's. The groping words I heard from other women, on quiet afternoons when the children were at school, or on quiet evenings when husbands worked late, I think I understood first as a woman long before I understood their larger social and psychological implications.

Just what was this problem that has no name? What were the words women used when they tried to express it? Sometimes a woman would say "I feel empty somehow ... incomplete." Or she would say, "I feel as if I don't exist." . . .

It is no longer possible to ignore that voice, to dismiss the desperation of so many American women. This is not what being a woman means, no matter what the experts say. For human suffering there is a reason; perhaps the reason has not been found because the right questions have not been asked, or pressed far enough. I do not accept the answer that there is no problem because American women have luxuries that women in other times and lands never dreamed of; part of the strange newness of the problem is that it cannot be understood in terms of the age-old material problems of man: poverty, sickness, hunger, cold. The women who suffer this problem have a hunger that food cannot fill. It persists in women whose husbands are struggling interns and law clerks, or prosperous doctors and lawyers; in wives of workers and executives who make $5,000 a year or $50,000. It is not caused by lack of material advantages; it may not even be felt by women preoccupied with desperate problems of hunger, poverty or illness. And women who think it will be solved by more money, a bigger house, a second car, moving to a better suburb, often discover it gets worse.

It is no longer possible today to blame the problem on loss of femininity; to say that education and independence and equality with men have made American women unfeminine. I have heard so many women try to deny this dissatisfied voice within themselves because it does not fit the pretty picture of femininity the experts have given them. I think, in fact, that this is the first clue to the mystery: the problem cannot be understood in the generally accepted terms by which scientists have studied women, doctors have treated them, counselors have advised them, and writers have written about hem. Women who suffer this problem, in whom this voice is stirring, have lived their whole lives in the pursuit of feminine fulfillment. They are not career women (although career women may have other problems); they are women whose greatest ambition has been marriage and children. For the oldest of these women, these daughters of the American middle-class, no other dream was possible. The ones in their forties and fifties who once had other dreams gave them up and threw themselves joyously into life as housewives. For the youngest, the new wives and mothers, this was the only dream. They are the ones who quit high school and college to marry, or marked time in some job in which they had no real interest until they married. These women are very "feminine" in the usual sense, and yet they still suffer the problem....

If I am right, the problem that has no name stirring in the minds of so many American women today, is not a matter of loss of femininity or too much education, or the demands of domesticity. It is far more important than anyone recognizes. It is the key to these other new and old problems that have been torturing women and their husbands and children, and puzzling their doctors and educators for years. It may well be the key to our future as a nation and a culture. We can no longer ignore that voice within women that says: "I want something more than my husband and my children and my home."

National Organization for Women, *Statement of Purpose* (1966)

We, men and women who hereby constitute ourselves as the National Organization for Women, believe that the time has come for a new movement toward true equality for all women in America, and toward a fully equal partnership of the sexes, as part of the world-wide revolution of human rights now taking place within and beyond our national borders.

The purpose of NOW is to take action to bring women into full participation in the mainstream of American society now, exercising all the privileges and responsibilities thereof in truly equal partnership with men.

We believe the time has come to move beyond the abstract argument, discussion and symposia over the status and special nature of women, which has raged in America in recent years; the time has come to confront, with concrete action, the conditions that now prevent women from enjoying the equality of opportunity and freedom of choice which is their right as individual Americans, and as human beings.

NOW is dedicated to the proposition that women first and foremost are human beings, who, like all other people in our society, must have the chance to develop their fullest human potential. We believe that women can achieve such equality only by accepting to the full the challenges and responsibilities they share with all other people in our society, as part of the decision-making mainstream of American political, economic and social life.

We organize to initiate or support action, nationally or in any part of this nation, by individuals or organizations, to break through the silken curtain or prejudice and discrimination against women in government, industry, the professions, the churches, the political parties, the judiciary, the labor unions; in education, science, medicine, law, religion and every other field of importance in American society....

There is no civil rights movement to speak for women, as there has been for Negroes and other victims of discrimination. The National Organization for Women must therefore begin to speak.

WE BELIEVE that the power of American law, and the protection guaranteed by the U.S. Constitution to the civil rights of all individuals, must be effectively applied and enforced to isolate and remove patterns of sex discrimination, to ensure equality of opportunity in employment and education, and equality of civil and political rights and responsibilities on behalf of women, as well as for Negroes and other deprived groups.

We realize that women's problems are linked to many broader questions of social justice; their solution will require concerted action by many groups. Therefore, convinced that human rights for all are indivisible, we expect to give active support to the common cause of equal rights for all those who suffer discrimination and deprivation, and we call upon together organizations committed to such goals to support our efforts toward equality for women.

WE DO NOT ACCEPT the token appointment of a few women to high-level positions in government and industry as a substitute for a serious continuing effort to recruit and advance women according to their individual abilities. To this end, we urge American government and industry to mobilize the same resources of ingenuity and command with which they have solved problems of far greater difficulty than those now impeding the progress of women....

WE REJECT the current assumptions that a man must carry the sole burden of supporting himself, his wife, and a family, and that a woman is automatically entitled to lifelong support by a man upon her marriage; or that marriage, home and family are primarily a woman's world and responsibility—hers, to dominate, his to support. We believe that a true partnership between the sexes demands a different concept of marriage, an equitable sharing of the responsibilities of home and children, and of the economic burdens of their support. We believe that proper recognition should be given to the economic and social value of homemaking and child care. To these ends, we will seek to open a reexamination of laws and mores governing marriage and divorce, for we believe that the current state of "half-equality" between the sexes discriminates against both men and women, and is the cause of much unnecessary hostility between the sexes.

WE BELIEVE that women must now exercise their political rights and responsibilities as American citizens. They must refuse to be segregated on the basis of sex into separate-and-not-equal ladies' auxiliaries in the political parties, and they must demand representation according to their numbers in the regularly constituted party committees—at local, state, and national levels—and in the informal power structure, participating fully in the selection of candidates and political decision-making, and running for office themselves.

IN THE INTERESTS OF THE HUMAN DIGNITY OF WOMEN, we will protest and endeavor to change the false image of women now prevalent in the mass media, and in the texts, ceremonies, laws and practices of our social institutions. Such images perpetuate contempt for women by society and by women for themselves. We are similarly opposed to all policies and practices—in church, state, college, factory or office—which, in the guise of protectiveness, not only deny opportunities but also foster in women self-denigration, dependence, and evasion of responsibility, undermine their confidence in their own abilities and foster contempt for women....

Frances Sugre, Diary of a Rent Striker (1964)

Wednesday, Feb. 5: I got up at 6:45. The first thing to do was light the oven. The boiler was broke so not getting the heat. All the tenants together bought the oil. We give $7.50 for each tenant. But the boiler is old and many things we don't know about the pipes, so one of the men next door who used to be superintendent is trying to fix. I make the breakfast for the three children who go to school. I give then orange juice, oatmeal, scrambled eggs, and Ovaltine. They have lunch in school and sometimes they don't like the food and won't eat, so I say you have a good breakfast. Miss Christine Washington stick her head in at 7:30 and say she go to work. I used to live on ground floor and she was all the time trying to get me move to third floor next door to her because this place vacant and the junkies use it and she scared the junkies break the wall to get into her place and steal everything because she live alone and go to work.

I'm glad I come up here to live because the rats so big downstairs. We all say the "rats is as big as cats." I had a baseball bat for the rats. It's lucky me and the children never got bit. The children go to school and I clean the house and empty the pan in the bathroom that catches the water dripping from pipe into the big hole in the ceiling. You have to carry umbrella to the bathroom sometimes. I got to the laundry place this afternoon and I wash again on Saturday because I change my kids' clothes every day because I don't want them dirty to attract the rats....

After I go out to a rent strike meeting at night, I come home and the women tell me that five policemen came and broke down the door of the vacant apartment of the ground floor where we have meetings for the tenants in our building. They come looking for something—maybe junkies, but we got nothing in there only paper and some chairs and tables. They knocked them all over. The women heard the policemen laughing. When I came up to my place the children already in bed and I bathe myself and then I go to bed and read the newspaper until 11:30.

Thursday, Feb. 6: I wake up at six o'clock and I went into the kitchen to heat a bottle for my baby. When I put the light on in the kitchen I yelled so loud that I don't know if I disturbed the neighbors. There was a big rat coming out from the garbage pail.

Friday, Feb. 7: This morning I woke up a little early. The baby woke up at five o'clock. I went to the kitchen but this time I didn't see the rat.

After the girls left for school I started washing the dishes and cleaning the kitchen. I am thinking about their school. Today they ain't teaching enough. My oldest girl is 5.9 in reading. This is low level in reading. I go to school and English teacher tell me they ain't got enough books to read and that's why my daughter behind. I doesn't care about integration like that. It doesn't bother me. I agree with boycott for some reasons. To get better education and better teachers and better materials in school. I don't like putting them in buses and sending them away. I like to stay here and change the system. Some teachers has to be changed. My girl take Spanish in junior high school and I say to her, "Tell your teacher I'm going to be in school one day to teach him Spanish because I don't know where he learns to teach Spanish but it ain't Spanish."

I'm pretty good woman. I don't bother anyone. But I got my rights. I fight for them. I don't care about jail. Jail don't scare me. If I have to go to jail, I go. I didn't steal. I didn't kill nobody. There's no record for me. But if I have to go, I go.

Saturday, Feb. 8: A tenant called me and asked me what was new in the building because she works daytimes. She wanted to know about the junkies. Have they been on the top floor where the vacant apartment is? That's why I have leaking from the ceiling. The junkies on the top floor break the pipes and take the fixtures and the sink and sell them and that's where the water comes ... I'm not ascared of the junkies. I open the floor and I see the junkies I tell them to go or I call the police. Many people scared of them, but they scared of my face. I got a baseball bat for the rats and the junkies.... I know my rights and I know my self-respect. After supper I played cards (casino) for two hours with the girls and later I got dressed and I went to a party for the rent strike. This party was to get funds for the cause. I had a good time....

Sunday, Feb. 9: I dressed up in an hurry to got to church. When I got to church I pray for to have better house and have a decent living. I hope He's hearing. But I don't get discouraged on Him. I have faith. I don't care how cold I am I never lose my faith. When I come out of church I was feeling so good.

Monday, Feb. 10: At 9:30 a man came to fix the rat holes. He charged me only $3. Then one of the tenants came to tell me that we only had oil for today and every tenant would have to give $7.50 to send for more oil. I went to see some tenants to tell them there is no more oil. We all have to cooperate with money for the oil....

Tuesday, Feb. 11: This morning was too cold in the house that I had to light the oven and heat hot water. We had no steam, the boiler is not running good. I feel miserable. You know when the house is cold you can't do nothing. When the girls left for school I went back to bed. I just got up at 11:30 and this house is so cold. Living in a cold apartment is terrible....

Wednesday, Feb. 12: I wake up around 5 o'clock and the first thing I did was light the oven and the heater so when the girls wake up is a little warm. I didn't call them 'til 11 because they didn't have to got to school. It is still so cold they trembling. You feel like crying looking your children in this way.

I think if I stay a little longer in this kind of living I'm going to be dead duck. I know that to get into a project you have to have somebody prominent to back you up. Many people got to the projects and they don't even need them. I had been feeling applications I don't know since when. This year I feel another one. This year I *don't vote* for nobody. Maybe my vote don't count, but don't forget if you have fourteen cents you need another penny so you take the bus or the subway. At least I clean my house and you could eat on the floor. The rest of the day I didn't do nothing. I was so mad all day long. I cooked a big pot of soup. I leave it to God to help me. I have faith in Him.

Thursday, Feb. 13: I couldn't get up this morning. The house was so cold that I came out of bed at 7:15.... Later on, the inspector came. They were suppose to come to every apartment and look all violations. They knock at the door and asked if anything had been fixed. I think even the inspectors are afraid of this slum condition and that's why they didn't dare to come inside. I don't blame them. They don't want to take a rat or any bug to their houses or get dirty in this filthy houses. My little girl came from school with Valentine she made for me. Very pretty. At 8:30 I went downstairs to a meeting we had. We discuss about why there is no heat. We agreed to give $10 to fix the boiler for the oil....

Friday, Feb. 14 I didn't write this about Friday in my book until this Saturday morning, because Friday night I sick and so cold. It is really hard to believe that this happens here in New York and richest city in the world. But such is Harlem and hope. Is this the way to live. I rather go to the Moon in the next trip.

1. Although based upon surveys of upper middle-class women, *The Feminine Mystique* express the views of many women. What exactly was the "problem that has no name"?

2. For women like Betty Friedan what are the shortcomings of required domesticity?

3. From the *Statement of Purpose* what were the goals of the National Organization for Women?

4. How radical do the goals of NOW seem to you? Do they extend beyond equal opportunity, equal pay for equal work, and shared domestic responsibilities?

5. To what extent would the problems of women like Frances Sugre be solved by achieving the NOW goals?

CHAPTER 31

To a New Conservatism, 1969–1988

SUMMARY

The charismatic Ronald Reagan led a conservative resurgence that culminated in his two terms as president during the 1980s. Conservatives rejected the Cold War liberalism of Truman and Johnson, calling instead for less government, a balanced budget, family values, and peace through strength.

The Tempting of Richard Nixon

Nixon's controversial presidency included a shift in liberal reform measures to the states, an easing of tensions with the Soviet Union, new relations with China, and an end to the unpopular war in Vietnam. He also resigned in disgrace after the Watergate scandal.

Détente

Strongly influenced by National Security Adviser Henry Kissinger, Nixon pursued a foreign policy of détente—a relaxation of tension—with the Soviet Union and with China. Nixon signed the Strategic Arms Limitation Talks (SALT) treaty in 1972. Following his plan to use American trade to thaw relations, the president engineered sales of grain and technology to the Soviet Union.

Ending the Vietnam War

After a secret bombing campaign against communist supply lines in neutral Cambodia resulted in increased anti-war protests at home, Nixon called for secret negotiations between Kissinger and North Vietnam's Le Duc Tho. This meeting produced a truce, signed in January 1973. Accepting what amounted to a disguised surrender, the United States agreed to remove its troops in return for the release of all American prisoners of war, and the American role in Vietnam was over.

The Watergate Scandal

The president's attempt to cover up his administration's illegal actions unraveled in early 1973. After the House Judiciary Committee voted three articles of impeachment and the Supreme Court ordered the release of the tapes of presidential conversations, Nixon chose to resign on August 9, 1974. The Watergate Scandal revealed the strengths and weaknesses of the American political system, and prodded many to question the nation's political leadership.

Oil and Inflation

While the Watergate scandal raged in Washington, war in the Middle East threatened the flow of oil into the United States. The 1970s also witnessed changes in the American economy: inflation rose dramatically, heavy industry jobs left the country, union membership fell, and environmentalists called for cleaner energy.

War and Oil
In October 1973, Arab nations imposed an oil embargo against the United States to force American pressure on Israel to return Arab lands taken from Egypt, Syria, and Jordan during the Six Day War of 1967. Henry Kissinger soon negotiated an end to the embargo, but dramatic increases in oil prices remained and alerted Americans to an energy crisis.

The Great Inflation
The startling price increases of the 1970s resulted from swollen deficits from the Vietnam War, a worldwide shortage of food, and especially the six-fold increase in oil prices. Wages for many Americans failed to keep pace, and actions by the Federal Reserve Board increased interest rates.

Private Lives, Public Issues
American families and the private lives of individuals changed beginning in the 1970s and continuing throughout the century.

The Changing American Family
During the 1970s, families became smaller, divorce rates increased, female-headed households increased, unmarried couples doubled, and married couple households with children decreased. These changes, among others, strongly chipped away at the traditional nuclear family perceived by many as the norm.

Gains and Setbacks for Women
Women made dramatic strides in the last third of the 1970s, but still faced discrimination and lower pay. The Equal Rights Amendment failed to pass, and women have found their right to choose under attack as *Roe* v. *Wade* was assaulted in the courts. The most encouraging development for women came in business ownership.

The Gay Liberation Movement
A new pride movement, in some ways modeled after the ethnic pride movements of the same period, emerged as homosexual men and women across the country fought against discrimination based on sexual orientation and for acceptance. Violence and discrimination against gays and lesbians has diminished, but continues. The AIDS epidemic that began in the 1980s shifted earlier gay rights groups to focus on health and sex education.

Politics and Diplomacy after Watergate
Conflicts between the president and Congress hastened ineffective leadership and hampered the necessary handling of the many 1970s crises.

The Ford Administration
Ford's popularity rapidly declined with a pardon of Nixon and a seeming ineptitude in dealing with Congress. When congressional investigations revealed excesses by the CIA, Ford approved reform of the agency and appointed George H. W. Bush as its new director.

Carter and American Malaise
Former Georgia Governor Jimmy Carter won the Democratic nomination by portraying himself as an honest and candid "outsider," untainted by Washington politics. Although an intelligent politician initially, Carter never offered the public a clear sense of direction. Tension and conflict among his officials, among numerous other problems, doomed the administration to failure.

Trouble Abroad
Carter held out the lure of American economic aid in hopes of moderating the leftist Sandinista regime in Nicaragua as well as the right-wing military junta in El Salvador. Neither venture proved successful. The Camp David accords of 1978 led ultimately to a peace treaty between Egypt and Israel, but left the problems of the Palestinian Arabs unsettled. In 1979, Iranian mobs in Teheran seized the American embassy and fifty-eight American hostages. The failure of diplomacy, economic reprisals, and a military rescue mission to free the hostages steadily eroded the nation's confidence in Carter's leadership.

The Reagan Revolution
Despite Nixon's troubles during Watergate, Republicans regained power in 1980 behind the charismatic leadership of Ronald Reagan. The unrest of the 1960s and economic troubles of the 1970s had many Americans yearning for conservatism.

The Election of 1980
The failure of Carter's economic policies and America's weak image abroad were issues seized by Reagan in the 1980 campaign. Reagan captured 51 percent of the popular vote and Republicans made major gains in the congressional elections. The election also signaled the demise of the New Deal coalition as blue collar workers and Jews increasingly embraced the Republicans.

Cutting Taxes and Spending
Reagan supported supply-side economics, seeking to diminish the tax burden on the private sector and enhance investment-oriented growth. Reduction of government spending would hopefully ease inflation. Major congressional victories gave Reagan a 30 percent cut in income taxes over three years and significant reduction of domestic appropriations for social services.

Reagan and the World
Determined to alter America's shattered image abroad, Reagan continued the hard line adopted toward Russia and the massive military buildup begun by Carter. New military expenditures went to develop new weapons systems, and to an expanded navy.

Challenging the "Evil Empire"
Denouncing Soviet- sponsored terrorism and human rights violations, Reagan depicted the Soviet Union as the "evil empire" and pushed for the deployment of additional missiles in European NATO locations. Prompted by Soviet intransigence on arms control, the United States quickened the pace of Strategic Defense Initiative ("Star Wars") research and development. The nuclear arms race reached an unprecedented level.

Confrontation in Central America

In Nicaragua, the Sandinistas overthrew the Somoza regime in 1979. Carter had previously authorized economic aid for the Sandinistas; Reagan reversed that policy. Accusing the Sandinistas of accepting Cuban and Soviet military assistance, the president opted for covert support for the anti-government Contras.

Trading Arms for Hostages

An initiative in 1985 aimed at improving American influence in the Middle East by establishing contact with moderates in Iran deteriorated into an arms for hostages deal. In 1986, members of the National Security Council staff tied this initiative to an illegal and unconstitutional scheme to funnel arms profits to the Contras in Nicaragua. Although Reagan was never personally tied to the diversion of funds, his popularity dropped rapidly.

Reagan the Peacemaker

Mikhail Gorbachev's ascendancy as the Soviet leader in 1985, offered hope for improved U.S.-Soviet relations. With Reagan hoping to rebound from the Iran-Contra affair and Gorbachev anxious to repair the Soviet economy, the two world leaders held a series of meetings during Reagan's second term. The resulting treaty, signed in late 1987, banned intermediate nuclear missiles. U.S.-Soviet cooperation eased tensions in global hot spots, further enhancing Reagan's reputation.

Conclusion: Challenging the New Deal

The Reagan Revolution left a deep imprint on the American political landscape. The New Deal coalition had broke down, the welfare state was slashed, and the private sector was freed of government regulation and taxes. An era of "small government" had begun.

LEARNING OBJECTIVES

After mastering this chapter, you should be able to:

1. Explain Nixon's first-term goals and accomplishments in domestic affairs.

2. Discuss the objectives of Nixon's foreign policy and his strategy for ending the Vietnam War.

3. Explain the causes of the Watergate scandal and the role played by President Nixon in it. What were the effects on the American political system?

4. Describe the causes of the energy crisis as well as its impact on the American economy and political scene.

5. Describe changing family patterns, the "gains and setbacks" for women, and the rise of the Gay Liberation Movement.

6. Compare and contrast the approaches taken by presidents Ford and Carter to correct America's economic problems.

7. Account for the public disenchantment with Carter that resulted in his one-term presidency.

8. Analyze Carter's successes and failures in dealing with foreign affairs.

9. Discuss the reasons for a conservative resurgence and the election of Ronald Reagan in 1980.

10. Identify the victories as well as the disappointments of Reagan's first-term domestic policies.

11. Discuss Reagan's first-term approach to the Soviet Union, the arms race, and options for the future.

12. Analyze Reagan's foreign policies in Central America.

13. Explain the events of the Iran-Contra affair.

14. Analyze the motivations and results of Reagan's attempts at peacemaking during his second term.

GLOSSARY

To build your social science vocabulary, familiarize yourself with the following terms:

1. **strident** harsh; shrill. "In contrast to Goldwater's strident rhetoric, Reagan used relaxed, confident, and persuasive terms."

2. **ideologue** an adherent of a particular set of ideas. "without appearing to be a rigid ideologue of the right."

3. **think tanks** associated researchers who study and report on important questions of public policy. "Scholars and academics on the right flourished in new 'think tanks.'"

4. **détente** a relaxation of strained tensions or relations. "Nixon and Kissinger shrewdly played the China card as their first step toward achieving détente with the Soviet Union."

5. **scapegoat** person upon whom the blame for the mistakes or crimes of others is thrust. "… Nixon was compelled to fire aide John Dean, who had directed the cover-up but who now refused to become a scapegoat."

6. **executive privilege** authority of the president to refuse to divulge conversations among members of the executive branch, presumably to provide protection on matters of national security. "At first the president tried to invoke executive privilege to withhold the tapes."

7. **embargo** governmental order prohibiting outgoing shipments. "The Arab oil embargo had a disastrous effect on the American economy."

8. **tight-money** an economic policy in which credit is difficult to secure and interest rates are high. "The new tight-money policy served only to heighten inflation."

9. **Third World** countries of the world plagued by poverty, particularly in Africa, Asia and South America. "New steel producers in western Europe, Japan, and the Third World …"

10. **nuclear family** a family consisting of a father, a mother, and their children. "The traditional nuclear family of the 1950s no longer prevailed in America …"

11. **malaise** a generalized, nonspecific feeling of discomfort. "… a week after what his critics called the 'national malaise' speech …"

12. **deterrence** the act or process of discouraging or preventing. "the deadly trap of deterrence, with its reliance on the threat of nuclear retaliation to keep the peace."

13. **covert** hidden; secret. "Reagan opted for covert action."

IDENTIFICATION

Briefly identify the meaning and significance of the following terms:

1. Henry Kissinger _____

   _____

2. SALT I _____

   _____

3. the "plumbers" _____

   _____

4. OPEC _____

   _____

5. The Stonewall riots _____

   _____

6. Camp David accords _____

   _____

7. the Iranian hostage crisis _____

   _____

8. the Moral Majority _____

   _____

9. Sandra Day O'Connor _____

   _____

10. Oliver North _____

    _____

MATCHING

A. Match the following nations with the appropriate description:

_____1. China

_____2. Cambodia

_____3. Israel

_____4. Iran

_____5. El Salvador

Israel **a.** following the Six Day War of 1967, this nation took possession of the Golan Heights, the Sinai Peninsula, and the West Bank

Panama **b.** nation with which the United States agreed in 1977 to a later return of land and a canal

Cambodia **c.** secret bombings of this nation in 1970 sparked massive antiwar demonstrations

China **d.** Nixon's tour of this nation in 1972 marked first step in ultimate U.S. recognition

Iran **e.** 1979 revolution in this nation sparked deep resentments that later turned on the United States

El Salvador **f.** nation offered U.S. economic aid by Carter in attempt to encourage democratic reforms

B. Match the following Watergate figures with the appropriate description:

_____1. John J. Sirica

_____2. John Dean

_____3. John Mitchell

_____4. James McCord

_____5. Archibald Cox

a. attorney general and head of Nixon's reelection committee later receiving a jail term for his role in Watergate

b. Watergate special prosecutor, fired by Nixon for demanding release of presidential tapes

c. White House counsel who refused to play the role of scapegoat and revealed the president's involvement in the cover-up

d. chair of the House Judiciary Committee, which conducted impeachment proceedings

e. judge presiding over the trial of the Watergate burglars

f. first Watergate burglar to break his silence and expose the cover-up

COMPLETION

Answer the question or complete the statement by filling in the blanks with the correct word or words.

1. Student protest over Nixon's bombing of Cambodia in 1970 ended in tragedy at _____ when four students were killed by National Guardsmen breaking up a demonstration.

2. After the October War of 1973, Arab members of _____ cut oil production until Israel agreed to return disputed lands.

3. The 1973 Supreme Court decision *Roe v. Wade* stated that women had the Constitutional right to abortion during the early stages of pregnancy.

4. During the Ford administration, a Senate committee headed by Frank Church of Idaho investigated the actions of the _____, a federal agency involved in plots to assassinate foreign leaders.

5. In mid-1979, dictator Anastasio Somoza of _____ capitulated to the Sandinistas, the leaders of a leftist regime that developed close ties with Castro's Cuba.

6. The Cold War resumed with full fury in December 1979 when the Soviet Union invaded _____, a move designed to ensure a regime friendly to the USSR.

7. Reagan's policy of *Supply-side economics* called for massive tax cuts to promote investment by the private sector.

8. Popularly known as "Star Wars," the _____ this antimissile defense system escalated the arms race .

9. The _____ was a secret government program that used the money from arms sales to Iran to finance Contra rebels in Nicaragua.

10. Gorbachev was intent upon improving Soviet relations with the United States as a part of his new policies of _____ (restructuring the Soviet economy) and _____ (political openness).

TRUE/FALSE

Mark the following statements either T (True) or F (False).

_____1.   Rising prices during the early 1970s was solely a result of the oil embargo.

_____2.   Although a symbolic first step toward nuclear arms control, the United States Senate bitterly opposed the SALT I treaty because it allowed the Soviets a strategic advantage by recognizing their existing lead in numbers of missiles.

_____3.   Nixon's determination to stonewall the public on any White House involvement in the Watergate burglary proved successful in the short run, but eventually the cover-up led to his downfall.

_____4.   The Equal Rights Amendment (ERA) was never approved by Congress.

_____5.   In January 1979, the United States and China exchanged ambassadors, thereby completing the reconciliation that Nixon had begun in 1971.

_____6.   President Clinton fulfilled a campaign promise by passing legislation allowing gays to openly serve in the military.

_____7.   President Carter avoided military means while successfully negotiating a diplomatic resolution to the Iranian hostage crisis.

_____8.   In the election of 1980, the only group of traditional Democrats to remain loyal to the party was that of African Americans.

_____9.   President Reagan favored an increase in federally funded domestic programs to improve the American economy.

_____10.   The central tenet of Reagan's foreign policy was that the Soviet Union was a deadly enemy that threatened the well-being and security of the United States.

MULTIPLE CHOICE

Circle the one alternative that *best* completes the statement or answers the question.

1. Since 1970, the American family changed in that
   a. the number of married couples with children increased.
   b. the number of adults living alone surpassed the number of married couples with children.
   c. the number of unmarried couples declined.
   d. there was a sharp decline in the number of children born to women over the age of thirty.

2. Henry Kissinger, Nixon's chief foreign policy advisor
   a. viewed the Cold War as an ideological struggle against communism.
   b. saw the Cold War as great-power rivalry that should be managed, not won.
   c. disliked academic approaches to international affairs.
   d. opposed U.S. recognition of China.

3. The most successful tactic employed by Nixon in calming American protest as he sought an end to the Vietnam War was his
   a. renewed bombing of communist supply lines.
   b. hard-line negotiations with Hanoi.
   c. gradual withdrawal of American troops.
   d. order for the mining of Haiphong harbor.

4. The truce ending the Vietnam War did *not* require or allow which of the following provisions?
   a. the release of all American prisoners of war
   b. U.S. removal of its troops from South Vietnam within sixty days
   c. North Vietnamese troops to remain in South Vietnam
   d. the removal of all communist troops from South Vietnam

5. The most damaging evidence against Nixon in the impeachment proceedings was the
   a. existence of taped conversations implicating him in attempts to cover up details of the Watergate break-in.
   b. testimony of John Dean revealing Nixon's personal involvement.
   c. record of orders by Nixon to use government agencies to "punish" his enemies.
   d. illegal campaign contributions made to the Committee to Re-Elect the President.

6. Unlike prior executive branch scandals, Watergate
   a. resulted in the impeachment of a president.
   b. led to a decline in power exercised by Congress.
   c. involved a lust for power rather than money.
   d. All of the above.

7. The Yom Kippur or October War of 1973
   a. lasted only six days, as Israeli military dominance prevailed over Arab aggression.
   b. resulted in Israeli seizure of the Golan Heights from Syria, the Sinai Peninsula from Egypt, and Jerusalem and the West Bank from Jordan.
   c. led to American demands for a strong pro-Israeli peace settlement.
   d. led to the Arab oil embargo, imposed to pressure Israel to return Arab lands seized in 1967.

8. The rampant inflation of the 1970s was caused by all of the following *except* the
   a. heavy government expenditures on the Vietnam War.
   b. heavy tax increases imposed by the Carter administration.
   c. worldwide shortage of food.
   d. six fold increase in petroleum prices.

9. By 1990, women achieved
   a. ratification of the Equal Rights Amendment.
   b. earning the same amount as men.
   c. a dramatic increase in the number of females serving as corporate officers.
   d. None of the above.

10. Jimmy Carter attracted votes in the election of 1976 with his
    a. self-portrayal as a candid and honest "outsider" offering fresh leadership.
    b. forceful stands on the major issues.
    c. calculated appeals to the affluent, the well-educated, and conservative suburbanites.
    d. well-reasoned political philosophy and clear sense of direction.

11. In the Camp David Accords, President Carter mediated a peace agreement between
    a. Egypt and Israel.
    b. the Soviet Union and the United States.
    c. Nicaragua and El Salvador.
    d. Cuba and the United States.

12. During the 1970s and 1980s, gay rights activists achieved
    a. laws forbidding discrimination in housing and employment based on sexuality.
    b. a gay rights plank in the Democratic National Platform.
    c. the American Psychological Association no longer classifying homosexuality as a mental disorder.
    d. All of the above.

13. The Intermediate Nuclear Forces (INF) Treaty was
    a. one of the few foreign policy successes of the Carter administration.
    b. designed to keep nuclear weapons out of Cuba.
    c. the most significant arms-control agreement since SALT I in 1972.
    d. All of the above.

14. The Reagan administration policy to trade arms for hostages was flawed in that it
    a. was criminal because of the Boland Amendment.
    b. failed to win compliance from the Iranians.
    c. led to the seizure of American soldiers.
    d. encouraged an end to the war between Iran and Iraq.

15. The summit meetings between Reagan and Gorbachev led to an agreement in 1987 to
    a. abolish all nuclear weapons in a decade.
    b. ban all intermediate nuclear weapons.
    c. abandon plans for any "star wars" projects.
    d. reduce conventional force around the world.

THOUGHT QUESTIONS

To check your understanding of the key issues of this period, solve the following problems:

1. How did Nixon and Kissinger effectively reshape American foreign policy?

2. The text argues that the Watergate episode "revealed both the weaknesses and strength of the American political system." Explain.

3. What caused the "energy crisis" of the 1970s? Discuss the political as well as economic consequences of the energy crisis.

4. Discuss the successes and failures of the Carter administration in terms of foreign policy. What problems eroded the policy of détente and renewed a Cold War atmosphere during Carter's administration?

5. Did Reagan's victory in 1980 signal a major realignment in American politics with the Republicans becoming the majority party?

6. Analyze the success of the Reagan administration in curing the nation's economic woes.

7. Reagan began his administration by characterizing the Soviet Union as a deadly enemy and the "evil empire." By the end of his presidency, however, he had assumed the role of peacemaker and pointed to the end of the Cold War. Trace the evolution of events that allowed this change.

8. The deal to trade United States arms to Iran for hostages was bad policy, but the Iran-Contra affair was criminal. Explain.

CRITICAL THINKING QUESTIONS

Read the following selections: "Conclusion on Impeachment Resolution" (1974) by the House Judiciary Committee and "The 'Malaise' Speech" (1979) by President Jimmy Carter. Answer the questions following the reading selections.

House Judiciary Committee, "Conclusion on Impeachment Resolution" (1974)

After the Committee on the Judiciary had debated whether or not it should recommend Article I to the House of Representatives, 27 of the 38 Members of the Committee found that the evidence before it could only lead to one conclusion: that Richard M. Nixon, using the powers of his high office, engaged, personally and through his subordinates and agents, in a course of conduct or plan designed to delay, impede, and obstruct the investigation of the unlawful entry on June 17, 1972, into the headquarters of the Democratic National Committee; to cover up, conceal and protect those responsible; and to conceal the existence and scope of other unlawful activities.

This finding is the only one that can explain the President's involvement in a pattern on undisputed acts that occurred after the break-in and that cannot otherwise be rationally explained.

1. The President's decision on June 20, 1972, not to meet with his Attorney General, his chief of staff, his counsel, his campaign director, and his assistant, John Ehrlichman, whom he had put in charge of the investigation-when the subject of their meeting was the Watergate matter.

2. The erasure of that portion of the recording of the President's conversation with White House chief of staff H. R. Haldeman on June 20, 1972, which dealt with Watergate-when the President stated that the tapes had been under his "sole and personal control."

3. The President's public denial on June 22, 1972, of the involvement of members of the Committee for the Re-election of the President [CREEP] or of the White House staff in the Watergate burglary, in spite of having discussed Watergate, on or before June 22, 1972, with Haldeman, special counsel Charles Colson, and former attorney general John Mitchell [head of CREEP]—all persons aware of that involvement.

4. The President's directive to Haldeman on June 23, 1972, to have the CIA request the FBI to curtail its Watergate investigation.

5. The President's refusal, on July 6, 1972, to inquire and inform himself what Patrick Gray, Acting Director of the FBI, meant by his warning that some of the President's aides were "trying to mortally wound him."

6. The President's discussion with Erlichman on July 8, 1972, of clemency for the Watergate burglars, more than two months before the return of any indictments.

7. The President's public statement on August 29, 1972, a statement later shown to be untrue, that an investigation by [White House counsel] John Dean "indicates no one in the White House staff, no one in the Administration, presently employed, was involved in this very bizarre incident."

8. The President's statement to Dean on September 14, 1972, the day that the Watergate indictments were returned without naming high CRP [CREEP] and White House officials, that Dean had handled his work skillfully, "putting your fingers in the dike every time that leaks have sprung here and sprung there," and that "you just try to button it up as well as you can and hope for the best." ...

In addition to this evidence, there was before the Committee the following evidence:

1. Beginning immediately after June 17, 1972, the involvement of each of the President's top aides and political associates, Haldeman, Mitchell, Ehrlichman, Colson, Dena, LaRue, Mardinan, Magruder, in the Watergate coverup....

Finally, there was before the Committee a record of public statement by the President between June 22, 1972 and June 9, 1974, deliberately contrived to deceive the courts, the Department of Justice, the Congress and the American people.

President Nixon's course of conduct following the Watergate break-in, as described in Article I, caused action not only by his subordinates but by the agencies of the United States, including the Department of Justice, the FBI, and the CIA. It required perjury, destruction of evidence, obstruction of justice, all crimes. But, most important, it required deliberate, contrived, and continuing deception of the American people.

President Nixon's actions resulted in manifest injury to the confidence of the nation and great prejudice to the cause of law and justice, and was subversive of constitutional government. His actions were contrary to his trust as President and unmindful of the solemn duties of his high office. It was this serious violation of Richard M. Nixon's constitutional obligations as President, and not the fact that violations of Federal criminal statutes occurred, that lies at the heart of Article I.

The Committee find, based upon clear and convincing evidence, that this conduct, detailed in the foregoing pages of this report, constitutes "high crimes and misdemeanors" as that term is used in Article II, Section 4 of the Constitution. Therefore, the Committee recommends that the House of Representatives exercise its constitutional power to impeach Richard M. Nixon.

Jimmy Carter, "The 'Malaise' Speech" (1979)

Good evening.

This is a special night for me. Exactly three years ago, on July 15, 1976, I accepted the nomination of my party to run for President of the United States. I promised you a President who is not isolated from the people who feels your pain, and who shared your dreams and who draws his strength and his wisdom from you....

Ten days ago I had planned to speak to you again about a very important subject—energy. For the fifth time I would have described the urgency of the problem and laid out a series of legislative recommendations to the Congress. But as I was preparing to speak, I began to ask myself the same question that I now know has been troubling many of you. Why have we not been able to get together as a nation to resolve our serious energy problem?

It's clear that the true problems of our Nation are much deeper-deeper than gasoline lines or energy shortages, deeper even than inflation or recession. And I realize more than ever that as President I need your help. So, I decided to reach out and listen to the voices of America.

I invited to Camp David people from almost every segment of our society-business and labor, teachers and preachers, Governors, mayors, and private citizens. And then I left Camp David to listen to other Americans, men and women like you. It has been an extraordinary ten days, and I want to share with you what I've heard....

These ten days confirmed my belief in the decency and the strength and the wisdom of the American people, but it also bore out some of my long-standing concerns about our Nation's underlying problems.

I know, of course, being president, that government actions and legislation can be very important. That's why I've worked hard to put my campaign promises into law-and I have to admit, with just mixed success. But after listening to the American people I have been reminded again that all the legislation in the world can't fix what's wrong with America. So, I want to speak to you first tonight about a subject even more serious than energy or inflation. I want to talk to you right now about a fundamental threat to American democracy.

I do not mean our political and civil liberties. They will endure. And I do not refer to the outward strength of America, a nation that is at peace tonight everywhere in the world, with unmatched economic power an military might.

The threat is nearly invisible in ordinary ways. It is a crisis of confidence. It is a crisis that strikes at the very heart and soul and spirit of our national will. We can see this crisis in the growing doubt about the meaning of our own lives and in the loss of a unity of purpose for our Nation.

The erosion of our confidence in the future is threatening to destroy the social and the political fabric of America....

The symptoms of this crisis of the American spirit are all around us. For the first time in the history of our country a majority of our people believe that the next five years will be worse than the past five years. Two-thirds of our people do not even vote. The productivity of American workers is actually dropping, and the willingness of Americans to save for the future has fallen below that of all other people in the Western world....

Often you see paralysis and stagnation and drift. You don't like it, and neither do I. What can we do?

First of all, we must face the truth, and then we can change our course. We simply must have faith in each other, faith in our course. We simply must have faith in each other, faith in our ability to govern ourselves, and faith in the future of this Nation. Restoring that faith and that confidence to America is now the most important task we face. It is a true challenge of this generation of Americans....

We are at a turning point in our history. There are two paths to choose. One is a path I've warned about tonight, the path that leads to fragmentation and self-interest. Down that road lies a mistaken idea of freedom, the right to grasp for ourselves some advantage over others. That path would be one of constant conflict between narrow interests ending in chaos and immobility. It is a certain route to failure.

All the traditions of our past, all the lessons of our heritage, all the promises of our future point to another path, the path of common purpose and the restoration of American values. That path leads to true freedom for our Nation and ourselves. We can take the first steps down that path as we begin to solve our energy problems....

1. What was the conclusion of the House Judiciary Committee regarding Nixon's role in the Watergate affair? How did he escape impeachment?

2. Upon what evidence did the House Judiciary Committee base their conclusion?

3. What does Carter perceive as the most fundamental threat to American democracy?

4. How do you think Americans responded to Carter's speech? Explain.

5. To what reasons did Carter attribute this threat or problem? What solutions did Carter propose?

CHAPTER 32

To the Twenty-first Century, 1989–2006

SUMMARY
With the collapse of the Soviet Union during the early 1990s, the United States emerged as the world's only superpower. With that title came awesome responsibility in world affairs. At home, the ebb and flow of the economy, changing demographics, and technological innovations challenged politicians and ordinary people alike.

The First President Bush
George Bush became president basking in the popularity of his predecessor, Ronald Reagan. Bush continued Reagan's domestic policy and found himself embroiled in complex foreign affairs as unforeseen events transpired around him.

Republicans at Home
George Bush sponsored few initiatives in education, health care, or environmental protection and maintained Reagan's theme of limited federal interference. He did, however, support the Americans with Disabilities Act (ADA). This act prohibited discrimination against the disabled in hiring, transportation, and public accommodations. Otherwise, Bush focused on two pressing problems: the nation's savings and loan industry and the nation's budget.

Ending the Cold War
An attempt at internal liberation by Chinese students proved tragically premature, while communist regimes in eastern Europe collapsed with surprising speed in mid-1989 once it became apparent that Gorbachev would not use Soviet power to support them. By late 1991, both Gorbachev and the Soviet Union became victims of the demise of communism. Bush negotiated first with Gorbachev, then with Russian President Boris Yeltsin on the START I and II treaties, significantly reducing nuclear weapons on each side.

The Gulf War
The end of the Cold War did not mean a world free of violence. In January 1991, the United States began an aerial assault leading to a ground offensive the next month against Iraq, aiming to free Kuwait and protect the vital oil resources of the Persian Gulf. Kuwait was liberated, but Iraq's brutal dictator, Saddam Hussein, remained in power in Iraq.

The Changing Faces of America
In the 1970s and 1980s, Americans moved internally at a significant rate, especially to the south and to the west and to urban areas. An influx of immigrants, primarily from developing nations, also changed the country's demographics, making the nation more ethnically diverse while creating social unrest.

A People on the Move
The flourishing of the Sunbelt states of the south and west that began during World War II with war industry continued during the Cold War as industries moved to areas with lower labor costs and better climates. Americans also increasingly moved to urban areas, enjoying better education and higher incomes, but also suffering from rising crime rates, traffic congestion, and higher costs of living. Another striking population trend was the marked increase in the number of elderly, many of whom suffered from health problems, lived in poverty, and voted regularly.

The Revival of Immigration
The number of immigrants to the nation rose sharply in the 1970s and 1980s, as millions arrived primarily from Latin America and Asia. The rising numbers of foreigners not only indicated the emergence of an increasingly diverse American society, but put pressure on public services and threatened to create a permanent underclass.

Emerging Hispanics
Hispanics, including Mexican Americans, Puerto Ricans, Cuban Americans, and other immigrants from Latin America, became the nation's largest ethnic group. Though differences among these groups exist, they are characterized by many similarities including their relative youth, high fertility rates, poverty, lack of education, and employment in low-paying jobs. The large number of undocumented aliens, primarily from Mexico, contributes to the exploitation of Hispanic Americans. The illegal immigration issue is further clouded by fears of porous borders in the age of terrorism.

Advance and Retreat for African Americans
The second largest of the nation's ethnic groups, African Americans, made some economic gains during the era (especially among educated, middle-class blacks), but still did not share proportionately in the nation's wealth. The acquittal of several white policemen who had beaten black motorist Rodney King led to an eruption of a bloody race riot in South Central Los Angeles in 1992. The aftermath of Hurricane Katrina in New Orleans in 2005 raised other racial issues. Although northern cities still claimed the heaviest concentration of African Americans, many migrated back to the south seeking a re-establishment of family ties or economic opportunity.

Americans from Asia and the Middle East
By the 1980s, Asian Americans were the nation's fastest-growing minority group, although they still only comprised a little over 3 percent of the total population. Compared to other minority groups, Asian Americans became relatively well educated and affluent, making remarkable progress and striking contributions to American culture. The major exception to this generalization was refugees from southeast Asia. Immigration from the Middle East followed the same trends as Asian immigration during the period, although Arab Americans often faced hatred following September 11.

The New Democrats
Democrats campaigned hard on the issue of the economy and were able to capture the White House in 1992 and keep it in 1996 (despite a Republican sweep in the midterm elections). They

gained political strength by moving away from their traditional reliance on big government, choosing moderate candidates, and tailoring programs to appeal to the middle class. The major figure in this Democratic revival was Bill Clinton.

Clinton and Congress

Despite struggling with Congress over many of his policies, Clinton won approval of the North American Free Trade Association (NAFTA) in 1993. Unresolved political and personal scandals for Clinton contributed to an overwhelming victory for Republicans in 1994 as they took control over both houses of Congress. Conservative Newt Gingrich introduced his Contract with America, which promoted traditional conservative ideology. Clinton managed to win re-election in 1996 as he blamed the Republican Congress for gridlock in government.

Scandal in the White House

The special prosecutor from the Whitewater investigation uncovered a sexual affair between Clinton and White House intern Monica Lewinsky. The House passed two articles of impeachment based on Clinton's denial of the affair, but the Senate acquitted him. The event tarnished Clinton's image and outraged the public, both for Clinton's actions and the public nature of this seemingly private affair.

Republicans Triumphant

A booming economy and no obvious threats to American security gave Democrats hope that they could retain the White House in 2000. A disputed election dashed their hopes.

The Disputed Election of 2000

The election of 2000 was dominated by two themes: the economic boom and prosperity of the 1990s and the sense of unrest spawned by the scandals of the Clinton administration, the Oklahoma City bombing, and Columbine. The entrance of consumer advocate Ralph Nader into the race on the Green Party ticket complicated the tight race between Democrat Al Gore and Republican George W. Bush. When charges of voter fraud emerged in Florida, the electoral decision rested with the courts, which declared Bush the victor five weeks later. Though election revealed splits in the electorate based on region, gender, race, ethnicity, and urbanity.

George W. Bush at Home

In an attempt to face the stalling economy head on, Bush pushed through significant tax cuts that turned the budget surplus into a sky rocketing annual deficit. Despite these cuts, the country entered an economic recession in 2001 coupled with extremely high unemployment rates and public disgust over corporate scandals and corrupt business practices that enabled CEOs to get rich while the rank and file lost their jobs, retirement funds, and savings. Though the economy began to recover in 2003, unemployment remained high as did America's lack of economic confidence.

The War on Terrorism

On September 11, 2001, Islamic militant terrorists killed over 3,500 people during attacks within the United States. President Bush provided the nation with comfort and leadership in the tragedy's wake and declared a war on terrorism. Osama bin Laden and his terrorist organization al Qaeda became the focal point, leading to an invasion of Afghanistan that ousted the extremist regime of the Taliban, but failed in capturing bin Laden. The establishment of the new Department of Homeland Security to guard against future attacks succeeded in upgrading airport security, but confronted a contradiction in the relentless detaining and questioning of Muslim Americans and the American commitment to civil liberties. Bush's handling of the war on terrorism netted him high approval ratings that obscured some Americans' doubts over his economic program.

A New American Empire?

The events of September 11 caused a shift in American foreign policy that rejected traditional forms of international cooperation, resting instead on a policy of American preeminence. As part of the continuing war on terrorism, President Bush identified Iran, Iraq, and North Korea as part of an "axis of evil." The new National Security Strategy included the United States' full acceptance of the role of global police and the assertion that the use of preemptive force was justified in order to maintain world peace. The first test for the NSS was Iraq where Saddam Hussein allegedly possessed weapons of mass destruction (WMDs) that were an immediate danger to the U.S. and the world. Failing to find any evidence of these weapons, the UN Security Council vetoed Bush's resolution authorizing force to compel Iraq's disarmament. The Bush administration ignored the veto and proceeded on its own with Britain as its major ally. The ground war ended quickly and Saddam was captured. With the failure to find WMDs, questions about the validity of the war arose, but were quieted with assertions of Saddam's brutal history as a dictator. Winning the peace was elusive as sectarian violence continued.

Bush Re-elected

Bush portrayed himself as an effective wartime leader to win re-election over Democrat John Kerry in a vitriolic election. Despite the close race, Bush declared a mandate and unsuccessfully sought to privatize Social Security.

Challenges of the New Century

The war in Iraq, a growing gap between rich and poor, health care woes, and environmental concerns all posed significant challenges as the nation entered a new century.

The Culture Wars Continue

The 1990s witnessed a re-invigoration of old controversial issues like affirmative action, abortion, gay rights, and evolution being taught in schools.

Prosperity—for Whom?

The economy recovered slightly after the recession during Bush's first term, but disturbing trends continued. The median family income declines, corporate executives received lavish salaries while the wages of ordinary workers remained flat, benefits fell, and nearly 13 percent of Americans lived in poverty. Americans also suffered from jobs going overseas and the increasing price of oil.

Doubting the Future

Americans became increasingly doubtful about the future as foreign investors held more of America's debt, health care costs rose, immigration destabilized the economy, and the environment seemed in peril.

Conclusion: The Paradox of Power

Never before has America been so powerful relative to the rest of the world, yet Americans felt increasingly at risk.

LEARNING OBJECTIVES

After mastering this chapter, you should be able to:

1. Explain the pressing domestic problems that preoccupied the Bush administration.

2. Discuss the reasons for and results of the Persian Gulf War in 1991.

3. Describe the series of events that signaled an end to the Cold War.

4. Analyze the causes and the results of those changes in the American population during the latter twentieth century and early twenty-first century.

5. Discuss the movement of the U.S. population during the latter twentieth century and early twenty-first century.

6. Assess the debate surrounding the revival of immigration to the U.S. during the latter twentieth century and early twenty-first century.

7. Discuss how demographic, economic, social, and political changes during this era impacted African Americans, Hispanics, Asian Americans and Middle-Eastern Americans.

8. Evaluate the performance of Bill Clinton as president in terms of domestic affairs.

9. Explain the controversies and scandals that swirled around the Clinton White House, and explain how and why Clinton survived these scandals.

10. Explain the significance of the Contract with America for the Republican party and its impact on the Clinton administration.

11. Account for the close election in 2000, and identify some of the challenges that Bush faced because of the narrow and controversial election returns.

12. Evaluate the performance of George W. Bush as president in terms of both domestic and foreign affairs.

13. Assess the impact of the events of September 11, 2001 on the U.S. and the world.

14. Analyze the ongoing culture wars in America.

15. Assess the gap in prosperity experienced by Americans and explain why many Americans are fearful of the future.

GLOSSARY

To build your social science vocabulary, familiarize yourself with the following terms:

1. **de facto** means in fact or in reality, even if not officially sanctioned. "During the Cold War, a de facto division of labor had developed."

2. **recriminations** bitter responses; retaliations. "Not only did Bush face recriminations from voters for breaking a campaign pledge…"

3. **repression** a state of forcible subjugation. "…full scale repression swept over China."

4. **martial law** a state in which all civil laws, rights and liberties are suspended and the military has direct rule. "Chinese leaders imposed martial law to quell the dissent…"

5. **undocumented aliens** illegal immigrants. "The entry of several million illegal immigrants…now known as undocumented aliens…"

6. **affluent** having an abundant supply of money or possessions of value "Compared to other minorities, Asian Americans were well educated and affluent."

7. **free trade** trade among countries that occurs without barriers such as tariffs or quotas. "Critics complained that free trade would cost American workers their jobs…"

8. **line-item veto** the power of an executive to veto parts of a bill. "The contract consisted of familiar conservative goals… a line-item veto for the president…"

9. **malfeasance** wrongful conduct by a public official. "The special prosecutor…turned over stone after stone in search of evidence of malfeasance…"

10. **affirmative action** a policy or program for correcting the effects of past discrimination in the employment or education of members of certain groups, as women, or African Americans. "…as affirmative action policies came under increasing scrutiny."

IDENTIFICATION

Briefly identify the meaning and significance of the following terms:

1. Americans with Disabilities Act (ADA)_____

_____

2. Operation Desert Storm_____

_____

3. Tiananmen Square _____

_____

4. Saddam Hussein_____

_____

5. undocumented aliens _____

_____

6. Rodney King_____

_____

7. Monica Lewinsky_____

_____

8. Contract With America_____

_____

9. election of 2000_____

_____

10. war on terrorism_____

_____

MATCHING

A. Match the following world leaders with the appropriate description:

_____1. Lech Walesa

a. leader of Iraq in 1990 when Kuwait was invaded and the subsequent First Gulf War

_____2. Boris Yeltsin

b. mastermind of the bombing of a federal building in Oklahoma City

_____3. Saddam Hussein

c. elected president of Russian Republic in 1991 after fall of communism

_____4. Mikhail Gorbachev

d. leader of the Polish solidarity movement that came to power in 1989

_____5. Osama bin Laden

e. Soviet leader who replaced the Brezhnev Doctrine with one that allowed Eastern Europeans to decide their own fate

f. leader of the terrorist organization al Qaeda that claimed responsibility for the September 11 attacks

B. Match the following political figures with the appropriate description:

_____1. Newt Gingrich

a. president at end of Cold War, suffered political defeat due to subsequent economic stagnation

_____2. Robert Dole

b. presidential candidate in 1996, lacked charisma and public sensitivity

_____3. H. Ross Perot

c. presidential candidate in 2004, seen as wavering on issues and disloyal for protesting Vietnam War after his return from combat

_____4. Ralph Nader

d. eccentric Texas billionaire, sought to focus attention of Americans on the dangers of the federal deficit

_____5. George H.W. Bush

e. consumer advocate, presidential candidate of the Green Party in 2000

f. Speaker of the House, sought to unite Republicans in support of conservative, ideological issues

COMPLETION

Answer the question or complete the statement by filling in the blanks with the correct word or words.

1. In June 1989, Lech Walesa and his Solidarity movement came to power in free elections in _____.

2. Newly elected president of the Russian Republic, _____ helped break up a military coup and secure the release of Gorbachev from right-wing plotters.

3. The _____, best defined as a broad band running across the country below the 37th parallel from the Carolinas to southern California, had begun to flourish with the buildup of military bases and defense plants during World War II.

4. In 2002, people of _____ origin became the nation's largest ethnic group.

5. The effects of _____ of August 2005 explicitly showed that poverty in America disproportionately affected African Americans.

6. Critics of _____ argued that it would undermine small American companies and send millions of American jobs to exploited and underpaid workers overseas.

7. The election of 2000 was decided when the _____ overruled the Florida Supreme Court's decision to recount the vote in that state, thus declaring George W. Bush the victor.

8. After the September 11 attacks, President Bush ordered an invasion of _____ to destroy the extremist Muslim government of that nation and al Qaeda too.

9. In declaring war against Saddam Hussein in 2003, the Bush administration justified their actions by alleging that Iraq had_____.

10. After the terrorist attacks of September 11, 2001, President Bush created the _____ to secure the nation against future attacks.

TRUE/FALSE

Mark the following statements either T (True) or F (False).

_____1.   President George H.W. Bush kept his campaign promise of "no new taxes" when he struck a deal with Congress to lower the federal budget deficit.

_____2.   The First Gulf War quickly moved from an operation to liberate Kuwait to an offensive to overthrow the regime of Saddam Hussein in Iraq.

_____3.   Compared to other minorities, Asian Americans were well educated and affluent.

_____4.   Perhaps the key factor in slow economic progress by Hispanic immigrants to the United States is lack of education.

_____5.   The debate over immigration has become more complicated since the events of September 11, 2001.

_____6.   During his first term President Clinton secured new taxes and spending cuts that created a deficit reduction helped fuel the economic boom of the 1990s.

_____7.   Clinton was impeached by the House and Senate for his action during the Monica Lewinsky affair.

_____8.   After Republicans gained control of Congress in 1994, they achieved almost all of the goals articulated in the Contract with America, despite the efforts of President Clinton to hinder them.

_____9.   George W. Bush won the popular vote in 2000, giving him the presidency.

_____10.   Upon invading Iraq in 2003, the American military found huge stockpiles of weapons of mass destruction.

MULTIPLE CHOICE

1. As president, George H.W. Bush
   a. signed the Americans with Disabilities Act.
   b. issued no new taxes.
   c. fought for family leave legislation.
   d. sponsored many initiatives in education.

2. The first president Bush refused to topple the regime of Saddam Hussein in Iraq for all of the following reasons except
   a. the stated purpose of the engagement was to only liberate Iraq.
   b. it was doubtful American forces could have conquered Iraq.
   c. he fear getting mired in a guerilla war.
   d. he was advised against it by Chairman of the Joint Chiefs of Staff, Colin Powell.

3. During the 1970s and 1980s, the American population was characterized by
   a. an internal movement of people to the Sunbelt region of the south and west.
   b. a remarkable influx of immigrants from Japan and Germany.
   c. an exodus of people moving away from congested urban areas.
   d. All of the above.

4. Which of the following minority groups enjoys a median family income higher than the national level?
   a. African Americans
   b. Hispanics
   c. Asian Americans
   d. Vietnamese Americans

5. The majority of immigrants to the United States during the latter third of the twentieth century came from
   a. Latin America and Eastern Europe.
   b. Asia and the Middle East.
   c. Latin America and Africa.
   d. Latin America and Asia.

6. As the United States entered the twenty-first century, African Americans
   a. had been moving south during the prior thirty years.
   b. increasingly earned high school diplomas.
   c. had a median family income less than two-thirds that of whites.
   d. All of the above.

7. Regarding the Monica Lewinsky affair, President Clinton was
   a. open and honest from the beginning.
   b. removed from office by the U.S. Senate.
   c. impeached by the House on two charges.
   d. All of the above.

8. All of the following candidates lost a presidential election between 1988 and 2000 EXCEPT
   a. George H.W. Bush.
   b. Robert Dole.
   c. Bill Clinton.
   d. Al Gore.

9. During his first term as president, Bill Clinton succeeded in having Congress approve
   a. the North American Free Trade Association.
   b. national health care reform.
   c. lower taxes for the wealthy.
   d. the largest tax cut in American history.

10. In his Contract with America, Newt Gingrich supported a
    a. balanced budget amendment to the Constitution.
    b. term limit for members of Congress.
    c. line-item veto for the president.
    d. All of the above.

11. What problems unnerved voters before the 2000 presidential election?
    a. President Clinton's perceived moral failings during his last term
    b. the Oklahoma city bombing
    c. the Columbine High School shooting
    d. All of the above.

12. George W. Bush's domestic policies have included
    a. a series of tax cuts to stimulate the economy.
    b. the appointment of the extremely conservative John Ashcroft as Attorney General.
    c. the No Child Left Behind program to reform education.
    d. All of the above.

13. George W. Bush's foreign policies have included
    a. the assertion of American preeminence.
    b. the full acceptance of the role of global police.
    c. the assertion of the right of preemptive use of force.
    d. All of the above.

14. Recent court cases have challenged
    a. affirmative action laws.
    b. abortion laws.
    c. gay rights.
    d. All of the above.

15. Since the beginning of the twenty-first century
    a. medical and retirement benefits for American workers have grown.
    b. the median family income declined.
    c. the poverty rate increased.
    d. All of the above.

THOUGHT QUESTIONS

To check your understanding of the key issues of this period, solve the following problems:

1. Discuss the events that signaled an end to the Cold War during the Bush administration.

2. In what ways did "Desert Storm" bring mixed blessings to the Bush administration? Why did Bush lose the election of 1992?

3. Who gains and who loses from illegal immigration? What immigration policies should the nation enforce?

4. Do you favor or oppose policies of affirmative action? Explain.

5. Is America today a "melting pot" or a "mosaic" of multiethnic diversity? What difference does it make which analogy is used?

7. Contrast American economic policies during the Clinton years and those of the George W. Bush administration. Which seemingly worked better? Explain.

8. In your opinion, how will history judge Bill Clinton as president? Explain.

9. Discuss the controversy in the election of 2000. Consider the impact the race had on George W. Bush's administration. Has he acted without a mandate? Explain.

10. Discuss George W. Bush's foreign policies. What have the ramifications been for the U.S. and the world?

11. What is the paradox of power?

CRITICAL THINKING QUESTIONS

Read Chapter 32 of the text and the following selections: "Address to the Nation Announcing Allied Military Action in the Persian Gulf" (1991) by President George H. W. Bush and "State of the Union Address" (2002) by President George W. Bush. Answer the questions following the reading selections.

George H. W. Bush, Address to the Nation Announcing Allied Military Action in the Persian Gulf (1991)

Just 2 hours ago, allied air forces began an attack on military targets in Iraq and Kuwait. These attacks continue as I speak. Ground forces are not engaged.

This conflict started August 2nd when the dictator of Iraq invaded a small and helpless neighbor. Kuwait, a member of the Arab League and a member of the United Nations, was crushed; its people, brutalized. Five months ago, Saddam Hussein (President of Iraq) started this cruel war against Kuwait. Tonight, the battle has been joined.

This military action, taken in accord with United Nations resolutions and with the consent of the United States Congress, follows months of constant and virtually endless diplomatic activity on the part of the United Nations, the United States, and many, many other countries. Arab leaders sought what became known as an Arab solution, only to conclude that Saddam Hussein was unwilling to leave Kuwait. Others traveled to Baghdad in a variety of efforts to restore peace and justice. Our Secretary of State, James Baker, held an historic meeting in Geneva, only to be totally rebuffed. This past weekend, in a last-ditch effort, the Secretary-General of the United Nations went to the Middle East with peace in his heart—his second such mission. And he came back from Baghdad with no progress at all in getting Saddam Hussein to withdraw from Kuwait.

Now the twenty-eight countries with forces in the Gulf area have exhausted all reasonable efforts to reach a peaceful resolution—have no choice but to drive Saddam from Kuwait by force. We will not fail.

As I report to you, air attacks are underway against military targets in Iraq. We are determined to knock out Saddam Hussein's nuclear-bomb potential. We will also destroy his chemical-weapons facilities. Much of Saddam's artillery and tanks will be destroyed. Our operations are designed to best protect the lives of all the coalition forces by targeting Saddam's vast military arsenal. Initial reports from General Schwarzkopf are that our operations are proceeding according to plan.

Our objectives are clear: Saddam Hussein's forces will leave Kuwait. The government of Kuwait will be restored to its rightful place, and Kuwait will once again be free. Iraq will eventually comply with all relevant United Nations resolutions, and then, when peace is restored, it is our hope that Iraq will live as a peaceful and cooperative member of the family of nations, thus enhancing the security and stability of the Gulf.

Some may ask: Why act now? Why not wait? The answer is clear: The world could wait no longer. Sanctions, though having some effect, showed no signs of accomplishing their objective. Sanctions were tried for well over five months, and we and our allies concluded that sanctions alone would not force Saddam from Kuwait.

While the world waited, Saddam Hussein systematically raped, pillaged, and plundered a tiny nation, no threat to his own. He subjected the people of Kuwait to unspeakable atrocities—and among those maimed and murdered, innocent children.

While the world waited, Saddam sought to add to the chemical weapons arsenal he now possesses, and infinitely more dangerous weapon of mass destruction—a nuclear weapon. And while the world waited, while the world talked peace and withdrawal, Saddam Hussein dug in and moved massive forces into Kuwait...

The United States, together with the United Nations, exhausted every means at our disposal to bring this crisis to a peaceful end. However, Saddam clearly felt that by stalling and threatening and defying the United Nations, he could weaken the forces arrayed against him.

While the world waited, Saddam Hussein met every overture of peace with open contempt. While the world prayed for peace, Saddam prepared for war.

I had hoped that when the United States Congress, in historic debate, took its resolute action, Saddam would realize he could not prevail and would move out of Kuwait in accord with the United Nation resolutions. He did not do that. Instead, he remained intransigent, certain that time was on his side.

Saddam was warned over and over again to comply with the will of the United Nations: Leave Kuwait, or be driven out. Saddam has arrogantly rejected all warnings. Instead, he tried to make this a dispute between Iraq and the United States of America.

Well, he failed. Tonight, twenty-eight nations—countries from five continents, Europe and Asia, Africa, and the Arab League—have forces in the Gulf area standing shoulder to shoulder against Saddam Hussein. These countries had hoped the use of force could be avoided. Regrettably, we now believe that only force will make him leave.

Prior to ordering our forces into battle, I instructed our military commanders to take every necessary step to prevail as quickly as possible, and with the greatest degree of protection possible for American and allied service men and women. I've told the American people before that this will not be another Vietnam, and I repeat this here tonight. Our troops will have the best possible support in the entire world, and they will not be asked to fight with one hand tied behind their back. I'm hopeful that this fighting will not go on for long and that casualties will be held to an absolute minimum.

This is an historic moment. We have in this past year made great progress in ending the long era of conflict and cold war. We have before us the opportunity to forge for ourselves and for future generations a new world order—a world where the rule of law, not the law of the jungle, governs the conduct of nations. When we are successful—and we will be—we have a real chance at this new world order, an order in which a credible United Nations can use its peacekeeping role to fulfill the promise and vision of the U.N.'s founders.

We have no argument with the people of Iraq. Indeed, for the innocents caught in this conflict, I pray for their safety. Our goal is not the conquest of Iraq. It is the liberation of Kuwait. It is my hope that somehow the Iraqi people can, even now, convince their dictator that he must lay down his arms, leave Kuwait and let Iraq itself rejoin the family of peace-loving nations.

Thomas Paine wrote many years ago: "These are the times that try men's souls." Those well-known words are so very true today. But even as planes of the multinational forces attack Iraq, I prefer to think of peace, not war. I am convinced not only that we will prevail but that out of the horror of combat will come the recognition that no nation can stand against a world united. No nation will be permitted to brutally assault its neighbor.

No president can easily commit our sons and daughters to war. They are the Nation's finest. Ours is an all-volunteer force, magnificently trained, highly motivated. The troops know why they're there. And listen to what they say, for they've said it better than any president or prime minister ever could.

Listen to Hollywood Huddleston, marine lance corporal. He says, "Let's free these people, so we can go home and be free again." And he's right. The terrible crimes and tortures committed by Saddam's henchmen against the innocent people of Kuwait are an affront to mankind and a challenge to the freedom of all.

Listen to one of our great officers out there, Marine Lieutenant General Walter Boomer. He said: "There are things worth fighting for. A world in which brutality and lawlessness are allowed to go unchecked isn't the kind of world we're going to want to live in."

Listen to Master Sergeant J. P. Kendall of the 82d Airborne: "We're here for more than just the price of a gallon of gas. What we're doing is going to chart the future of the world for the next 100 years. It's better to deal with this guy now than five years from now."

And finally, we should all sit up and listen to Jackie Jones, an army lieutenant, when she says, "If we let him get away with this, who knows what's going to be next?"

I have called upon Hollywood and Walter and J. P. and Jackie and all their courageous comrades-in-arms to do what must be done. Tonight, America and the world are deeply grateful to them and to their families. And let me say to everyone listening or watching tonight: When the troops we've sent in finish their work, I am determined to bring them home as soon as possible.

Tonight, as our forces fight, they and their families are in our prayers. May God bless each and every one of them, and the coalition forces at our side in the Gulf, and may He continue to bless our nation, the United States of America.

George W. Bush, State of the Union Address (2002)

"…As we gather tonight, our nation is at war, our economy is in recession, and the civilized world faces unprecedented dangers. Yet the state of our Union has never been stronger.

We last met in an hour of shock and suffering. In four short months, our nation has comforted the victims, begun to rebuild New York and the Pentagon, rallied a great coalition, captured, arrested, and rid the world of thousands of terrorists, destroyed Afghanistan's terrorist training camps, saved a people from starvation, and freed a country from brutal oppression.

The American flag flies again over our embassy in Kabul. Terrorists who once occupied Afghanistan now occupy cells at Guantanamo Bay. And terrorist leaders who urged followers to sacrifice their lives are running for their own.

America and Afghanistan are now allies against terror. We'll be partners in rebuilding that country. And this evening we welcome the distinguished interim leader of a liberated Afghanistan: Chairman Hamid Karzai.

The last time we met in this chamber, the mothers and daughters of Afghanistan were captives in their own homes, forbidden from working or going to school. Today women are free, and are part of Afghanistan's new government. And we welcome the new Minister of Women's Affairs, Doctor Sima Samar.

Our progress is a tribute to the spirit of the Afghan people, to the resolve of our coalition, and to the might of the United States military. When I called our troops into action, I did so with complete confidence in their courage and skill. And tonight, thanks to them, we are winning the war on terror. The man and women of our Armed Forces have delivered a message now clear to every enemy of the United States: Even 7,000 miles away, across oceans and continents, on mountaintops and in caves—you will not escape the justice of this nation.

For many Americans, these four months have brought sorrow, and pain that will never completely go away. Every day a retired firefighter returns to Ground Zero, to feel closer to his two sons who died there. At a memorial in New York, a little boy left his football with a note for his lost father: Dear Daddy, please take this to heaven. I don't want to play football until I can play with you again some day.

Last month, at the grave of her husband, Michael, a CIA officer and Marine who died in Mazur-e-Sharif, Shannon Spann said these words of farewell: "Semper Fi, my love." Shannon is with us tonight.

Shannon, I assure you and all who have lost a loved one that our cause is just, and our country will never forget the debt we owe Michael and all who gave their lives for freedom.

Our cause is just, and it continues. Our discoveries in Afghanistan confirmed our worst fears, and showed us the true scope of the task ahead. We have seen the depth of our enemies' hatred in videos, where they laugh about the loss of innocent life. And the depth of their hatred is equaled by the madness of the destruction they design. We have found diagrams of American nuclear power plants and public water facilities, detailed instructions for making chemical weapons, surveillance maps of American cities, and thorough descriptions of landmarks in America and throughout the world.

What we have found in Afghanistan confirms that, far from ending there, our war against terror is only beginning. Most of the 19 men who hijacked planes on September the 11th were trained in Afghanistan's camps, and so were tens of thousands of others. Thousands of dangerous killers, schooled in the methods of murder, often supported by outlaw regimes, are now spread throughout the world like ticking time bombs, set to go off without warning.

Thanks to the work of our law enforcement officials and coalition partners, hundreds of terrorists have been arrested. Yet, tens of thousands of trained terrorists are still at large. These enemies view the entire world as a battlefield, and we must pursue them wherever they are. So long as training camps operate, so long as nations harbor terrorists, freedom is at risk. And America and our allies must not, and will not, allow it.

Our nation will continue to be steadfast and patient and persistent in the pursuit of two great objectives. First, we will shut down terrorist camps, disrupt terrorist plans, and bring terrorists to justice. And, second, we must prevent the terrorists and regimes who seek chemical, biological or nuclear weapons from threatening the United States and the world.

Our military has put the terror training camps of Afghanistan out of business, yet camps still exist in at least a dozen countries. A terrorist underworld—including groups like Hamas, Hezbollah, Islamic Jihad, Jaish-i-Mohammed —operates in remote jungles and deserts, and hides in the centers of large cities.

While the most visible military action is in Afghanistan, America is acting elsewhere. We now have troops in the Philippines, helping to train that country's armed forces to go after terrorist cells that have executed an American, and still hold hostages. Our soldiers, working with the Bosnian government, seized terrorists who were plotting to bomb our embassy. Our Navy is patrolling the coast of Africa to block the shipment of weapons and the establishment of terrorist camps in Somalia.

My hope is that all nations will heed our call, and eliminate the terrorist parasites who threaten their countries and our own. Many nations are acting forcefully. Pakistan is now cracking down on terror, and I admire the strong leadership of President Musharraf.

But some governments will be timid in the face of terror. And make no mistake about it: If they do not act, America will.

Our second goal is to prevent regimes that sponsor terror from threatening America or our friends and allies with weapons of mass destruction. Some of these regimes have been pretty quiet since September the 11th. But we know their true nature. North Korea is a regime arming with missiles and weapons of mass destruction, while starving its citizens.

Iran aggressively pursues these weapons and exports terror, while an unelected few repress the Iranian people's hope for freedom.

Iraq continues to flaunt its hostility toward America and to support terror. The Iraqi regime has plotted to develop anthrax, and nerve gas, and nuclear weapons for over a decade. This is a regime that has already used poison gas to murder thousands of its own citizens—leaving the bodies of mothers huddled over their dead children. This is a regime that agreed to international inspections—then kicked out the inspectors. This is a regime that has something to hide from the civilized world.

States like these, and their terrorist allies, constitute an axis of evil, arming to threaten the peace of the world. By seeking weapons of mass destruction, these regimes pose a grave and growing danger. They could provide these arms to terrorists, giving them the means to match their hatred. They could attack our allies or attempt to blackmail the United States. In any of these cases, the price of indifference would be catastrophic.

We will work closely with our coalition to deny terrorists and their state sponsors the materials, technology, and expertise to make and deliver weapons of mass destruction. We will develop and deploy effective missile defenses to protect America and our allies from sudden attack. And all nations should know: America will do what is necessary to ensure our nation's security.

We'll be deliberate, yet time is not on our side. I will not wait on events, while dangers gather. I will not stand by, as peril draws closer and closer. The United States of America will not permit the world's most dangerous regimes to threaten us with the world's most destructive weapons.

Our war on terror is well begun, but it is only begun. This campaign may not be finished on our watch—yet it must be and it will be waged on our watch.

We can't stop short. If we stop now—leaving terror camps intact and terror states unchecked—our sense of security would be false and temporary. History has called America and our allies to action, and it is both our responsibility and our privilege to fight freedom's fight...

1. What objectives does George H. W. Bush offer for the 1991 allied military action in the Persian Gulf and why does he feel the action was necessary at that time?

2. Why does George H. W. Bush assure the American people that the Persian Gulf action "will not become another Vietnam"? How might such a concern of Bush have affected the outcome of the action?

3. What did George W. Bush mean in 2002 when he referred to an "axis of evil?" Why do you think he chose those words and how did it affect his foreign policy?

4. How does each president use fear, hope, strength, peace, and comments by average Americans in delivering their message?

5. What role does each president see for allied nations in diplomacy and resolving world problems?

ANSWER KEY

CHAPTER 16

Matching A
1. c
2. a
3. d
4. e
5. b

Matching B
1. c
2. e
3. a
4. b
5. d

Completion
1. *Birth of a Nation*
2. Thirteenth Amendment
3. pocket veto
4. investment capital
5. Fourteenth
6. sharecropping
7. greenbacks
8. Ku Klux Klan
9. businessmen, poor White farmers, Blacks
10. spoilsmen

True/False
1. T
2. F
3. F
4. T
5. F
6. T
7. F
8. T
9. T
10. F

Multiple Choice
1. d
2. a
3. c
4. d
5. d
6. b
7. c
8. b
9. a
10. a
11. d
12. c
13. c
14. b
15. d

CHAPTER 17

Matching A
1. b
2. a
3. c
4. d
5. e

Matching B
1. c
2. d
3. e
4. f
5. b

Completion
1. land, water, timber
2. Ghost Dance
3. buffalo
4. "Buffalo Bill" Cody
5. Missouri
6. National Reclamation Act (Newlands Act)
7. barbed wire
8. Grange
9. Oklahoma
10. Exodusters

True/False
1. F
2. F
3. F
4. T
5. T
6. F
7. T
8. F
9. T
10. T

Multiple Choice

1. d
2. c
3. a
4. c
5. d
6. a
7. d
8. d
9. c
10. c
11. c
12. b
13. b
14. d
15. a

CHAPTER 18

Matching A

1. b
2. f
3. c
4. a
5. e

Matching B

1. e
2. a
3. b
4. c
5. d

Completion

1. Corliss engine
2. J.P. Morgan
3. American Railway Association
4. Chinese
5. U.S. Steel Corporation
6. trust
7. two thousand, twenty-one thousand
8. mail-order
9. vertical integration
10. Homestead Strike

True/False

1. T
2. F
3. F
4. F
5. F
6. T
7. T
8. T
9. F
10. F

Multiple Choice

1. b
2. c
3. a
4. d
5. c
6. c
7. d
8. c
9. b
10. b
11. d
12. c
13. d
14. a
15. a

CHAPTER 19

Matching A

1. b
2. e
3. c
4. a
5. f

Matching B

1. d
2. b
3. a
4. c
5. f

Completion

1. Louis Sullivan
2. Mugwumps
3. dumbbell tenements
4. Louis Pasteur
5. ragtime
6. football
7. fifteen
8. Atlanta Compromise
9. William M. Tweed

10. National American Woman Suffrage Association (NAWSA)

True/False
1. F
2. F
3. T
4. T
5. T
6. T
7. T
8. T
9. T
10. F

Multiple Choice
1. d
2. c
3. b
4. d
5. a
6. d
7. c
8. b
9. d
10. d
11. a
12. c
13. b
14. a
15. b

CHAPTER 20

Matching A
1. d
2. a
3. e
4. f
5. b

Matching B
1. c
2. e
3. f
4. a
5. b

Completion
1. Bland-Allison Silver Purchase Act
2. Pendleton

3. subtreasury system
4. grandfather clause
5. 79 percent
6. Eugene V. Debs
7. James Weaver
8. Ocala Demands
9. Wilson-Gorman Tariff
10. League for the Protection of the Family

True/False
1. T
2. F
3. T
4. F
5. F
6. F
7. F
8. T
9. T
10. T

Multiple Choice
1. d
2. a
3. b
4. a
5. b
6. c
7. a
8. b
9. a
10. c
11. c
12. a
13. a
14. d
15. c

CHAPTER 21

Matching A
1. c
2. f
3. b
4. e
5. a

Matching B

1. b
2. f
3. e
4. c
5. a

Completion

1. Rough Riders
2. Charles Darwin
3. Josiah Strong
4. Crossroads of the Pacific
5. Hawaii
6. Alfred Thayer Mahan
7. Benjamin F. Tracy
8. George Dewey
9. Samuel Gompers
10. "Yellow Journalism"

True/False

1. T
2. F
3. T
4. T
5. F
6. F
7. F
8. F
9. T
10. T

Multiple Choice

1. c
2. d
3. c
4. c
5. b
6. d
7. c
8. b
9. c
10. d
11. a
12. d
13. b
14. a
15. d

CHAPTER 22

Matching A

1. b
2. d
3. a
4. c
5. f

Matching B

1. b
2. d
3. e
4. a
5. c

Completion

1. Theodore Roosevelt
2. "Tin Lizzie"
3. General Electric
4. hookworm
5. W.E.B. Du Bois
6. rural free delivery
7. literacy test
8. Industrial Workers of the World (IWW)
9. jazz
10. Ashcan School

True/False

1. T
2. F
3. F
4. F
5. T
6. T
7. T
8. F
9. T
10. F

Multiple Choice

1. b
2. b
3. d
4. d
5. c
6. c
7. a
8. b
9. b

10.	d		5.	b
11.	c		6.	a
12.	b		7.	c
13.	c		8.	a
14.	a		9.	d
15.	b		10.	c
			11.	a
			12.	d
			13.	c
			14.	b
			15.	a

CHAPTER 23

Matching A
1. c
2. d
3. b
4. e
5. a

Matching B
1. e
2. f
3. c
4. b
5. d

Completion
1. "bully pulpit"
2. Commerce and Labor
3. referendum, initiative, recall
4. Payne Aldrich Act
5. New Nationalism
6. WCTU or Anti-Saloon League
7. Pure Food and Drug Act
8. "Wisconsin Idea"
9. free
10. optimism

True/False
1. T
2. F
3. F
4. F
5. F
6. T
7. T
8. F
9. T
10. T

Multiple Choice
1. a
2. a
3. d
4. c

CHAPTER 24

Matching A
1. d
2. e
3. a
4. b
5. c

Matching B
1. d
2. f
3. c
4. b
5. a

Completion
1. William Jennings Bryan
2. an isthmian canal
3. Root-Takahira Agreement
4. moral diplomacy
5. Portfirio Diaz
6. neutrality
7. submarine
8. peace or preparedness
9. Victoriano Huerta
10. "New Negro"

True/False
1. F
2. T
3. F
4. F
5. T
6. F
7. F
8. F
9. T

10.   F

Multiple Choice
1. c
2. b
3. a
4. d
5. a
6. d
7. c
8. a
9. c
10. a
11. a
12. b
13. b
14. a
15. c

CHAPTER 25

Matching A
1. c
2. d
3. f
4. e
5. b

Matching B
1. d
2. a
3. b
4. e
5. c

Completion
1. Model T
2. *Amos 'n' Andy*
3. marketing
4. Charles Lindbergh
5. flapper
6. Calvin Coolidge
7. A. Mitchell Palmer
8. Scopes Trial
9. Albert Fall
10. Al Smith

True/False
1. F
2. F
3. F
4. T

5. T
6. T
7. F
8. F
9. T
10. F

Multiple Choice
1. c
2. c
3. a
4. d
5. d
6. c
7. c
8. b
9. c
10. a
11. b
12. a
13. a
14. c
15. c

CHAPTER 26

Matching A
1. c
2. e
3. f
4. b
5. a

Matching B
1. d
2. f
3. e
4. a
5. b

Completion
1. New Deal
2. General Douglas McArthur
3. labor
4. National Recovery Association
5. Henry A. Wallace
6. Father Charles Coughlin
7. Wagner Act
8. Huey Long
9. Congress of Industrial Organizations

10. Burton Wheeler

True/False
1. F
2. F
3. T
4. T
5. F
6. F
7. F
8. T
9. T
10. F

Multiple Choice
1. c
2. a
3. b
4. a
5. b
6. d
7. b
8. d
9. c
10. b
11. d
12. c
13. d
14. c
15. c

CHAPTER 27

Matching A
1. b
2. d
3. e
4. f
5. c

Matching B
1. c
2. f
3. a
4. e
5. d

Completion
1. Kellogg-Briand Treaty
2. Axis Powers
3. *blitzkrieg*
4. Nazi-Soviet Pact

5. Holocaust
6. General Erwin Rommel
7. Admiral Chester Nimitz
8. Willow Run
9. Battle of the Bulge
10. Henry Stimson

True/False
1. F
2. T
3. T
4. T
5. F
6. F
7. T
8. F
9. T
10. F

Multiple Choice
1. b
2. a
3. d
4. c
5. a
6. b
7. a
8. b
9. c
10. a
11. d
12. a
13. b
14. b
15. d

CHAPTER 28

Matching A
1. e
2. c
3. d
4. f
5. b

Matching B
1. e
2. a
3. b
4. d
5. f

Completion
1. Russia (Soviet Union)
2. Greece, Turkey
3. Thomas E. Dewey
4. hydrogen
5. North Korea
6. Dixiecrats
7. Alger Hiss
8. Joseph McCarthy
9. Army-McCarthy
10. Korea

True/False
1. F
2. T
3. F
4. T
5. T
6. F
7. T
8. F
9. T
10. F

Multiple Choice
1. b
2. a
3. a
4. b
5. d
6. a
7. c
8. d
9. c
10. b
11. b
12. a
13. d
14. d
15. a

CHAPTER 29

Matching A
1. c
2. e
3. d
4. b
5. a

Matching B
1. b
2. c
3. e
4. d
5. a

Completion
1. suburbs
2. sunbelt
3. armed forces
4. *Twenty-One*
5. television
6. Fourteenth Amendment
7. Montgomery Bus Boycott
8. passive resistance
9. segregation
10. Jackson Pollock

True/False
1. F
2. T
3. F
4. F
5. F
6. T
7. F
8. F
9. T
10. F

Multiple Choice
1. c
2. a
3. c
4. c
5. a
6. b
7. c
8. a
9. c
10. a
11. d
12. c
13. a
14. d
15. b

CHAPTER 30

Matching A
1. d
2. c
3. a
4. f
5. b

Matching B
1. a
2. c
3. e
4. d
5. f

Completion
1. "the best and the brightest"
2. Bay of Pigs
3. Alliance for Progress
4. Viet Cong
5. "hot line"
6. *The Arrogance of Power*
7. Great Society
8. Civil Rights Act of 1964
9. Office of Economic Opportunity
10. Medicare, Medicaid

True/False
1. F
2. T
3. F
4. F
5. F
6. F
7. F
8. T
9. T
10. F

Multiple Choice
1. b
2. d
3. c
4. a
5. d
6. b
7. a
8. d
9. a
10. b
11. a
12. a
13. d
14. d
15. c

CHAPTER 31

Matching A
1. d
2. c
3. a
4. e
5. f

Matching B
1. e
2. c
3. a
4. f
5. b

Completion
1. Kent State University
2. OPEC (Organization of Petroleum Exporting Countries)
3. *Roe v. Wade*
4. CIA
5. Nicaragua
6. Afghanistan
7. supply-side economics
8. Strategic Defense Initiative (SDI)
9. Iran-Contra affair
10. *perestroika, glasnost*

True/False
1. F
2. F
3. T
4. F
5. T
6. F
7. F
8. T
9. F
10. T

Multiple Choice
1. b
2. b
3. c

4.	d
5.	a
6.	c
7.	d
8.	b
9.	d
10.	a
11.	a
12.	d
13.	c
14.	a
15.	b

CHAPTER 32

Matching A

1.	d
2.	c
3.	a
4.	e
5.	f

Matching B

1.	f
2.	b
3.	d
4.	e
5.	a

Completion

1. Poland
2. Boris Yeltsin
3. Sunbelt
4. Hispanic
5. Hurricane Katrina
6. North American Free Trade Agreement (NAFTA)
7. United States Supreme Court
8. Afghanistan
9. weapons of mass destruction (WMDs)
10. Department of Homeland Security

True/False

1.	F
2.	F
3.	T
4.	T
5.	T
6.	T
7.	F
8.	F
9.	F
10.	F

Multiple Choice

1.	a
2.	b
3.	a
4.	c
5.	d
6.	d
7.	c
8.	c
9.	a
10.	d
11.	d
12.	d
13.	d
14.	d
15.	b